THE POLITICAL GEOGRAPHIES OF PREGNANCY

LAURA R. WOLIVER

The Political Geographies

of Pregnancy

UNIVERSITY OF ILLINOIS PRESS

URBANA AND CHICAGO

♾ This book is printed on acid-free paper.

Library of Congress Cataloging-in-Publication Data
Woliver, Laura R., 1954–
The political geographies of pregnancy / Laura R. Woliver.
p.   cm.
Includes bibliographical references and index.
ISBN 0-252-02778-7
1. Pregnancy—Political aspects. 2. Human reproduction—
Political aspects. 3. Human reproductive technology—
Political aspects. I. Title.
RG556.w655   2002
305.48—dc21   2002003599

To my gorgeous babies,
Paul and Sarah Woliver Binkley

Contents

Acknowledgments

Once again, the University of Illinois Press has welcomed my multidisciplinary, boundary-violating work. Richard Martin's support for work like mine (feminist, theoretical, empirical, eclectic, difficult to pigeonhole) is a refreshing reminder of tp ideals of intellectual curiosity and expanded visions. The reviewers he selected for this book helped me enormously, enhancing my reading, strengthening my voice, and clarifying my points.

My colleagues and fellow travelers in the Women's Studies Program at the University of South Carolina at Columbia nurture me and one another in our teaching, scholarship, activism, and sustenance of our families in all their diversities. Their wicked witticisms, infectious, uproarious laughter, and skewering insights on the patriarchal foibles in our lives brace me to keep doing the feminist work that is the archaeology of our futures.

The Women's Studies Program is blessed with two brilliant, dedicated, and gracious administrators, Rosa Thorn and Jacqueline McClary, who execute their feminist praxis deftly, subtly, and effectively. They are faithful supporters of my work and make all of our wonderful students feel included, welcomed, and valued.

My students in my women and politics courses at the undergraduate and graduate levels teach me every semester new ways to weave, spin, and cook up imaginary domains of possible social justice. Their courage and wisdom make me proud and full of hope for future iterations of feminist practices, movements, and paradigm shifts. I thank in particular my teaching and research assistants who have made my work much easier.

Wesley H. and Phyllis M. (Taeschner) Woliver, my parents, taught me to relish knowledge and explore the world. Mark Washburn Binkley, my husband and best friend, as always supports my work and dreams. Our children, Paul and Sarah, inspired me to write this book. Their births altered me profoundly for the better. Maybe some day all the babies will be wanted, healthy, nurtured, valued, loved, and safe. To work toward that goal, we must begin by really valuing women and all the labors of love, decades of nurturing, and care of dependents performed on the distaff side of life.

THE POLITICAL GEOGRAPHIES OF PREGNANCY

1 *Feminist Praxis, Reproductive Powers, and Medical Models*

> Given the very geography of pregnancy, questions as to
> the status of the fetus must follow, not precede, an ex-
> amination of the rights of the woman within whose
> body and life the fetus exists.
> —Janet Gallagher, "Fetus as Patient"

The context in which women become mothers in Western societies is changing, reshaping and sharpening issues of power and control over women's reproductive agency. Having babies and building families are being "enterprised up" in our times (Strathern, 1992). More money is being invested in reproductive technologies, the management of pregnancy and birth, and medicine aimed at the fetus. The investments, like all business transactions, are suppose to provide future profits and benefits. This book is an analysis of the broad spectrum of reproductive political issues, from abortion politics to surrogacy, the impact of the new reproductive technologies and cloning, adoption practices and powers, and the political and reproductive impact of mapping the human genome. These shifting terrains of reproductive power alter familial and social relationships, increase professional and social monitoring of women's reproductive lives, and echo social values of the worth and "worthlessness" of various people.

Women's reproductive potentials place them in the center of these shifting terrains of power. Families, siblings, fathers, and larger communities are also affected by these changes in reproductive contexts. Framing reproductive issues predominantly within a medical and scientific domain draws our attention away from the social and political forces (such as discrimination, pollution, iatrogenesis, poverty, violence, and exploitation) that also impact the health of women, babies, children, and families. There are other or additional ways to improve the health of women, babies, and children. The relatively low-tech program of adding folic acid to flour, for instance, has been linked to a 19 percent drop in the number of children born with certain spinal and brain defects (Webber, 2001). "As with most technologies," Sue Rosser points out, "intrinsically the new reproductive technologies are neither good nor bad; it is the way they are used that determines their potential for benefit or harm" (1986: 40). Introduced into sexist, racist, homophobic, and class-based cultures, these technologies raise serious issues of eugenics, the specter of abortions for sex selection or the elimination of people with disabilities, and the diminution of women's relation to reproduction.

Reproductive technologies, such as ultrasound, amniocentesis, in vitro fertilization, and embryo transfer, are altering women's experiences of gestation and birth while increasing the medicalization of women's lives. These technologies bring new policy issues to the courts and legislatures as they address how to incorporate new reproductive arrangements into our legal system. In the meantime, disputes arising from new reproductive technologies are forced to fit into old legal codes of paternity, maternity, baby-selling, adoption, and contracts. The new reproductive technologies and arrangements, such as surrogacy, are increasingly in conflict with old legal precedents and assumptions. Given the track record of the American legal system's treatment of women and the enormous importance of new reproductive technologies to all women, this new policy domain engenders considerable concern about women's reproductive rights and the lack of empowerment for mothers in family law.

In reproductive politics, inserting the experiences, voices, and desires of women into policy-making, legal theory, and practice is a new, incomplete, and radical move. It is radical because it subverts the status quo. This threatens authority figures because of their hierarchical thinking and beliefs in zero-sum games. If women's voices are allowed within society and the polity, dominant males fear they will be silenced. Feminist criticism and analysis include the experiences of girls and women, not to silence the dominant canonical paradigms but to add to the discourse viewpoints that are often overlooked (Heilbrun, 1990: 30–31; Minnich, 1990). Part of the tension and threat to the status quo is the dichotomy in our culture between male and female, dependency and independence, and nurture and masculinity. Jessica Benjamin explains that such gender polarity results in symptoms of discontent, such as:

contempt for the needy and dependent, emphasis on individual self-reliance, rejection of social forms of providing nurturance—[which] are not visibly connected to gender. Yet in spite of the fact that these attitudes are almost as common among women as they are among men, they are nevertheless the result of gender polarity. They underlie the mentality of opposition which pits freedom against nurturance: either we differentiate or remain dependent; either we stand alone or are weak; either we relinquish autonomy or renounce the need for love. No doubt many individuals are flexible enough to forge less extreme solutions, but the polarities tug mightily whenever dependency is an issue. (1988: 171–72)

Praxis, Approach, Method

Materials for my study of these issues were gathered from a variety of sources: interviews, participant observation, and analysis of texts. I interviewed more than sixty attorneys, lobbyists, interest group directors, and activist leaders in the pro-life and pro-choice movements. Interviews were also conducted with people involved in reproductive politics more generally, such as attorneys for the American Medical Association and lobbyists for the American College of Obstetricians and Gynecologists. The interviews were conducted from 1991 to 2000. Individuals in Chicago and Washington, D.C., involved in reproductive politics at the national level were interviewed and their groups and coalition activities examined. The local nature of reproductive politics, particularly abortion conflicts, is folded into one section of my book by an in-depth examination of the abortion wars and punitive surveillance of pregnant women in South Carolina. Interviews with South Carolina activists, providers, and politicians help illuminate the local impact of these political conflagrations.

My experiences of pregnancy, birth, and motherhood are also incorporated into this book. Birthing my two children was the best thing I have ever done. Many of my friends say the same about their birthing experiences. I have told many students, "I had my first child when I was starting my dissertation. It was not the smartest thing I've ever done, but it was the best." When I first read *Bearing Meaning: The Language of Birth* by Robbie Pfeufer Kahn, I was stunned by her use of the same phrase to describe giving birth, "the best thing I ever did." "In giving birth," Kahn reflects, "I found out I had a *woman's* body, not a body that wasn't a man's, and I could do things with my body that were fundamental to human existence" (1995: 38; see also Nedelsky, 1999).[1] Most birthgivers allow that the experiences of pregnancy and birth are intellectually transformative (Ruddick, 1994: 41). Many of the women with whom I have discussed birth are amazed at what our bodies can do. Repeatedly they quip, "And women are suppose to be the weaker sex!" with much chuckling. At the same time, many women lament the intrusive, patronizing, and alienating medical protocols and authoritative knowledge imposed on them while they labor and give birth.

With my second child, I was considered an "older" mother and thus a candidate for all the tests and machines at the doctors' disposal. Although my doctors were kind women, their assumptions about the protocols I would "of course" follow intrigued me. The concept of older mother is a social definition and varies over generations and across countries (Rapp, 1994a: 205). In Western medicine, expanding indicators for use of tests and machines and doctors' practice of defensive medicine mean that many women are now considered "older" mothers at an age when their own mothers would not have been. Their mothers might have been having their last children at an age when they are birthing their first and second. Our mothers' later pregnancies, however, were not considered unusual and in need of hypermedicalization.

Being pregnant also made me think deeply about abortion politics. My generation remembers illegal, clandestine abortions and has adjusted to legal choices derived from *Roe v. Wade* (1973). My students at the University of South Carolina sometimes discuss with me their struggles as they negotiate their reproductive decisions. Some of them are blessed by being able to choose legal, safe abortions. At the same time, others are equally blessed by being able to choose, rather than being coerced and shamed, to continue their unplanned pregnancies.

I have also watched as many colleagues, neighbors, friends, and relatives have entered and negotiated the adoption market. Adoption is a normal part of my life. I was raised in a U.S. military family and saw many families with adopted children from many of the countries to which the U.S. military regularly sends troops. When I was in high school and lived in Pusan, South Korea, on a U.S. military base, adoption of Korean children by American families seemed to be easy, smooth, and routine. Only later, as an adult, professor, and mother, did I begin to think about the social structures on which such practices were built. Friends and students of mine who are adult adoptees have taught me the complexities of being an adopted child. My research on abortion politics, in turn, drew me toward adoption politics because of the links often made, such as the slogan "Adoption, Not Abortion." Research I did on surrogacy contracts and women's rights also reminded me of the need to study adoption because supporters of surrogacy often made analogies to our adoption system and practices.

In my work on abortion and my preliminary readings on adoption history and practices, I was struck immediately by how little was ever done about the impact adoption has on birthmothers. Several years ago my graduate student, Kathryn Bryant, wrote a terrific master's thesis on adoption and feminist theory, from which I learned a lot. I hope that future researchers will explore even further the complexities of adoption practices and behaviors. The new laws on open records and open adoptions provide fascinating material for future scholarship on how we knit together our families in a world where birthmothers are no longer automatically erased as families are cobbled together.

At the same time, international adoption markets continue, for the most part, to erase birthmothers and other relatives from the child's life. The relative powerlessness of women in many countries makes it impossible for them to request open adoptions. International adoptions now resemble American adoptions from the 1940s through the 1970s, which erased a child's past and made every legal and social effort to create one nuclear, traditional family out of the arrangements.

I have also observed dozens of pro-life, pro-choice, and reproductive politics marches, court hearings, rallies, meetings, church revivals, movies, videos, slides, and other visual displays at the national and local levels. Analysis of the amicus curia briefs that interest groups and coalitions submitted to the U.S. Supreme Court in the *Webster* (1989), *Bray* (1993), *Whitner* (1997), and *Ferguson* (2001) cases is also threaded throughout the study. The briefs are examined for their rhetoric, their images of girls and women, and their standpoints vis-à-vis the fetus, born people, and state power and responsibilities. These observations, fieldwork, interviews, and readings led me to see the interconnected nature of abortion, adoption, surrogacy, the new reproductive technologies, the mapping of the human genome, and police monitoring of pregnant women. Although modern changes in all these domains can be beneficial, they are also riddled with dangers to the dignity and agency of women.

In 1996, I was invited to attend a week-long convention of the Human Genome Project's Ethical, Legal, and Social Implications of Human Genome Research (ELSI) program. The program was aimed at assessing the impact of mapping the human genome from a women's studies perspective. My observations, readings, and participation in that multidisciplinary week-long exploration of the human genome's potential social impact are also woven throughout this book. At the ELSI sessions I was struck that, for instance, the Canadian participants had a different view of the diffusion of genetic knowledge in society, partly because they operate in a country with universal health care.

My evaluation of these politics is nested within feminist legal and political theories, particularly feminist standpoint theory, the ethic of care, and new and exciting work on human dependency and social theory. My study is also enriched by my decades-long teaching and reading in political science and women's studies.

My orientation is macro, to consider the impact of new reproductive practices on the larger institutions and structures of our society. The individual biological bench scientist working away in a laboratory, I realize, is not deliberately engaged in an effort to transform in a manner meant to harm the way women put together their families. The micro work of the scientists is often aimed at helping people negotiate their fertility and family relations more easily. However, the diffusion of new procedures, information, and technology and their expansion into the medical standard of care are done in a society and culture with a long history of race, class, gender, and sexual orientation inequalities. If implemented sensitively by incorporating the experiences of women, people with disabilities, those that do most of the nurturing work in a society, and people who raise disabled and differently abled children, the innovations might enhance the lives of many families.

My book is not the final word on these matters, by any means. Reproductive options, legal decisions on human reproduction, scientific discoveries, and medical practices are changing us so rapidly that the study of the politics and ethics of reproduction is a constant, never ending struggle. No one universal covering law or conclusion would do justice to new ethical dilemmas created by science, technology, law, and human desire to form families in all their diversities.

Shifting Powers in Women's Reproduction

Motherhood should be placed within the context of women's lives as one of the greatest pleasures, worries, and burdens of females (Quindlen, 2001; Maushart, 2000; Layne, 1999b; Cornell, 1998: 27–28; Ladd-Taylor and Umansky, 1998; Hays, 1996; Bassin, Honey, and Kaplan, 1994; Tong, 1998: chap. 3; Sevenhuijsen and de Vries, 1984; Martin, 1987; Belenky et al., 1986; Dworkin, 1983: 173–88; Chodorow, 1978; O'Brien, 1981; Ruddick, 1980; Rich, 1976; Bernard, 1974; S. Firestone, 1970). The experience of motherhood is powerfully shaped by culture, but it is also profoundly affected by race, social class, and sexuality (P. Collins, 1994: 56–74). Even though mothers have never had much power and prestige in many societies (despite the sweet talk about "motherhood and apple pie"), women alone have had the power to gestate and birth babies. The nurturing that people sometimes experience in families preserves us from the unbearable moral and physical solitude of much of modern life (Hays, 1996: 175). Conservative, moderate, and liberal political debates about families are often impassioned and fierce, partly because of the value we place on families. There also seems to be an abundance of mother-blaming, while father-blaming rarely occurs (see, for example, Caplan, 1993: 127–44; and Terry, 1998: 169–90). Some of the heat and acrimony is also a backlash against feminism.

Modern society's medicalization of pregnancy and birth, the permutations possible through new reproductive technologies, and the impact of new genetic knowledge and mappings are subtly altering women's role in reproduction by making conception, gestation, birth, and genetic inheritance something that predominately male scientists monitor, examine, and control. Many feminist theorists and scholars of women and public policy are very wary of these arrangements because of the disappointing track record of the medical and legal professions' treatment of women (Hirshman and Larson, 1998; Corea, 1985a and 1985b; M. Daly, 1978; Dutton, Preston, and Pfund, 1988; M. Edwards and Waldorf, 1984; Ehrenreich and English, 1978; Farrant, 1985: 103; Fisher, 1986; H. Graham and Oakley, 1981; Martin, 1987; Oakley, 1984; Pollock, 1984; B. Rothman, 1982; S. Rothman, 1978: 142–53; Rich, 1976). Feminist scholars are also justly skeptical about modern science because of its history and ethic of dominance, control, and insensitivity to women's lives (Davis-Floyd and Sargent, 1997; Arnold and Faulkner, 1985; Bleier, 1984; Gould, 1981; Griffin, 1978; Harding, 1986; Keller, 1985; Merchant, 1980; Rothschild, 1983; Rosser, 1986 and 1989). Nations shift and amend their statutes on abortion and birth control partly on the basis of their population needs during warfare or when threatened by growing, yet unwelcomed, birthrates within certain ethnic groups (Tobias, 1997: 67). Whether abortion is legal or criminal is affected by the nationalist and state-building needs and concerns of regimes. In postsocialist Eastern Europe, for instance, nationalist myths and rhetoric, ethnic hatreds, and patriotic behaviors were, in part, discussed in terms of women's birth patterns. Regimes that had legal abortion often recriminalized abortion out of the desire to increase births within privileged nationalist and ethnic groups, to meet labor force needs, and to reinforce views of the "natural" role for women. For the most part, women had little voice in these abortion reforms (Ferree, 1997: 48; Fuszara, 1997: 134; Gaber, 1997: 146; Gal, 1997: 41; Knezevic, 1997: 70; Lang, 1997: 110; Salecl, 1997: 83–87).

As 250 historians argued in their amicus brief to the U.S. Supreme Court in the 1992 case *Planned Parenthood of Southeastern Pennsylva-*

nia v. Casey, "Opposition to abortion and contraception were closely linked, and can only be understood as a reaction to the uncertainties generated by changes in family function and anxieties created by women's challenges to their historic roles of silence and subservience" (Amicus Brief of 250 Historians in *Planned Parenthood of Southeastern Pennsylvania v. Casey,* 1992: 18). Historically, birth control and abortion laws were intended to restrain and control women. Legal restrictions on abortion in our past, the brief continued, "did not stop abortions, but made it humiliating and dangerous" (20).

In addition, normal, natural childbirth is problematized "for women's own good" as new reproductive technologies frame women's bodily functions as, in Hilary Rose's words, "both distressingly 'natural' and undercapitalized" (1994: 73). Reproduction is being enterprised up. Donna Haraway ponders these developments while "[r]eading and writing on the razor edge between paranoia and denial" (1997: 7). The biological sciences smoothly segue from explaining and understanding life to manipulating and controlling it, partly by rationalizing reproduction (Clarke, 1998: 24–27). The medical profession's gatekeeping role and monopoly over birth control information and services already manifest these tendencies (Jordan, 1997; Jaquette and Staudt, 1985; Hartman, 1987; Petchesky, 1984). Today, many women feel obligated to use genetic tests and fetal monitoring machines and technologies. Increasingly explicit is the underlying message that this is the only way to be a good mother and have a healthy baby. During my own pregnancies, these forces came into play. The compartmentalization of pregnancy and childbirth manifest in modern medical practices (Trevathan, 1997; Kahn, 1995; Woliver, 1989a) evolves into even smaller disaggregation and alienation through the minute examination and reduction of human reproduction into bits of genetic code. Professional power and financial markets intercede into people's reproductive choices, then, even prior to conception. One observer notes that "because in the practice of biomedicine a reductionistic style of reasoning is frequently dominant, medicalization and geneticization are often the end results of visits to physicians" (Lock, 1998: 49). The ties to financial markets and biomedical institutions mean that "geneticization, like medicalization, not only is blind to issues of equity and justice with respect to health but erases them from the public mind" (Lippman 1998, 64; see also Diamond, 1990; and Elkington, 1985). Although many medical advances, genetic discoveries, and scientific findings help many people and empower them to make satisfactory reproductive choices for themselves, it must also be acknowledged that these events are altering the terrains of reproductive power and are "mixed blessings" (Woliver, 1989a, 1989c, 1990a, 1990c, 1991a, 1995, 1999b, and 1999c; McGee, 1997).

The surveillance of pregnant women or those who want to become pregnant insinuates the medical industry and the state into very private dimensions of women's lives. At this point, however, if the tests, monitors, and oversight reveal "problems" with the fetus, the women can either prepare themselves for the birth of an unhealthy or different baby or seek an abortion; there are very few treatments or cures for what the monitoring reveals. If a woman chooses abortion (which is legal in the United States), she is often abandoned by the very same intrusive, intimate health industry personnel who often do not provide abortion services. A legal abortion, however, is a logical consequence for some people considering the information the industry sells them. The reassurance many women seek during their pregnancies is available from many avenues, not just medical doctors. Being enmeshed in medical surveillance during a pregnancy can increase anxiety and decrease the pleasure of the pregnancy. The medical surveillance can create dis-ease, as Abby Lippman points out: "It hides the iatrogenic nature of 'need' by failing to ask whether reassurance would be sought if an outsider had not first decided that certain women were at risk and that the condition for which the risk existed warranted diagnosis before a baby with it was born. It hides the need to consider the possibility that reassurance is a biomedical fix disempowering women and increasing their dependency on technology" (1994a: 16). Women's stories from these perspectives, however, are rarely heard and often discredited.

Many legal systems have already displayed a marked tendency to devalue and belittle the experiences and desires of women (Baer, 1999; Bumiller, 1988; Eisenstein, 1988; Estrich, 1987; Fineman, 1988; Finley, 1986; MacKinnon, 1987; Pateman, 1988; Woliver, 1988 and 1993a). The enterprising up of human reproduction therefore has real potential to decrease women's power over their own bodies. The shifting terrain of reproductive power, with predictions based on genes, is also framed as enhancing women's choices. However, the emphasis is on the individual as the sole determinant of health (Lippman, 1998: 66). The market for babies manifest in adoption practices, surrogacy arrangements, and the selling of eggs is often presented as a seemingly neutral situation resulting in fair policies and happy family outcomes. Again, however, this glosses over women's relative poverty and powerlessness in society, which skews these arrangements toward the abuse and heartbreak of certain women. Changes in American divorce and child custody policies, for example, have actually harmed many women because reformers did not consider women's economic and emotional circumstances but instead adopted an ostensibly neutral stance, which actually favored men (Cornell, 1999a; Fineman, 1983 and 1988).

Supposedly neutral medical technologies have similarly engendered debate about their disproportionate economic, legal, and ethical effects on women (see, for example, Browner and Press, 1997; Lazarus, 1997; Spallone and Steinberg, 1987; Hanmer, 1984; Hubbard, 1984; Kishwar, 1987; Raymond, 1984; St. Peter, 1989; Stanworth, 1987; Wikler, 1986; Saxton, 1984; S. Cohen and Taub, 1989; Teich, 1990; Elshtain, 1989; Diamond, 1988; and Glover et al., 1989, to name just a few). Enterprised-up reproduction, the medicalization of pregnancy and childbirth, and the rational economic decision making expected from the human genome project chafe against many women's experiences of the nurturing, interwoven lives of families. Sharon Hays explains:

> Mothers, in other words, are engaged in an explicit and systematic rejection of the logic of individualistic, competitive, and impersonal relations. This final analysis, emphasizing opposition, underlines and embraces the tensions that mothers experience, just as it embraces the tension between arguments about love and self-interest and arguments about those who have power over mothers and the ways mothers themselves are powerful. When these four analyses are taken together, it becomes clear that the beliefs of today's mothers and the cultural contradictions of motherhood point to a persistent, wide-spread, and irreducible cultural ambivalence about a social world based on the motive of individual gain, the impersonality of bureaucratic and market relations, and the calculating behavior of *homo economicus.* (1996: 154)

Motherhood is one of the central areas in which our society's ambivalence about the wisdom of basing a society on the competitive pursuit of rational self-interest alone is played out (Hays, 1996: 18).

Reproductive Frames: Populations, Resources, Women's Agency

On Earth Day 2001, the media highlighted the fact that the population of the earth had doubled since 1970. The continuing redistribution of the earth's resources since 1970 went unreported. A 1998 cover story in *National Geographic* declares, "Of all the issues we face as the new millennium nears, none is more important than population growth" (Swerdlow, 1998: 4). While this frames the issue exclusively in terms of birthrates rather than the distribution of resources, this popular, mainstream magazine, to its credit, devotes a whole separate article to the roles women as decision makers play in reproductive decisions (Zwingle, 1998). Pollution, development of arable land, and problems in the distribution of food are also discussed in this cover story (Reid, 1998), but population growth remains central. In the same *National Geographic* issue, an article by Michael Parfit (1998) on human migration patterns documents the political upheavals, struggles, and oppressions that push many people to migrate. Yet the tone of the article appears as a neutral narrative that casts refugees, diasporas, and flight from terror and violence as inevitable aspects of human nature, thus diminishing the importance of politics. Human responsibility for forced or economic migration is not foregrounded in the article. However, an article on food production and human population growth in the same issue clearly states, "A major reason for the disparity between haves and have-nots is politics" (Reid, 1998: 64). Although the world's population is growing rapidly, a major problem for people is resource distribution, not simply production. Whether the earth can feed all its people is therefore a political issue.

Echoing what many people wondered about concerning whose births we celebrate and whose we disapprove of, the *National Geographic* writer Erla Zwingle notes in an article on women and population issues, "On a certain November day an obscure woman in Iowa gives birth to seven babies; we marvel and rejoice. On the same day an obscure woman in Nigeria gives birth to her seventh child in a row; we are distressed and appalled" (1998: 38). She does not explore this juxtaposition but goes on to examine the individualized reasons people all over the world have children, think about limiting the size of their families, and negotiate their reproductive decisions. Evidence of the extent of the impact of the women's movement on culture and politics is that this popular mainstream (many say conservative) magazine centers on the lives of women, their choices, travails, power, and powerlessness in choosing their own destiny (Zwingle, 1998).

Worldwide reductions in birthrates are ascribable to contraception, health care, and culture, with contraception as central (Zwingle, 1998: 39). "'There isn't any place where women have had the choice that they haven't chosen to have fewer children,' says Beverly Winikoff at the Population Council in New York City. 'Governments don't need to resort to force.'" (quoted in Zwingle, 1998: 39). Women's agency, education, health, and empowerment are vital aspects of population politics. As Zwingle points out, "For birthrates to keep falling, experts say women must be offered opportunities beyond motherhood and given the authority to choose whether to bear children" (1998: 44). Many feminist health activists worldwide oppose mainstream population and family planning programs ethically and politically. Rosalind Pollack Petchesky maintains "that their failure to treat women's health and wellbeing as ends in themselves (rather than as means toward lowering or raising numbers) and their disregard for women as reproductive decision makers constitute violations of women's human rights" (1998b: 2). Or, as one Population Council official is quoted as saying, "One can promote a smaller world by promoting a more just world" (quoted in Zwingle, 1998: 43).

The vision of a just world, however, must not leave men out by treating women like the "disease vector," as Winikoff of the Population Council put it (quoted in Zwingle, 1998: 46). "Men," Zwingle observes, "are the point at which family planning leaves the realm of mechanics and enters the mysterious territory of behavior. Contraceptives themselves are simple—it's the users that are complicated, caught up in the volatile dynamics of human relationships" (1998: 47). One comparative study of seven countries found "that it is not a lack of will or access to methods of contraception that keeps women from preventing unwanted pregnancies successfully, but rather a lack of methods that meet their *social* as well as their biological needs *as they define them*" (Petchesky, 1998a: 300; see also Russell and Thompson, 2000).

The dominant frame is one of population crisis and overpopulation, particularly of poor people and within third and fourth world countries. An additional, but less popular, frame is one that stresses the crisis of resource allocation and the need to ensure women's well-being, bodily autonomy, and health so that they can have healthy babies, families, and futures.

Framing environmental problems with population issues as central contributes to perpetuating injustices worldwide and acute harm to women (Sen, 1998). As one scholar cautions regarding dominant views of recent environmental crises, "As ordinary people try to reclaim local lands, forests and waters from the depredations of business and the state, and work to build democratic movements to preserve the planet's health, those in power continue to occupy themselves with damage control and the containment of threats to the way power is currently distributed and held" (Lohmann, 1998: 240). Environmental scarcities have already contributed to violent political conflicts worldwide. These environmental scarcities (renewable resource scarcities), however, should be carefully defined from three sources: environmental changes, population growth, and unequal resource distribution (Homer-Dixon, 1998: 287–90; see also J. Cohen, 1995: 50).

Genetics has affected world trade and agriculture, sometimes to the detriment of indigenous populations. The same indigenous people preserved genetic varieties of plants or lived in harmony with the unexploited genetic varieties of plants and animals that only now have become valuable in a strict market term. One of the perils of free trade for undeveloped countries is the new genetic marketplace. The future market for corn displays some of these dynamics as corn varieties diminish under the onslaught of genetically enhanced Western seed production (H. Daly, 1998: 191). Perhaps too late, questions of the ownership and benefits of genetic materials have been raised on behalf of poor communities, where many of the varieties of plants and animals have not been made extinct. That the indigenous communities should be entitled to returns from the genetic wealth is an emerging issue in genetic politics. As Mahathir Mohamad puts it, "But now we are told that the rich will not agree to compensate the poor for their sacrifices. The rich argue that the diversity of genes stored and safeguarded by the poor are of no value until the rich, through their superior intelligence, release the potential within. It is an intellectual property and must be copy-righted and protected" (1998: 326).

Unmet Needs Taken Out of Context

Often family planning programs, birth control clinics, new reproductive technologies, surrogacy brokers, and such are justified as attempts to satisfy the unmet needs of women (and men) for biological children. However, that justification is taken out of context. The resources expended on these programs and innovations are often disproportionate to any unmet need, considering all the other preconditions for maternal and family health that are not met and not based on the needs of the women as they might see them. Jyotsna Agnihotri Gupta points out how population planners in many developing countries use maternal mortality figures and high abortion rates to justify aggressive and sometimes coercive family planning programs (2000: 590). "Reproductive health programmes," Gupta argues, "should not become top-down targeted programmes of public health investment in which they are narrowed down to meet the 'unmet need' for contraception alone, instead of incorporating all aspects of health delivery" (2000: 591). As Gupta writes, "Different demographic goals of countries apparently call for different population or social policies; in both, women are instrumentalised" (2000: 605; see also Scheper-Hughes and Sargent, 1998).

Feminist Analysis of Modern Reproduction

A feminist approach to analyzing the impact of these changes is very apt because the method incorporates gender, race, class, and sexuality powers into the analysis. Feminist approaches do not subsume the female experience and perspective into the male. As Susan Behuniak explains in her study of abortion and doctor-assisted suicide cases, feminist theory is particularly well suited to her (and my) inquiry because it challenges mainstream legal norms: "The questions that feminists raise concerning the societal division of labor, the privileging of knowledge, and the dynamics of oppression shed light as to why patients' knowledge and concerns for caring are diminished by the Court" (1999: 106–7). Feminist theorists press for the voices of people affected by political decisions and policies to be heard and integrated into decision making. For instance, the feminist theorist Iris Marion Young argues in her study of American welfare reform debates in the U.S. Congress from 1993 to 1996 that the requirements of democratic ethics were violated when poor, single mothers were not heard from throughout the entire deliberation (1999: 103–14). In previous studies, Kathryn Bryant and I found that the stories, voices, experiences, and contexts for girls and women involved in relinquishing children for adoption or deciding whether to have an abortion or continue a pregnancy are rarely included in media accounts of these issues (Woliver and Bryant, 1997a and 1997b). Similarly, in reproductive politics, the women profoundly affected by the developments in science, politics, and law are often not heard.

Feminist theorists have diverse and nuanced views on the role women's reproductive power has played in history, politics, and culture. They also have varied opinions on the impact new reproductive technologies might have on women's power in society. Rosemarie Tong puts it this way, "[R]adical-libertarian feminists are convinced the less women are involved in the reproductive process, the more time and energy they will have to engage in society's productive processes. In contrast, radical-cultural feminists are convinced the ultimate source of women's power rests in their power to gestate new life. To take this power from a woman is to take away her trump card and to leave her with an empty hand, entirely vulnerable to men's power" (1998: 71–72). Feminists like Shulamith Firestone and Marge Piercy view natural reproduction as the cause of women's oppression and celebrate the unshackling potentials of new reproductive technologies. In contrast, other feminist thinkers argue that natural human reproduction is the source of women's liberation and efforts to medicalize and control reproduction artificially will harm women (Tong, 1998: 72–87).

Women's Struggles for Reproductive Agency

Women's history is replete with our efforts to control our own bodies. The history of birth control, the development of various methods of birth control, and the creation of the field of reproductive science were aimed at making contraception more scientific and thus a more legitimate career field for male researchers. Since women were perceived as the implicated actors, birth control methods were directed exclusively at females. The hope of early feminist birth control movement activists was for simple contraceptives that would enhance women's autonomy. Instead, the field developed toward scientific expertise, medical control, and dissemination of birth control information and devices only through the discretion of predominately male doctors (Clarke, 1998: 200).

The development of birth control from 1925 to 1945 involved, in Adele Clarke's words, a pronounced shift "from commitments to birth control as a means of enhancing reproductive and sexual autonomy for women to contraception within an economic ethic of childbearing—economic planning, eugenics, and population control, often with racialized agendas" (1998: 201). The shift meant that many birth control advocates began to see the wisdom of modern scientific means of contraception that could be "'done to the people'" (Clarke, 1998: 201). The effectiveness of modern scientific birth control could be counted on because instead of relying on women's own motivations and decision making, the methods were biological and under expert medical control. By the mid-1960s, reproductive science had obtained more legitimacy, securing public and foundation grants to address population problems. Reproductive science gained prestige as a discipline within the overarching scientific culture, and women were reduced to the "configured users" (Clarke, 1998: 202). But, as Loretta Ross points out, during the 1960s "African-American women were not blind to the irony of a government plan to make contraceptives free and extremely accessible to Black communities that lacked basic health care" (1998: 177). What was not funded or was underfunded is also telling. Even though Margaret Sanger and others had campaigned for such simple means of contraception as diaphragms and spermicides since 1915, the emphasis was on more scientific endocrinological research on hormonal interventions less dependent on women's own control and discretion. Admonitions to improve women's health in general to effect their reproductive lives made by several organizations, including the American Medical Women's Association and the U.S. Department of Labor's Children's Bureau, also went unheeded (Clarke, 1998: 230). Between 1915 and 1945, the disciplinary structuring of reproduction took shape by recruiting scientists into the birth control arena, with reassurances that it was a new, legitimate scientific discipline. In the end, Clarke observes, "[r]eproductive scientists ultimately captured definitional authority as physicians, eugenicists, and neo-Malthusians conservatized the birth control movement into one for family planning and population control, displacing feminists from key organizational positions" (1998: 262–63).

Shifts within the birth control movement also facilitated this disciplinary structuring of reproduction for laypeople as well as scientists. Lay birth control activists themselves succumbed to the allure of more scientific means of contraception. The birth control movement moved from a commitment to simple means of contraception under individual choice and control to a more social vision of reproduction. The movement focused on qualities of populations and professional medical control over reproduction. Diminished, then, were visions of individual control and the health and well-being of individual women (Clarke, 1998: 263). The history of reproductive science shows a distancing and objectification of the "implicated actors" in human reproduction, especially the women directly affected (Clarke, 1998: 273).

Narratives or stories of women's reproductive experiences are also powerful public rhetorical forms. Breaking the silence and telling the stories of women's reproductive history place legal abortion choice or oppositely fetal rights within ideographs conjuring up emotive public values of the legal, constitutional commitments of a society. Ideographs are characters or symbols that represent ideas, things, or concepts without having to verbalize or expressly pronounce words for it. An example would be the pro–legal abortion ideograph of the metal coat hanger with an "X" marked over it. In abortion politics, battles over proper symbols, phrases, and nomenclature have been central. In American pro–legal abortion efforts, for instance, the larger, more inclusive ideograph "Reproductive Freedom" for women was not utilized as often as the more particular ideographic justification and slogan "Right to Choose." Given the delicacy, denial, and criminality surrounding women's abortion experiences during the illegal period, the first breaks in the silences were from women narrating their stories. When repeated frequently, narratives can take on aspects of myths. Celeste Condit notes evocative narratives of the back-alley abortion as examples of these rhetorical powers (1990: 13–14). As these narratives were told and retold, they established enough familiarity in the public that "back-alley abortions," "the coat hanger," and the "illegal abortionist" became ideographs that worked and altered the political discourse about abortion. More recently, I have noticed the narratives of "partial-birth abortions" where "babies are killed within seconds of their births" have similar force.

Reproductive policy-making interacts with feminist and postmodern critiques of objective knowledge and skepticism about the scientific establishment. Women and other people without power have experienced the power of scientific theories aimed at justifying economic and political status quos (Gould, 1981). One of the intellectual contributions of the second-wave women's movement has been the debunking of the mystiques of pure objectivity within the scientific enterprise and exposure of how scientists can easily interpret data through the lenses of preconceived notions, dominant paradigms, and ideologies. A succinct summation of these points might be, in Emmanuele de Lesseps's words, "one can always 'find' what one is looking for; but, above all, the interpretation of data is strongly susceptible to ideological interference" (1981: 83; see also Rose, 1994). Questions concerning women's biology and reproductive power, then, are seen as political and social issues, not just biological, scientific ones.

Often women's reproductive power and biological distinctions from men lead to an essentialist view of women, the old Freudian notion that "biology is destiny." Explication of the social construction of male and female helps expose the often political purposes these constructions hold for human subjects (see, for example, Butler, 1990; Digeser, 1994; Flax, 1990; and Hekman, 1990). The biological differences between men and women are used to create and justify false hierarchies. Cynthia Fuchs Epstein's *Deceptive Distinctions* (1988) reviews social science and educational research where failure to reject the null hypothesis (of no gender difference) means the research will most likely not be published. Preconceived notions about ineluctable gender differences (with males coming out better) mean that research showing no male or female differences is not published as often as those studies that confirm male and female differences (and in the expected male-is-superior direction). Small differences, however, between males and females are published and become part of our cultural lexicon justifying many gender inequalities.

Controversial, Heartfelt, Reproductive Politics

The meaning of human reproduction is socially and culturally constructed. The politics of reproduction is so controversial because it touches some of the most important and heartfelt issues in a social system. "Issues so central to life itself," Adele Clarke points out, "tend to be contested with a stunning extremity" (1998: 20). The history and disciplinary structure of reproductive science display how illegitimate and marginalized reproductive scientists and researchers have been. Sex and reproduction's cultural primacy involve manhood, womanhood, adulthood, kinship—concerns at the heart of social life. Clarke explains that "these are not easy issues, and in modernity anxieties about sexuality, reproduction, and families abound" (1998: 20).

Women's birth power, for instance, can be challenging to males. The history of obstetrics, when seen from the women's point of view, seeks to problematize, pathologize, and then control and rescue reproductive power. Western culture and medical protocols and practices disfigure birth. To develop a language of birth now requires reconfiguring the human body and restoring the intact integrity of the maternal body and its connection to nature (Kahn, 1995: 5). Obstetrics reduces women to their bodies alone, as Robbie Pfeufer Kahn points out: "Not only is her body denied consciousness, but her elemental physical powers are also suppressed. Consciousness *and* physical prowess reside in the doctor who works upon the body of the mother, as if he or she were mining ore from the earth" (1995: 94).[2]

Women's experiences of sexual relations, pregnancy, birth, and motherhood are enormously shaped by the social meanings constructed around them in different cultures, times, and societies. Nancy Hartsock observes that feminists might benefit from utilizing a "historical materialist approach to understanding phallocratic domination" (1998: 105). The epistemological tools such a feminist standpoint theory offers help us understand and resist forms of domination. Feminist standpoint theory seeks, in Hartsock's words, "to show how just as Marx's understanding of the world from the standpoint of the proletariat enabled him to go beneath bourgeois ideology, so a feminist standpoint can allow us to understand patriarchal institutions and ideologies as perverse inversions of more humane social relations" (1998: 107). Feminist standpoint theory uncovers the assumptions of power in the structures of patriarchy over time. Incorporating social class into social theory recognizes that the category of labor interacts with both other humans and the natural world. The standard dichotomy of nature and culture is severed in the Marxian category of labor, for instance. Feminist standpoint theory similarly permits feminist theorists to avoid the false choice of analyzing women's lives as either completely natural or social. As embodied humans, women (and men) are both natural and social, an insight feminist standpoint theory helps us incorporate into our politics (Hartsock, 1998: 106). As Hartsock notes, the nature of a standpoint "is not simply an interested position (interpreted as bias) but is interested in the sense of being engaged" (1998: 107).

Patriarchal power is so embedded in our legal system, language, science, and imaginations that we see our socioeconomic and sexual context as ineluctable fate. "The tragedy is in the fate that is not necessary but which," Drucilla Cornell points out, "at the same time, is imposed so that it appears as fate" (1999a: 199).

Jessica Benjamin contends that the ideal of self-sufficient individuals in our culture is "the chief manifestation of male hegemony, far more pervasive than overtly authoritarian forms of male domination" because it is framed as rational, objective, scientific, mature, and ineluctable (1988: 172). The concept of rationality linked with rampant individualism is, in her words, "the hallmark of modernity—the rationality that reduces the social world to objects of exchange, calculation, and control" and a concept of the male subject (1988: 184). The rational individual, she explains, denies dependency by "an act of abstraction, which denies his real dependency and social subordination. Consequently, his freedom consists of protection from the control or intrusion of others. It is a *negative* ideal of freedom: freedom as release from bondage, individuality stripped bare of its relationship with and need for others" (1988: 187–88). Rational, economic individualism also sees caring as a weakness by linking it to privacy, emotion, and the needy (Tronto, 1993: 117). We imagine ourselves as never needing care in our autonomous lives, so we pity those who do need care (Tronto, 1993: 123). We also devalue the caregivers.

A feminist ethic of care revolves around responsibility and relationships rather than rights and rules; the moral basis is tied to concrete circumstances rather than abstractions; and it is more an activity, a practice, than a set of theorized moral principles (Tronto, 1993: 79). Standard political ethics and rationalizations for an economic utilitarian moral life function to preserve the positions of the powerful (Tronto, 1993: 91). The marginalization of care and caregivers and the ethic of care now provides an ideological advantage to the powerful, as Joan Tronto points out: "By not noticing how pervasive and central care is to human life, those who are in positions of power and privilege can continue to ignore and to degrade the activities of care and those who give care. To call attention to care is to raise questions about the adequacy of care in our society. Such an inquiry will lead to a profound rethinking of moral and political life" (1993: 111). If care and dependency work were placed near the center of human life, instead of in the peripheral and silenced domain it now is in, the world would look very different (Tronto, 1993: 101). Instead of ratio-nalizing inattentiveness to the needs of others as a moral and rational choice, for example, we would see it as a moral evil (Tronto, 1993: 127–28).

Today, motherhood and nurturing are shaped by separate ideological worlds, one for mothers distinct from the social world, thereby making, in Sharon Hays's words, "women responsible for unselfish nurturing while men are responsible for self-interested profit maximization" (1996: 175). As Benjamin notes, questioning this polarity "challenges the repu-diation of femininity, and the equation of masculinity with humanity—and so it challenges men's right to make the world in their own image" (1988: 172).

Including women's voices within the shifting terrains of the new human reproduction is central to evaluating the ethics, politics, and jus-tice of these developments. Abstracting away human dependency and nurturing work, to borrow Hays's words, "tends to absolve the public world from responsibility for the values of unselfish care, commitment to the good of others, and willingness to carry out such obligations with-out direct or material remuneration" (1996: 175). The nurturing, self-sacrificing roles for women help ensure many male privileges. However, breaking those silences is fraught with difficulties, as this book will re-veal.

Additional Voices and Experiences

Raising critiques, questions, and cautions about new reproductive technologies, the uses to which genetic maps might be put, and related issues often results in ad hominem attacks on the messenger. Jeremy Rifkin, a well-known skeptic of some modern medical practices and re-search by the scientific establishment, summarizes some of his experi-ences: "Critics, myself included, have been attacked over and over again as Luddites, vitalists, fearmongers, and fundamentalists for broaching concerns over where the new science is heading, the implication being that any questioning of the 'conventional wisdom' is heresy or, even worse, lunacy" (1998: xi–xii). Pointing out that birth is not an illness and that women should have agency and control over their pregnancies and childbirths can make even the most mainstream and respectable public health professional an outcast dissident (Wagner, 1997).

One of the earliest actions for many second-wave American feminists involved reproductive politics. In 1969, several brave women disrupted hearings convened by Senator Gaylord Nelsen (a Democrat from Wisconsin) on the birth control pill. Their demands to be heard in that all-male enclave were, in the words of Alice Wolfson, "born out of a pure and burning anger over the lack of control women had over their bodies and their lives" (1998: 268). The Nelsen hearings have been characterized as "one of the most important feminist actions since the riots for the vote fifty years earlier" (L. Grant, 1994: 183). Feminist questioning of the male experts at the Nelsen hearings was a precursor to the emerging women's health movement, with such publications as *Our Bodies, Ourselves* teaching women about their bodies to make them more informed and empowered health care consumers (L. Grant, 1994: 183–92; see also Rose, 1994: 72).

Policy-making on reproductive politics, like all politics, is shaped within social systems noted for their lack of participation by women and failure to take the needs of women seriously. In the United States, for instance, there is a notable gender gap in political participation, which partly derives from persistent disparities between men and women in education, employment, and social status (Schlozman, Burns, and Verba, 1999). There is also the steady and powerful voice of neoconservatives and conservative Christian activists, with their tireless and growing opposition to legal abortion and lukewarm, at best, attitudes toward the women's movement (Wilcox, DeBell, and Sigelman, 1999). Indeed, issues of women's control of their reproductive lives is the crux of many political skirmishes over women's rights. As Linda Gordon observed, "The major reason for the heightened passion about reproductive issues is precisely that they seemed to express the core aims of the women's liberation movement, and for this reason became the major focus of the backlash against feminism" (1976: 29).

In addition, since abortion decisions and policy-making on new reproductive technologies involve the expert testimony of medical doctors, the voices of patients are muted. Susan Behuniak found that experts' knowledge (scientific, medical, and therefore objective) is empowered in U.S. court cases involving abortion and physician-assisted suicide, whereas patients' knowledge is discounted as hearsay, subjective, emotional, particularized, and personal. Biomedical cases in particular disregard patients' narratives and voices while validating physicians' stories. What courts regard as knowledge advantages medical experts and scientific method based on objective observations, statistical probability, hypothesis testing, and definitive (not ambiguous) results. Patients' knowledge, in contrast, does not fit the evidence template since it is characterized as particularistic, personal, experiential, biased, and nonprofessional (Behuniak, 1999: ix–x). I would add that patient stories often contain ambiguity instead of the requirement that the situation be either good or bad, one or the other, not both. Patients can feel ambiguous about physician-assisted suicide or abortion yet still want the courts to incorporate their stories. The ambiguity might be a natural standpoint in the situation, not an indication of lack of knowledge or ignorance on the part of the patients. Courts, however, pigeonhole the ambiguity of patients' narratives and favor the decisive, definitive findings of experts.

The preference for medical knowledge over patients' knowledge in court decisions results in an uncaring jurisprudence. As Behuniak observes, "The patient wants to add his or her story to the medical and legal records and urges the doctors and lawyers to 'Listen to what I know.' But it's hard for patients to be heard. Discredited for lacking objectivity, disregarded as having little reliable knowledge, and dismissed for lack of a disciplined method of study, patients struggle for recognition of their knowledge" (1999: 19). The consequences include shifting the courts' understanding of what constituency is at the center of the cases; skewing legal understanding of cases by leaving out the knowledge of patients; and pulling courts away from their own standards of justice (Behuniak, 1999: x–xi). Medicine, however, slips into the expertise aura of science even though, technically, medicine is an *"applied* science" (Behuniak, 1999: 3).

Marjorie Pryse contends that multidisciplinary, trans/feminist methods "for research and creative practice must attend above all to what the 'described and imagined' have to say to the 'describers and the imaginers'" (2000: 116). The approach pays homage to the "situated knowledge" of different groups in shifting positions of simultaneously expressed manifestations of race, gender, class, and sexuality (P. Collins, 1991: 129; see also Weber, 2000). The situated knowledge of people incorporates the context of their lives into their reproductive decision making. We can see, then, how these reproductive powers appear from the point of view of women. Yet, we also must be aware of the need to "get specific" about the differences within women (Phelan, 1994).

The rhetoric and public discourses surrounding reproductive politics have changed. Missing topics in reproductive discourse (such as birth-mothers in adoption stories or the women and girls choosing abortion in news articles about abortion politics) are just as telling as dominant frames, symbols, tropes, metaphors, and slogans. In a study of abortion rhetoric, Celeste Condit explains, "Charting the changes in the units of discourse that appear in a controversy across time and relating these changes to the general and specific forces of rhetoric can produce better explanations of the processes that operate to bring about the particular forms that social changes take" (1990: 11).

In an imperfect world, where economic and sexual oppression and exploitation of women leave many with few choices in life, figuring out what to do about marketing women's reproductive abilities through surrogacy, the selling of eggs, or other iterations creates a "double bind." If society permits the buying and selling of sex and reproduction, it threatens the personhood of women because women are the embodied owners of the desired commodities. Yet if society prohibits the buying and selling of sex and reproduction, women are denied the choice of engaging in these market exchanges. Given the oppressive circumstances in which women live worldwide, figuring out a fair system to deal with the reproductive marketplace has the potential of harming women instead of aiding them. Margaret Radin puts it in these terms: "For a group subject to structures of domination, all roads thought to be progressive can pack a backlash" (1990: 1701). The central importance of reproductive politics to women's rights and prospects is based on the fact that women embody human reproduction. Since only one-half of humans can directly experience menstruation, pregnancy, birth, and lactation, commodification of sex and reproduction is a central feminist issue because it incorporates "the instantiation of the perspective of female embodiment" (Radin, 1990: 1704).

Our social choices of where money, personnel, and research energy will be spent are also relevant here. Abby Lippman explains that "if healthy children really matter to us, their mothers must matter first. The well-being of children and the well-being of women are inseparable. Social, political, and economic neglect of women interferes with the physical and mental development of their children more than does the genetic variation they inherit" (1994a: 20). The surgeon general of the United States reports that battering by husbands, boyfriends, or ex-husbands is the single largest cause of injury to women and accounts for one-fifth of all emergency room cases. Some scholars estimate that one-half of all married women will be beaten at least once by their spouses (Zorza, 1992: 46–47). Historically, males have received more attention in medical research, funding decisions, and even selection as research subjects. This is doubly ironic and inequitable because women spend more money on health care than men do. Yet, in a culture that only recently tried to address the funding inequities for such female-dominant maladies as breast cancer, arthritis, and lupus, funding for new reproductive technologies and mapping the human genome is generous. The genetic focus also diminishes research efforts, social reform pressures, and community health foci to decrease environmental carcinogens and race, class, and age inequalities in access to health care (Eisenstein, 2001). It is understandable, then, if some scholars are skeptical that the motivations for these new innovations are the health and benefit of women and children.

Machines that permit visualization of the fetus internal to the mother are being used in our culture to sell Volvo automobiles and other products. In addition to the increased bonding these ultrasound pictures are supposed to provide for the pregnant woman, the marketing use of the images in our culture expands the supposed "bonding" effect of ultrasound "from the pregnant woman to the entire American public" (Taylor, 1998: 38).

Defiant Women

Women, however, are not simply passive subjects of medicalization, geneticization, and the enterprising up of reproduction. Feminist scholars and women through their personal behaviors are challenging the medicalization of pregnancy and birth. Disobedient women in doctors offices, often described as "noncompliant" and "difficult," are asserting their agency over reproduction when they refuse tests, question procedures and medical protocols, and try to shape their own reproductive and health experiences. Some women who "neglect" prenatal medical treatments (often poor teens, minorities, and immigrants) might also be making a political statement. From fieldwork with women in West Africa, Maria De Koninck observes, "The accounts all agree on one point: health personnel tend to be critical when women do not abide by their instructions, so women avoid consulting in order not to be blamed. I would add, they resist to protect their dignity" (1998: 170). A recent seven-country study of women's reproductive decision making found that "typically respondents became discouraged and alienated by insensitive, often abusive treatment and gave up on medical services rather than exposing themselves to such abuse" (Petchesky, 1998a: 315). Health providers' callous attitudes, often derived from class, race/ethnic, or gender biases, became barriers to access to health care. In Nigeria, Egypt, the Philippines, and rural Malaysia, for instance, women did not challenge callous health care providers but instead "[voted] with their feet": "refusing to go back to the clinic or hospital even if this jeopardizes their own health" (Petchesky, 1998a: 315). Use of alternative medicine, herbs, vitamins, and such might also be a political statement about disentangling oneself from the Western modern health care industry and asserting one's own agency.

The Plan of the Book

The next chapter discusses the impact of new reproductive technologies on women's experiences of pregnancy and birth. Chapter 3 examines the mega project to map the human genome and how, when combined with the new reproductive technologies now available, the genome maps might be used politically. The impact genetic information has on families, particularly on women, is also explored.

Abortion politics, central to new reproductive technologies, genetic screening, the state's interest in women's bodies, and much more is the topic of chapter 4. One section of the chapter examines how national abortion politics is played out in South Carolina within modern culture wars. The analysis covers various interest groups' framing of these reproductive arrangements, innovations, and practices. The ebbs and flows of abortion politics, for instance, draw in and exclude various groups that constitute shifting coalitions of interests at national and state levels in abortion jurisprudence and policy-making. The role of the American Medical Association, for example, is illustrative and developed in the chapter.

The history, laws, practices, and dynamics of adoption and surrogacy policies and politics are the topics of chapter 5. Continuing some of the discussion from chapter 4 on abortion politics, chapter 5 discusses how class, race, and gender in adoption and surrogacy practices shape the experiences of those involved. Glib statements from anti-abortion activists, such as "Adoption, Not Abortion," are constructed on the silencing and denial of the history, experiences, and lives of birthmothers and many adoptees. Research documenting how modern adoption laws seek to re-create a male-headed family is included. The ethics, practices, and controversies raised by surrogacy contracts are also incorporated in chapter 5. The chapter utilizes a woman-centered vision of pregnancy, birth, adoption, and abortion to discuss the race, class, and gender power evident in many adoption and surrogacy arrangements.

The policing of pregnant women by the state and the important *Whitner* (1997) and *Ferguson* (2001) decisions that deal with applying child abuse laws to women who use illegal drugs while pregnant are interwoven into the previous themes of adoption, abortion, reproductive technologies, and state powers in chapter 6. The pros and cons of this punitive monitoring of pregnant women while programs to help them are cut or not available are explored.

Finally, the conclusion utilizes a woman-centered view of "the language of birth" (Kahn, 1995), feminist theory, the ethic of care, new scholarship on dependency, community, and commitment in human nurturing to discuss how to evaluate the new and shifting geographies of reproductive power. I advocate a feminist standpoint predicated on the need to display the enhancement of human flourishing when human genome maps are used, when medical procedures become the standard of care, and when laws on adoption and abortion are revised and implemented. The feminist theories used stress the constant work and monitoring these visions of future justice require.

The title of my book attempts to draw our attention back to where pregnancy takes place: within women's bodies. We can discuss women's bodies as geographical spaces observed, mapped, dissected, and researched by others. Laws, policies, and medical practices, however, layer state political control over women's reproductive power. Herein lies a power shift in the geographies of pregnancy, with decision making concerning reproduction moving toward professionals, policymakers, genetic counselors, and others and away from women as agents of their bodies, themselves. The maps and boundaries of women's reproductive powers are being redrawn.

Notes

1. Kahn continues, "Freud thinks that a baby is a penis to a woman, but, on the contrary, a baby can stand for exactly the opposite. A baby may show a woman—in doubt of the worth of her body compared to a man's—that her body is complete already" (1995: 42).

2. Performing cesarean sections, for example, is akin to doctors' mining ore from the earth. Kahn repeats this powerful image later in her study: "The manipulation of childbirth, which is the customary practice today in medicine, is an attempt to 'act upon' nature, which is the woman's body. Medical representations of the birth process—and this is where representations are so important—now conceptualize childbirth by saying, as one of my obstetricians did, 'There is no such thing as a normal labor and delivery'; when nature has no norms, they need to be imposed. So physicians act upon women and deliver them of babies in the same way that people extract coal, say, from the earth" (1995: 127).

2 New Reproductive Technologies: Medicalizations of Pregnancy, Birth, Reproduction, and Infertility

A fashion photographer, hoping to cash in on would-be parents' wishes for a beautiful baby, is offering the eggs of eight models in an online auction set to start Monday. ... The Web site, <www.ronsangels.com>, has pictures of eight models offering their eggs for sale.

—*The State,* October 24, 1999

Genetics isn't just a science. It's becoming more than that. It's a way of thinking, an ideology. We're coming to see life through a "prism of heritability," a "discourse of gene action," a genetics frame.

—Barbara Katz Rothman, *Genetic Maps and Human Imaginations*

New reproductive technologies are a modern "mixed blessing." While they enhance choices for a few people, they might restrict options for most women and constrain women's bodily autonomy. History has taught us that control of women's bodies is often sold as being good for women. Behind seemingly benign, neutral, and objective scientific practices and research are often subtle systems of power. Murray Edelman (1977), for instance, reveals the way phrases implying progress, therapy, and empathy toward patients by mental health professionals disguise and justify systems of control and dominance. Similarly, modern feminists view medical and legal power in reproduction skeptically.

These technologies bring a new series of policy issues to courts and legislatures as they address how to incorporate new reproductive arrangements into our legal system (Harris and Holm, 1998). "Ethics has a kind of desperate post-hoc character these days," Jean Elshtain writes. "First, certain techniques are perfected or modeled; then, we consult professional ethicists to advise us on whether we ought to be doing what we are, in fact, already doing" (1989: 19).

Woven within efforts to develop such reproductive technologies as an artificial womb is a distrust of women and their bodily powers to reproduce humans without these technological devices and enterprises. Jeremy Rifkin notes that at least one prominent medical ethicist believes women's wombs are hostile, dark, dangerous environments where future children could not be adequately watched and monitored for their own safety (1998: 30; see also Corea, 1985b: 252; and Rowland, 1987: 524). I am reminded here of the bumper sticker against legal abortion that claims, "The most dangerous place in America is inside a womb." Ann Oakley found from her study of the history of the medical treatment of pregnant women in Britain that "if one single message emerged, it was that pregnant women were themselves deficient: they lacked the necessary intelligence, foresight, education or responsibility to see that the only proper pathway to successful motherhood was the one repeatedly surveyed by medical expertise" (1984: 72). Within this context, such new reproductive technologies as ultrasound seem revolutionary because, in Oakley's words, "for the first time, they enable obstetricians to dispense with mothers as intermediaries, as necessary informants on fetal status and life-style" (1984: 155). Dystopian visions, such as Huxley's *Brave New World*, decouple women from producing babies in order to enhance state power and control. Today ultrasound is like "a window on the womb," a long desired goal for the professional providers of maternity care (Oakley, 1984: 156). Research is progressing on artificial wombs (ectogenesis). Justifications for the new technologies often assume a male-standardized measure of what freedom and equality would be. For example, in discussing artificial wombs, John Robertson speculates, "A more revolutionary, though far distant, development would be the complete extracorporeal gestation of human beings. Perhaps ectogenesis is necessary to cut the female tie with childbearing, and thus provide full, substantive equality with men" (1986: 1032). The standard that women should aspire to, this viewpoint reveals, is male. "There is a pattern in Western culture," Robbie Pfeufer Kahn notices, "of trying to improve upon women by making them into men" (1995: 188). For many women, however, their experiences of pregnancy, birth, lactation, and nurturing, even in this imperfect world, are already invaluable and irreplaceable.

The new reproductive technologies are marketed as gifts to women because they appear to give infertile women the ability to reproduce. However, as Janice Raymond points out, "when women look this 'gift horse' in the mouth, they will see that it comes accompanied by the persistent *medicalization* of women's lives. This means that more and more areas of female living have been colonized by medical intervention, and staked out as medical territory" (1987: 12). The unwillingness of some scientists to consider the social implications of their work has allowed them to expand research in these areas without community debate.[1] However, the argument that they are addressing the needs of women looks less altruistic as efforts to generate profits intensify (Rowland, 1987: 518).

Researchers have noticed that many women going through ultrasound are excited to see their fetus, relieved to learn it appears normal, and lovingly affectionate toward their future baby. "Ultrasound must, therefore," Oakley writes, "take its place in a long line of other well-used strategies for educating women to be good mothers. . . . Antenatal care has finally discovered mother love. Along with postnatal bonding, prenatal bonding will now in the future be added to the repertoire of reproductive activities named and controlled by obstetricians" (1984: 185; see also B. Rothman, 1986: 78–85; and Martin, 1987: 145–48).

Standards of Care

Expanding indicators for these new technologies mean they are increasingly becoming part of women's experiences of motherhood. Where once they were used for emergencies and special cases, now many of them (ultrasound and fetal monitors, for example) are used routinely. Expanding indicators is partially fueled by the need to spread the costs of expensive equipment by using them on more patients. Health professionals' concern about protecting themselves from malpractice suits also pressures them to practice "defensive medicine" and use new tests and equipment on increasing numbers of patients. The tests and equipment become, then, the new standard of care.

Fetal monitors, for example, were invented for use in high-risk pregnancies where there is a real potential for fetal distress and damage. Now they are used routinely in many hospitals. High cesarean rates, the expanded use of ultrasound, and the lower age at which pregnant women are advised to have amniocentesis are further examples. I wonder what real choices women will have in a future filled with these technologies. As Judith Lasker and Susan Borg point out, "A woman does not have a free choice to use a technology if a physician tells her that it is for the good of her baby and she would be irresponsible not to use it. It will not be a choice whether or not to have our embryos or fetuses checked for abnormalities if society condemns women as irresponsible if they give birth to handicapped children" (1987: 188–89). Arguments might be presented by medical personnel that it is irresponsible or unethical for high-risk women (maybe even all women) to refuse prenatal diagnosis. Gena Corea presented an even more ominous possibility: "Arguing that it may have to pay for facilities or treatment for a physically or mentally disabled child, the state could maintain that it has an overwhelming interest in the matter" (1985a: 93). Jessie Bernard noted many years ago that although modern medicine makes giving birth safer now than in the past, new technologies also make it harder emotionally. If fate gave you a child with a disability, there was little guilt. Modern technologies give mothers choices so that the act of fate or nature is now an act of the mother's own choosing. Mothers are then faced with harrowing decisions (Bernard, 1974: 248).

Barbara Rothman, in her study of the effects of amniocentesis, genetic counseling, and selective abortion on women's experience of pregnancy, explains, as Bernard foreshadowed, that women are often placed in a quandary by these technologies. Women are not selfishly aborting fetuses it would be inconvenient or difficult to raise. Rather, the women "are the victims of a social system that fails to take collective responsibility for the needs of its members, and leaves individual women to make impossible choices. We are spared collective responsibility, because we individualize the problem" (B. Rothman, 1986: 189). Whatever the mother's choice is, we as a society are absolved of collective responsibility to better the lives of different children.

In these and many other ways, the naturalness of pregnancy and childbirth has been transformed into an illness, an unnatural condition, with an assumption of risk to fetal and maternal health that only the medical profession can rectify and control. Shifting control from the pregnant woman to doctors and other medical professionals brings with it increased power of "experts" at the expense of women. Experts define social issues in the arcane language of their professions, limiting the terms of debate and popular involvement. Issue control is maintained, then, by the experts when it is defined as technical or professional and should be left up to the professionals (Elder and Cobb, 1983: 130).

Eventually, it is feared, the definition of a "good mother" will include only women whose pregnancies and births are managed by the medical establishment using these technologies. At the same time, an "abusive" mother might include one who refuses to utilize the available technologies. In 1979, the president of the American College of Obstetricians and Gynecologists, for example, referred to home births as "the earliest form of child abuse" (quoted in Oakley, 1984: 219). There have already been cases where mothers have been reprimanded for staying away from doctors' prenatal care, having home births, and refusing caesarean sections.

Another impetus for expanding indicators for new reproductive technologies is the reluctance of doctors to listen and attach credibility to women's knowledge of their own bodies. Rather than accept women's information about their last menstruation date or their knowledge of when they might have become pregnant, doctors turn to an impersonal machine, conduct an ultrasound, and then present the woman with her due date as if it were information only a doctor and machines could determine.

New reproductive technologies illustrate such a power shift as they portend the high-tech management of all aspects of female reproduction (Goslinga-Roy, 2000; Taylor, 2000; Beaulieu and Lippman, 1995; Rapp, 1994a; St. Peter, 1989). The danger might be that reproductive technologies become more than treatments for infertility. According to some, "It is actually providing 'wombs with a view,' opening the door for advancement of genetic engineering as well as becoming a form of social control" (Solomon, 1988: 45).

Peripheral Women

Increased medicalization of pregnancy pushes the women involved to the periphery. Marginalization of the women involved in these reproductive technologies is clear in the language used to describe them. Women are discussed in the new reproductive literature by bodily parts: "maternal environment" replaces "women" or "women's wombs"; a pregnant woman becomes "an embryo carrier" (see, for example, Klein, 1987: 66). Surrogate mothers are likened to reproductive machines and are described as inanimate objects: "rented wombs," "incubators," "receptacles," "a kind of hatchery," "gestators," "a uterine hostess," or a "surrogate uterus" (Corea, 1985b: 222; Ince, 1984; Hollinger, 1985: 901, 903; Burfoot, 1988: 108, 110; and Laborie, 1987).

In vitro fertilization is sometimes described without once indicating that a human woman is involved. No woman, for example, is mentioned in the following overview of the 1978 birth of Louise Brown, the first "test-tube" baby: "After many years of frustrating research, Drs. Edwards and Steptoe had succeeded in removing an egg from an ovarian follicle, fertilizing it in a dish, and transferring the developing zygote to a uterus where it implanted and was brought to term" (Robertson, 1986: 943). The women involved are erased. It is important to recall that "test-tube" babies are born from women who carry them during pregnancy. The preparations, hormonal injections, and medical procedures they undergo are emotionally and physically arduous. In addition, these women are sometimes experimented on without their full consent, or they participate based on misleading information concerning the probability of actually having a baby (Carp, 1998; Corea, 1985b: 112–17, 166–85; Lasker and Borg, 1987: 53–55; Corea and Ince, 1987). Many are vulnerable to any hope presented that they can have a baby (Carp, 1998).

Prenatal Screening

Aborting a wanted fetus because of its disability is a traumatic "choice" for women. These decisions are partially based on expectant mothers' concerns about inadequate social services society provides the disabled and how hard life would be for the child in such a society (Rapp, 1984). Implicit in the discussion of aborting defective embryos is disparagement of handicapped people (Fitzgerald, 1998; C. Wang, 1992 and 1998; Finger, 1984; Saxton, 1984). Often, though, the emotional traumas of prenatal screening for the women involved are overlooked by the medical profession. Wendy Farrant argues, based on her study of British health practices, that the expansion of prenatal screening "was stimulated less by consumer demand than by initiatives from government, from interested sectors of the medical profession, and from the medical supply industry" (1985: 99). The government wanted to save money by reducing handicapped births. Obstetricians and geneticists wanted to increase their professional prestige, varieties of intervention, and control (and thus business) in pregnancies, and the medical supply business wanted increased profits (Farrant, 1985: 99–103). The medical supply industry, for example, found the market for ultrasound equipment to be "among the fastest growing medical instrumentation markets of all time" (Association for Improvements in the Maternity Services, quoted in Farrant, 1985: 102). In addition, counseling and information are severely inadequate for poor and minority women.

My experiences in the ELSI Women and Genetics in Contemporary Society Conference taught me to listen and incorporate the voices of people with disabilities into any analysis of reproductive politics. How do they feel about living their lives? What would they see as beneficial to people like them? How could their families be assisted? What social supports do the people (mostly women) who nurture them have available?

Particularly moving to me were the insights offered at the conference by representatives from Little People of America (sometimes they are called "dwarfs").[2] They are already seeing the results of new reproductive technologies and selective abortions. Fewer little people are being born in the West. Absorbing the knowledge that the majority culture believes and acts on the demand that people like you should not even be born is very difficult. At the Women and Genetics in Contemporary Society Conference, representatives from Little People of America also spoke of how they can feel the changes in acceptance, political power, treatments, and social programs as their numbers dwindle. Incredibly, as I will discuss further, scholarship is published about people with disabilities and the use of new reproductive technologies and genetic screening without including their perspectives or experiences at all.

"Increasingly, it is the contents of the container that matter, not the container herself," writes Corea. "Accordingly, obstetricians are coming to view themselves as 'physician to the fetus'" (1985b: 299). In much obstetric literature, babies are considered products, and the emphasis resembles quality control (Corea, 1985b: 17; Martin, 1987). However, contradictory results from prenatal screening and other reproductive technologies occur, and "for many women, particularly low risk women, prenatal screening has become yet another way in which medical care detracts from the possibility of pregnancy being experienced as a normal and enjoyable event," Farrant contends (1985: 117).

One consequence of prenatal testing is emphasis on technological fixes to prevent the birth of handicapped fetuses rather than attention to the social and political causes of some birth defects (such as inadequate nutrition, drug [legal and illegal] and alcohol abuse, domestic violence, environmental toxins, and unsafe working conditions). The technologies leave intact, though, the burden of women's responsibility if anything goes wrong and women's duty to nurse and nurture differently abled children with few handicapped programs to help them. In addition, focusing on a mother's behavior during pregnancy deflects attention from the social and economic conditions that structure women's choices (Woliver, 1989a). Given the prevalence of poverty, ill-health, and domestic violence women experience, deflections from larger social issues will not improve the health of children. State hypocrisy is manifest when, as Kelly E. Maier puts it, "[t]he true lack of concern for the welfare of children is evident in the social policies that determine the social conditions under which the poor must live" (1989: 17).

Rather than address these social conditions, the state might find it easier to prosecute pregnant women (especially poor and minority women) who harm their fetuses. This is an important social issue discussed further in chapter 6. To cite another example, genetic screening for abortion (for "defects," including being the "wrong" gender, in other words, female) has disturbing eugenic possibilities (see, for example, Elshtain, 1989; and Blank, 1981).

Concern over the changing experiences of pregnancy and childbirth caused by new reproductive technologies goes against the grain of the dominant image in the media of exciting, miraculous, beneficial scientific progress (St. Peter, 1989). Doubts about these new technologies also go against strong currents in our culture in favor of technological fixes instead of primary and preventive care. Our acceptance of medical technologies is also fed by our desire for control and reduction of uncertainty. "The result, unfortunately," Robert Blank observes, "has been an unrealistic dependence on technology to fix our health problems at the exclusion of nontechnological solutions" (1988: 4–5).

Given the general tendency to follow the doctor's advice, women might be pushed into prenatal diagnosis. Poor and minority women might face a heightened potential for misuse of these technologies since they generally receive less information from health professionals about procedures and more insensitive treatment by doctors (Cool, 1999; Fisher, 1986; Martin, 1987). Studies of the United States find that minority and poor women receive less quality health care, are subject to more intrusive medical procedures, and have limited "choice" to use expensive reproductive technologies (Nsiah-Jefferson, 1989; Martin, 1987; A. Davis, 1990: 53–65).

One observer predicts, "The failure of a woman to consent to fetal therapy is likely to lead to state intervention, primarily through court action" (Blank, 1988: 147). Mothers' concerns about the health of their fetus and the medical industry's emphasis on controlling pregnancy and birth, profit motives, and the desire to avoid malpractice and assist in the birth of healthy children all combine to channel women's choices toward the use of medical technologies (Cannold, 2000: 82–86; Birenbaum-Carmeli, 1998; E. Roberts, 1998; Rose, 1994: 49, 175; Hubbard, 1984; Farrant, 1985; B. Rothman, 1986; Rowland, 1987).

International "Choices"

Reproductive technologies used for contraception, sex selective abortions, and coerced sterilizations violate the rights, dignity, and indigenous cultures of poor women the world over while failing to address the underlying poverty and inequalities in their societies (Woliver and Tangney,

pushing back the gestational age when fetuses might be viable outside the womb (Blank, 1984a and 1988: 64–65). The result is to pit the woman's rights against those of her fetus. "When maternal actions are judged detrimental to the health or life of the potential child," Blank found, "the court has shown little hesitancy to constrain the liberty of the mother" (1984b: 150). In reality only a very small number of women and babies have access to these neonatal technologies, but the experience of a privileged few is generalized into the whole abortion debate. In addition to the attack by conservatives and anti-abortion activists on abortion choice (see the descriptions by Cohan, 1986; Condit, 1990; Ginsburg, 1989; Glendon, 1987; Luker, 1984; Himmelstein, 1990: 89–90; and Steiner, 1983, to name a few), feminists now must respond to the pressure the new technologies put on abortion politics.

Cultural Shifts

New reproductive technologies have been used to bolster conservatives' notions of what a family should be, reinforcing traditional family and kinship patterns. For instance, Adele Clarke points out that "conceptive technologies are often made inaccessible to homosexuals, inserting homophobia where it had not dwelt" (Clarke, 1998: 20; see also Shanley, 1999).

The new reproductive technologies, while marketed as offering choices to women, can also close off choices. Prenatal diagnosis presents the option of preventing the birth of children with disabilities. Women accept prenatal screening from a generalized willingness to do everything possible to ensure a healthy pregnancy rather than from a specific intention to avoid the birth of a baby with a disability (N. Press et al., 1998: 58). But at the moment that families are told from a "positive" amniocentesis test that their fetuses have a disability, their informed consent to terminating or continuing the pregnancy is limited by societal attitudes and prejudices about the disabled. We therefore need to reexamine these attitudes so that informed consent will include the social realities, not just the medical diagnosis of rearing a child with a particular condition (Rapp, 1994a: 215). The information parents receive should include the perspectives of people living now with those conditions. Today, with the ubiquity of new reproductive technologies of prenatal testing, "the routine offer of prenatal diagnostic screening implies that women *should* consider the possibility of disability for the fetus they are carrying" (N. Press et al., 1998: 63). Selective abortion is the clearly implied expectation for fetuses diagnosed with many types of disabilities.

In addition, patients having difficulties conceiving feel that they must try all the technologies, procedures, and options before they "give up." Infertility clinics perform rigorous and repeated invasions of women's bodies and hyperstimulate their hormones. These procedures, combined with a sales talk of perseverance by the clinic owners, have been much criticized, especially given the low success rates many clinics have. But it is so hard for patients to give up, partly because, in Charis Cussins's words, the "lack of alternative operationalizations and an epistemic culture based on statistics" contribute to a "culture of perseverance" in infertility clinics (1998: 75). Statistical probabilities discussed with patients exacerbate their dilemmas, according to Cussins: "Projections based on statistics license doing the same thing again in the face of failure. This is a distinctive epistemic element of treatment cultures based on statistics. In practice, it is an extremely difficult epistemic standard to live with because it disregards mechanism. If the very same thing only works one in five times, then there is no positive answer to the question of the cause and effect of the infertility. This epistemic difficulty is managed on a daily basis so that it doesn't interfere with practice" (1998: 76). These structures and decisions leave infertile patients with no choice. As Sarah Franklin found in her study of patients in an infertility clinic, "all the women interviewed for this study described not having any choice—they 'had to try' IVF [in vitro fertilization]" (1998: 107).

Paradoxically, the new technologies take choices away when people feel they cannot peacefully accept their infertility. Instead, infertility is described to patients as a tentative condition. The technological options create forced choices. Patients must now deliberately pursue or refuse the choices (Franklin, 1998: 108). They might wonder whether their infertility could have been gotten around if only they had tried every combination of treatments over and over again. "In contrast to the extensive media depiction of women choosing IVF because they are 'desperate' for a child," Franklin reports, "this study found that women were in fact often already resigned to the likelihood of not having children *before* undergoing IVF. Indeed, it was often this ability to live with the prospect of remaining childless that enabled women to undertake IVF, as they felt more protected from emotional overinvestment" (1998: 112). The ethnographic interviews one scholar did with infertile women revealed that the availability of IVF treatments produced a greater desire for children. It is misleading to justify IVF and other procedures as responding to the desperation of infertile women. Undergoing IVF treatments for many women does not even bring about peace of mind. Instead, over the course of treatment, a couple's involvement in the world of achieved conception grows, and the couple becomes more committed to trying anything new (Franklin, 1998: 112–13).

These technologies change the lives of the infertile. Trying all the available technologies might seem required before a person is allowed "to give up" and be eligible for adoption. Already researchers are finding evidence of this. Christine Gailey recently reported, "Infertility treatment, presented in the media as a benefit, was experienced by at least some of the adopters as an expectation, and by one as a punitive demand: 'They [the agency] wouldn't consider us for adoption unless we'd been through the gamut of treatments'" (2000: 43; see also G. Becker, 2000). The cost of infertility treatments also means that people with less money will be left out of these possible ways to become parents. Implicit in the experiences of infertile people who went through extensive infertility treatments is an expectation that white, middle-class, insured professionals should try these technologies in order to have their "own" children (G. Becker, 2000: 19–21). Sadly enough, because of the high cost of adoptions today, people who use up their financial resources first on futile infertility treatments might then find adopting beyond their financial means (G. Becker, 2000: 246).

Conclusion: Diminishing Pressures for Social Reforms

The modern women's movement includes a women's health component, disenchanted with many medical practices and seeking to empower women to be better informed and more assertive consumers of health care (see, for example, M. Edwards and Waldorf, 1984; Boston Women's Health Book Collective, 1971 and 1984; and Gardner, 1981). The potential power of the women's health movement to critique and change the medicalization of pregnancy and birth, though, has been partially co-opted by the doctors and clinics themselves. For example, exercise, nutrition, natural childbirth, and similar classes organized and staffed by community women have slowly been absorbed by the birthing centers of hospitals and outpatient services of large ob-gyn clinics. The original classes were alternatives to, if not in opposition to, the traditional doctor's institutionalized treatment of pregnancy and childbirth. Goals included encouraging mothers to keep healthy, strong, and fit, in body and mind, for the upcoming birth. Mothers were educated about their bodies, what to expect from doctors and hospital staff, what their rights as patients were, and how best to resist and avoid unnecessary and demeaning aspects of the usual medicalized childbirth. In contrast, the hospital and clinic classes, while trying to educate women a little and encourage them to keep healthy, do not train them to challenge doctors or hospital routines but instead prepare them to be compliant patients. Moreover, some health insurance policies might pay for doctor-organized and clinic-based prenatal classes but not for those based in community organizations.

The future role of mothers in a medical system oriented toward technological intervention and control in conception, gestation, and birth, where life itself is just another commodity and women's bodies producers of quality or flawed products, is very troubling. "To use the law for these complicated moral decisions," writes Barbara Rothman, "is to lose the nuances, the idiosyncrasies, and the individuality that protect us from fundamentally untrustworthy political institutions" (1989: 87). At the same time, regardless of whether new legal regulations are written, the new reproductive technologies are already stretching and altering the legal boundaries of American family law. In addition to marginalizing women in the reproductive arrangements, these technologies deflect pressures for social reforms by promising technological fixes for reproductive difficulties. Some women delay motherhood and possibly increase reproductive risks to conform to male career timetables (such as the tenure system in universities or the partner process in law firms). The reproductive technologies help allow this to continue by implying that women will suffer few consequences by delaying motherhood. As women delay motherhood longer and longer, their chances of becoming pregnant, gestating, and birthing a child without complications for their own health and the health of their baby diminish. Studies have also shown that older men also have less successful reproductive outcomes. Most of the research, however, remains focused on women. Women's delay of motherhood is also used to justify women's "demands" for the technologies. Pressures to change institutions (universities, law firms, medical schools, and others) or to assist and integrate the disabled, then, are blunted by the technological turn (Woliver, 1989a: 39, 1989b, and 1990a). Societal causes of infertility are seldom addressed. Machinery and technologies that often must intervene at the end of pregnancies to assist underweight or premature babies should also be seen in the context of societies that continue to underfund preventive programs for women's health and well-being. New reproductive technologies and surrogacy arrangements are increasingly making women marginal in the new politics of motherhood.

The new reproductive technologies might deflect attention from social and medical causes of infertility and disabilities. Genetic screening and abortion of handicapped fetuses, for example, have the potential of altering interest group pressure politics for handicapped services. Ovum transfer, for example, with its companion possibility of discarding defective fetuses, would more likely be used by insured, middle-class women. These parents are more active in communities pushing for better services for handicapped children. Judith Lasker and Susan Borg raise an important question: "When only poor and uneducated women have children with serious problems, how much influence will they have over the allocation of resources to help such children?" (1987: 102). Concern about the harm environmental toxins and unsafe working conditions pose for reproductive health is increasing (see, for example, Eisenstein, 2001; Elkington, 1985: 118; and Nelkin and Brown, 1984: 49). Instead of cleaning up the causes of birth defects in our environment and the social structure (poverty, violence), new reproductive technologies channel our efforts at treating outcomes.

New technologies add complications to the politics of reproduction. "For as technology allows God fewer and fewer Acts," Jessie Bernard writes, "motherhood itself becomes increasingly a matter of political as well as of individual decisions" (1974: 264). Yet much of the discussion of reproductive technologies by health and legal professionals downplays the political preconditions that channel choice. Although choices are always shaped by social conditions, the rhetoric surrounding reproductive technologies slights this. Sensitive policies for families absorbing the news of a "positive" amniocentesis or genetic test need to be built less on the admonitions of experts and more on the voices of the women involved in prenatal diagnosis themselves (Rapp, 1994a: 217). Reformers should continue to critique and attempt to change the social context in which these choices are made. In the future, though, this will be even more difficult because reproductive technologies have the potential of being substituted for social change and thus of increasing justifications for their use. Amniocentesis and future forms of prenatal screening, for example, seem to make it easier for more women to delay motherhood, ultimately increasing the demand for these tests. What is displaced is pressure to change institutional practices that encourage women to delay motherhood. When prenatal screening is used to abort handicapped fetuses, it will decrease pressure for handicapped services and thus increase pressure to abort handicapped fetuses because there might be worse social services for them.

An overemphasis on technology risks ignoring the politics and organization of health care in general, the legal system that frames our rights over our bodies and our children, political struggles over the nature of sexuality, parenthood, and the family, and the impact of the various material and cultural circumstances in which people create their personal lives (Stanworth, 1987: 4; see also Woliver, 1989a and 1989c). The variety of issues motherhood raises for the women's movement worldwide is further complicated by the challenges of new reproductive technologies. The women's movement should continue to include in its already overburdened agenda a political critique of the impetus of these new technologies. Introduced into cultures that devalue women, these technologies add further layers of distance between a woman's body and her reproductive power, while at the same time telling her that this is what she needs to be a good mother. In countries such as India, for instance, mobile ultrasound machines are used even in the most remote villages to abort healthy female fetuses. The end result might alter the experience of maternity for all women by making it more compartmentalized, tenuous, medicalized, artificial, commodity-oriented, and distant.

The women's movement should focus on two aspects of the new reproductive technologies: first, its displacement of social change; and second, its foundation in an apolitical rendition of individual choice arguments. Discussions about medical choices often proceed without acknowledging the economic, religious, community, and ethnic contexts of women's lives. Women do not come to these decisions as autonomous, rational, economic actors conducting cost benefit analysis in a fair world. Instead, any economic and social inequality the women must negotiate in their lives is also an element in their reproductive decision making and often bounds and constricts their choices. The economic and cultural conditions that structure women's choices must be included in the analysis of reproductive technologies. Instead of simply opening new choices for women, reproductive technologies also challenge women's power over their bodies and babies and increase the powers of a professional, hierarchical health care system where women have little influence.

Notes

A much earlier version of this chapter was presented at the 1990 Feminism and Legal Theory Conference at the University of Wisconsin Law School.

1. The hyperspecializations in modern academics influence this. Many bench scientists have very little college education in the humanities, ethics, or social sciences. At the same time, many humanities and social science scholars know little about laboratory science.

2. For further information, see the Web site for the Little People of America, <http://www.lpaonline.org>.

3   The Human Genome Project: Designer Genes

The Human Genome Project is a fifteen-year, $3 billion government project to catalog and analyze all of our genes. The project has generated a lot of controversy, debate, hopes, and fears. This chapter examines the social implications of mapping the human genome. Incorporating the Human Genome Project is central for analyzing the modern politics of reproduction and the impact of technological and medical power on people, especially women, making choices about their reproductive lives. Genetics is taking on an ideological quality, as well as being an embedded set of medical practices (B. Rothman, 1998; Lippman, 1998).

A Conceptual Shift

Framing reproductive issues primarily within a medical and scientific domain drains our attention away from the social and political forces that also affect the health of women, babies, children, and families. The sales pitch of the Human Genome Project not only promises the standard scientific benefits but also vows to solve many human problems: cure disease, improve intelligence, prevent crime, and even solve homelessness (Hubbard, 1995). A static biological, racial viewing of genes is political as well as scientific. In reactionary times, support for genetic

45

determinism is strong. Saying life is genetic alone, combined with a "privatized discourse of neoliberalism," as Zillah Eisenstein points out, "makes the individual responsible for his or her condition whether that be poverty or illness" (2001: 77). Invoking scientific expertise, however, renders genetic diagnostics regarding society compelling and difficult to critique culturally, legally, and politically (Nelkin, 1992: 186; see also Rose, 1994: 206).

The money involved in the genome project has restructured career paths for Ph.D.s in biology, the post-docs they can get, and the kind of grants that might be funded. At initial meetings where the enormous cost of the mapping project was discussed, one scientist worried that it meant "changing the structure of science in such a way as to indenture all of us, especially the young people, to this enormous thing like the Space Shuttle, instead of what you feel like doing" (David Botstein quoted in Cook-Deegan, 1994: 111; see also Kevles, 1992: 25–26). Many scholars have already noted the loss of a critical mass of independent, highly trained, commercially unaffiliated scientists with capacities and a willingness for social criticism as well as scientific research (Haraway, 1997: 93–94).

"Genes do not do everything," one historian of the Human Genome Project writes, "and the genetic approach must be wedded to biochemistry and physiology to complete understanding of a causal chain, but molecular genetics has been advancing more rapidly than these other fields. Technology emanating from molecular genetics will continue to shift the conceptual foundations of biology and medicine toward the study of DNA" (Cook-Deegan, 1994: 27–28). Molecular and genetic medicine's allure, grant potentials, and career-building possibilities for researchers pressure revision of undergraduate schooling, medical school curriculum, and postgraduate education (Caskey, 1992: 134). The immensity of the Humane Genome Project is already reshaping university research institutes and how biology will be taught in the future (Wheeler, 1999; see also Gilbert, 1992). The impact of the project is a profound conceptual shift in medicine and biomedical research (Keller, 1992: 292)

Donna Haraway notes that the genome project "in current biotechnical narratives regularly functions as a figure in a salvation drama that promises the fulfillment and restoration of human nature" (1997: 44). People working on the Human Genome Project have likened it to the search for the Holy Grail, an enduring rhetorical metaphor within the genome debate that perhaps conjures up more than the users of it intended (Cook-Deegan, 1994: 88, 316; Gilbert, 1992). Thomas Kuhn's concept of a "paradigm shift," here regarding the field of biology, seems apt (see

Cook-Deegan, 1994: 91 and 178, for instance). When genes are the accepted givens and all research questions worth grant money and publication revolve around genes and their derivatives, other questions and research projects are closed out of consideration. A paradigm shift involves patterns of thinking that never question current truths until another potential shift shakes up a discipline enough to open up new areas of inquiry. It reminds me of Michel Foucault's quip that academic disciplines are not called "disciplines" for nothing. "Genes are," to borrow Haraway's words, "a bit like the Eucharist of biotechnology" (1997: 44). Genetic screening and testing will most likely become part of the standard of care in Western medicine.

Geneticization and Topographies of Reproductive Power

Abby Lippman coined the phrase "[g]eneticization to capture the ever-growing tendency to distinguish people one from another on the basis of genetics; to define most disorders, behaviors, and physiological variations as wholly or in part genetic in origin" (1998: 64). Much controversy has arisen over the cost of the Human Genome Project (big science versus little science); the goals of the project; the possible social implications; whether this huge amount of money is being wisely allocated to improve our health; the potential conflicts of interest between gene researchers, the public that funds this research, and private research laboratories; and the potentially huge profits from patenting aspects of our genetic heritage (Martone, 1998; see also Abate, 2001). One scholar writes that the Human Genome Project is "the ultimate reductionist project," where even the soul has been moved into the genes (B. Rothman, 1998: 18).

Individual access to the results of the Human Genome Project are also ethically problematic. One threat is when genetic information is used contrary to the interests of individuals. A second concern is when individuals are denied access to genetic technologies that might benefit them because of insurance policies or their ability to pay (Mehlman and Botkin, 1998: 40). Enhancement genetic therapy, paid for by the individual's private funds, could, in the words of Maxwell Mehlman and Jeffrey Botkin, lead to a "'genobility,' already privileged by its wealth, [which] would experience an unprecedented burst of positive evolution. The privileged status of its members would become more and more unassailable, particularly if genetic enhancements were installed through germ cell manipulation and, therefore, were passed on from one generation to the next" (1998: 98–99).

Increasing Medicalization

The current "genomania" overvalues biological inheritance and makes us needlessly dependent on medical and scientific experts. A genetic focus also diverts our attention from major problems that needlessly threaten the health of huge segments of the world's population, such as hunger, malnutrition, urban squalor, infections, and dehydration that flourish under these conditions. Preventive and health care resources would be better spent, some assert, on these prevalent, pressing public health problems than on the ones that might lurk in our genes (Hubbard, 1995: 14). Western science, however, is based on "a corporate-consumer mentality set on efficiency, productivity, and profitability. This mental set draws the parameters for a particular kind of science. It makes it harder to get grant money for interdisciplinary research, which attempts to look at the multiple factors defining chemical risk [for cancers]," according to Zillah Eisenstein (2001: 89). Social and public health approaches to human illnesses are not the favored pathways to scientific research success, grantmanship, and fame. In addition, unlike genome discoveries, social, political, and communal health improvements cannot be patented by individuals and thus cannot produce profits for individuals.

Politically, genes have in the past been blamed for poverty, crime, and other troublesome circumstances. Recently, the new genetic discoveries are being once again linked to social problems. But genes alone cannot explain the different crime, poverty, or illiteracy rates between the United States and a country like Canada (Hubbard, 1995: 16).

Viewing all of human experience through the narrow lens of genetics poses acute dilemmas. Predictive diagnoses can make people worry and feel troubled about the future. The diagnoses do not help us understand the substance of our predicted future experiences. However, these predictive diagnoses, as Ruth Hubbard points out, "may indeed be useful to employers, insurers, and other forces in this society that can use the information to increase their profits or to discriminate against us and limit our lives in various ways" (1995: 20).

Many scholars of the Human Genome Project note the complexity of diseases and traits. Robert Cook-Deegan, in discussing the decades-long genetic research on Alzheimer's disease, discusses the many different genes that might be involved, humbly adding that "it remains unclear how many cases of Alzheimer's disease are genetic in origin, as opposed to other unknown causes (head trauma, viruses, environmental toxins, and other postulated agents)" (1994: 27). Nevertheless, "tests will predict behaviors as well as disease" some assert (Nelkin, 1992: 178). Increas-

ing leaps to biological assumptions in nonclinical settings and an actuarial mindset in our culture add to the genetic ideology and social power. The genetic tests create social categories that may be used to preserve
existing social and political hierarchies and to justify the controls and
advantages of some groups over others (Nelkin, 1992: 180). Dorothy
Nelkin explains: "Tests can be used to redefine socially derived syn-
dromes as problems of the individual, placing blame in ways that reduce
public accountability and protect routine institutional practices. The
availability of biological tests, in effect, gives an organization a scientific
means to deal with failures or unusual problems without threatening its
basic values or disrupting its existing programs" (1992: 183). For instance,
biological tests could reveal which job applicants are more susceptible
to certain diseases and exclude them from jobs that carry increased exposure. Workers' health would be protected, but at the workers' expense
by excluding the most vulnerable and avoiding costly environmental
workplace cleanups. Nelkin makes clear that "[i]t is the employee who
is burdened with responsibility; it is the employee who can be expected
to fit the environment or to move to another job" (Nelkin, 1992: 183).

The social impact of genome research will be based partly on whether
it recasts the debate about genetic determinism. The eugenics and racial
hygiene movements of the early and mid-twentieth century were aided
by the emergence of genetics as a science. It is now recognized that these
were virulent ideologies shaped by political expediency and the preconceived notions of researchers, where the backlash cast a long shadow over
genetic science itself. We must be humble and cautious about the new
genetics. As genetics turns up more knowledge about the role of genes
in diseases and other traits, we must be vigilant that genetic determinism and echoes of eugenics do not reappear. Claiming "it's genetic" might
mean "we can't do anything about it." We need a richer understanding
that embraces both genetic and environmental factors. The interesting
question is how nature and nurture interact (Cook-Deegan, 1994: 351).

Yet the growing genetic frame helps avoid explanations, as Eisenstein
suggests: "This autonomous and ahistorical viewing of genes reflects a
corporeal and physiological abstractness that disconnects bodies from
their cultural and economic moorings," whereas our bodies are partly
genetic and partly genetics awaiting proclivities from environments
(2001: 73; see also B. Rothman, 1998: 30). Subtly, our culture is turning
away from thinking, for instance, that cancer occurs because of many
factors, including carcinogens in our environment, to reframing it as a
"genetic disease." Breast tissue is vulnerable to the carcinogens in the
environment, our workplaces, and our food, yet most efforts to address

breast cancer focus on individuals. Individuals must cope with breast cancer, while groups of us will wear pink ribbons and walk and run in marathons to raise funds for a cure. Although the pink ribbons and fund-raisers are beneficial for raising awareness and bringing into the open this previously whispered about disease, we might be slighting environmental aspects of cancer patterns when we look for medical cures alone. A genetic focus shifts our efforts away from the environment, poverty, and lack of access to health care and centers our efforts on genes. Genetic discoveries, new medical protocols, and experimental drugs alone will not help us with breast cancer. The biomedical scientific method is, as Eisenstein notes, "the singularized causal sort that silences more than it reveals" (2001: 66).

According to Eisenstein, individualizing cancers and pinpointing genes "nibbles away at our ability to believe in and build political alternatives" (2001: 104), such as fighting carcinogens, eliminating poverty, and guaranteeing a fair and universal health care system. The Women's Community Cancer Project, founded in 1989, offers another vision. Project literature states, for instance, that Breast Cancer Awareness Month should be more accurately called National Cancer Industry Awareness Month (Eisenstein, 2001: 129). What a change in perspectives it would be if all the pink ribbons and fund-raisers were to curb carcinogenic pollutions. The amniotic fluid fetuses live in as their "first environment" contains the pollutions to which the mothers have been exposed because, as Eisenstein points out, "[w]omen's bodies absorb the political geographies of their local cultures" (2001: 148). Women who live in chemically polluted neighborhoods have higher rates of reproductive problems, miscarriages, infertility, and cancer. Our political geographies overlap with our social class and ethnicity. Research that places women's bodies within the social class, ethnic, and toxic environmental nexus of our lives, however, is not on the cutting edge of molecular and genetic science. Perhaps we could convince politicians that this was fetal abuse and get the environment cleaned up a bit. Instead, I am afraid, many politicians would see this as another reason to monitor pregnant women and fine them, punish them, for exposing themselves (and, most important, their fetuses) to carcinogens.

One leading cancer researcher, for instance, advocated mapping the human genome as part of a transition in cancer biology and suggested turning the focus of cancer research "inward" to find a cure (Cook-Deegan, 1994: 107). Hilary Rose explains this genetic turn: "In areas as diverse as explanations of schooling failure—the notorious IQ debate—

alcoholism, cancer, heart disease and psychiatric illness, there has been an immense turn away from the environment, particularly the social environment which had been addressed by governments in the sixties and by international agencies such as the World Health Organization in the seventies and early eighties, into a search within our genetic make-up to explain who will succeed and who will fail, who will get sick and who will die" (1994: 172).

Media attention to the so-called breast cancer gene includes this distortion. Most breast cancers are not linked to any gene.[1] An article in a popular magazine explains the differences this way: "When you hear about the discovery of the gene for breast cancer, Alzheimer's disease, or some other ailment, what is usually meant is that someone has found a gene implicated in some forms of the disease, in some people, some of the time. Rooting out the genetic component in most illnesses is still a dauntingly difficult task" (Shreeve, 1999: 57).

The metaphors for cancers, nonetheless, are changing to fit the new genetic ideologies (B. Rothman, 1998: 128–33; Eisenstein, 2001). This genetic emphasis lessens our attention to the social and environmental factors that affect our health in communities and starkly individualizes our health and welfare. When genetic screening is conducted, one Institute of Medicine committee recommended that it be done only when safeguards are in place that ensure informed consent to the testing, genetic education, and counseling. For prenatal screening and diagnosis, the standards of care should incorporate education and counseling before and after the test and ongoing counseling following the termination of pregnancies (Andrews et al., 1994: 7, 103). Most people's health coverage, however, does not cover these aspects of ethical and humane standards of care when genetic screening is used, leaving many people to cope alone with the news the genetic tests provide.

The paradigm shifting and almost hegemonic budgeting for the Human Genome Project have brought about public questioning of the results and thrust of the project. Large portions of scientific training and available grant money are connected to the huge Human Genome Project and its offshoots. The project raises questions about whether scientists are "playing God" (Boukhari and Otchet, 1999; T. Peters; Lin, 1998). The Ethical, Legal, and Social Implications of Human Genome Research (ELSI) program's open scrutiny of the ethics of the project explicitly attaches, in Robert Cook-Deegan's words, "public bioethics to the scientific research program . . . a new anharmonic in the cacophonous din of democracy" (1994: 255).

Eugenic Concerns

Features of the Human Genome Project not only have the potential to increase the medicalization of our lives but also hearken back to the dire consequences of previous scientific attempts to improve humans, explain human behaviors, and change social conditions. When the Human Genome Project is combined with previous ethical concerns about possible uses of the new reproductive technologies (see chapter 2) to shape human reproductive decisions in a less than perfectly ethical world, some scholars have pointed to "new eugenics," much of it "homegrown" from the reproductive decisions individual adults will make about the kind of babies they want to bring into this world (P. Williams, 2000; Kevles and Hood, 1992: 319). Similarly, Jeremy Rifkin posits, "Is it wrong, ask today's molecular biologists, to want healthier babies? The new eugenics is coming to us not as a sinister plot, but rather as a social and economic boon. Still, try as we will, there is simply no way to get around the fact that the fledgling commercial effort to redesign the genetic blueprints of life on Earth is bringing us to the threshold of a new eugenics century" (1998: 128). Some make a distinction between the old eugenics, which did not allow people to breed for themselves but imposed state breeding selections on people, and the new eugenics, where individuals can make private choices on the basis of genetic screening (Ridley, 1999: 299). However, the cumulative effect of these individual, private decisions can alter demographic patterns based on cultural hierarchies and prejudice. In India, for instance, as previously discussed, although governments have tried to stop the practice, private individuals' sex-based abortions have already skewed the birth ratios toward boys. Ultrasound machines help people make these sex-based abortion decisions. Height, weight, race, gender, and disability are not trivial characteristics in our culture and will be figured into many people's decisions about future children. Denial of this will not make it go away.

One Institute of Medicine committee worries that prospective parents in the United States might use genetic screening and prenatal diagnosis for such "trivial" reasons as sex selection. "The committee recommends that prenatal diagnosis only be used to assess genetic disorders and birth defects; it is concerned about the offering of prenatal diagnosis for trivial reasons" (Andrews et al., 1994: 295–96). The committee contends that the public must be involved in developing appropriate standards for using genetic technologies (Andrews et al., 1994: 296). Once medical tests, devices, and drugs are available, however, little can actually be done to monitor how, when, and why they are used.

Race, Class, and Genome Power

There are many reasons for African Americans and poor people to mistrust the motives and ethics of the scientific and medical communities (Dula, 1994). The Tuskegee syphilis experiments (government studies in which African Americans were deliberately not treated for syphilis so that researchers could study the progress and effects of the disease), involuntary sterilizations, and sickle cell screening in the 1970s are but three examples of how this mistrust built up (Dula, 1994: 349; see also Bowman, 1994). Large-scale sickle cell screening encouraged various forms of discrimination against the African American community on the part of insurance companies, school systems, and employers, to name a few (Dula, 1994). In the 1970s there was no treatment or cure for sickle cell, so the massive screening effort seemed to have few beneficial effects. While education and counseling would have been useful, they were rarely offered. Instead, the usual advice to sickle cell carriers was "not to have children," which some African Americans saw as "an attempt to reduce the black population" (Dula, 1994: 349). In addition, follow-up studies of the social impact of the sickle cell screening reveal how it increased African American suspicions of the motives of the medical profession. Damage to the black community also included reduced self-esteem of young blacks marked and stigmatized as carriers. Some families were harmed because of paternity issues revealed by the screening. At the same time, one study found that blacks did not change their reproductive behavior based on the screening and counseling programs (Dula, 1994: 349).

Nondirectiveness is an ethical mantra in genetic counseling. The specter of our eugenic past (and present?), however, makes implementing nondirectiveness essential to any just and humane utilization of genetic screening, diagnosis, and counseling. Even simple screening programs without implied pressures for abortions, such as the sickle cell program, can have widespread, unintended consequences for the targeted population.

Abilities and Diversities

The language used by genetic counselors should be carefully nondirective and not impart overt or hidden values. "Eradication" of genetic "imperfections" has a negative and forceful connotation, for instance. Saying "defect" instead of "condition" or "trait" is another of many possible pejorative expressions that push a eugenic and directive point of view. The language implies human perfection (by a nonobjective standard of perfect) as the goal. However, human diversity and difference are the norms. Our language is infused with eugenics. "Mutations" are actually just variety. For example, counselors should talk about the functioning status of different children or people rather than their "handicaps" or "disabilities" or "morbidity" (Andrews et al., 1994: 153). The social history of genetic explanations hovers over the Human Genome Project. "While those confronting human genetic disease in clinics day by day are unlikely to fall prey to simple genetic determinism," Cook-Deegan observes, "the culture is nonetheless vulnerable to muddle-headed claims about the genetics of intelligence and criminality" (1994: 254–55).

One problem with predicting so-called genetic conditions is that the severity of symptoms can vary from person to person and within one person over time. The impact of biochemical or environmental factors differs. Various "alleles" (mutations) of the same gene might lead to different outcomes. "A predictive diagnosis, or name, attached to a future genetic condition usually cannot take the effects of such variables into account," Ruth Hubbard points out (1995: 41). She continues, "When such diagnoses are used to characterize the future health of a fetus, they contain very little information about what kind of a person that fetus will become and what significance the condition in question will have in her or his life or in the lives of the people among whom she or he will live" (1995: 41). Hubbard cautions, and many others agree, that "there is always an interplay between numbers of genetic and environmental factors" (1995: 46).

Since the community of people with disabilities will no doubt feel the impact of the Human Genome Project, it is essential that genetic professionals, in the words of the People with Disabilities Caucus, "[b]ear in mind and learn more about the societal context of the development of new genetic technologies, namely the severe societal discrimination against people with disabilities" (1992: 84). Discrimination against people with disabilities is rampant in employment, education, and access to community resources and political power. The discrimination is bolstered by pervasive stereotyping and underestimating the capabilities and contributions of people with disabilities. The sad impact includes "making many genetically disabled people (particularly those with visible or severe disabilities) feel like we must defend our very existence" (People with Disabilities Caucus, 1992: 84; see also Saxton, 1998).

Disability rights activists want to guarantee "the right [of women] *not to have to have* an abortion. Disability rights advocates believe that disabled women have the right to bear children and be mothers, and that all women have the right to resist pressure to abort when the fetus is identified as potentially having a disability" (Saxton, 1998: 375; see also Callahan and Knight, 1992: 139). Adding to the potential for harm is the isolation of most of the able-bodied world from people with disabilities. Assumptions made about the disabled, even by medical professionals, and about the desirability of having or being someone with a disability skew people's choices. Some disability activists see selective abortion as "eugenic abortions" or part of the "new eugenics" (Saxton, 1998).

Genetic research oriented toward finding a genetic link to behaviors has many powerful social implications. A search for the gene for aggression, for instance, raised many alarms in the African American community, because of the possible glossing over of social, economic, and environmental influences on the behaviors of people and, instead, settling for a genetic explanation (Dula, 1994: 351–52). The reach of this is very broad, as Annette Dula observes: "Behavioral geneticists believe that genetic research can explain and eliminate society's problems, including violence and aggression, drug abuse, alcoholism, mental illness, homosexuality, and childhood hyperactivity" (1994: 351).

A huge controversy arose over a planned 1992 conference entitled "Genetic Factors in Crime: Findings, Uses and Implications," sponsored by the National Institutes of Health (NIH). The NIH withdrew funding after African American academics and politicians claimed "that merely holding the conference would lend credence to unproved theories on the relationship between genes and violence, thereby legitimizing beliefs that black males are genetically prone to violence" (Dula, 1994: 351). Indeed, there is a long and discredited history of scientists' asserting a biological basis for people's behavior and even intelligence that has strong racial implications (Gould, 1981; Boyd, 1996: D5). Nonetheless, research on behavioral genes, such as a violence gene, continues.

Even otherwise careful scholars can edge toward assuming that genetics determine or shape profoundly behavior. For example, in *Access to the Genome,* a measured and thoughtful book (partly funded by an ELSI grant), Maxwell Mehlman and Jeffrey Botkin speculate, "Prenatal or newborn genetic testing need not be limited to physical disorders. As we learn more about the human genome, we almost certainly will identify genetic tests to detect treatable psychological disorders. The government could require testing for these disorders, particularly if they cause affected persons to engage in violent or criminal behavior" (1998: 45). Unexamined is an assumption that success is at least partly genetically related. "In short," Mehlman and Botkin write, "providing access to genetic technologies according to current coverage policies would create a widening gulf between the genetically privileged and the genetic underclass" (1998: 99).

Genetic enhancements, stem-line genetic therapies, and other possible treatments from the Human Genome Project, if distributed by our current ability to pay system, would undermine societal faith in equality and equal opportunity (Mehlman and Botkin, 1998: 105, 117).

Furthermore, medical and scientific discussions of the ethics of government-mandated fetal testing and treatment do not address reproductive geography or physically how this would be achieved. They discuss "parental consent" but do not flesh out what is obviously in the foreground: these treatments would occur in a pregnant woman's body (see, for example, Mehlman and Botkin, 1998: 49–50).

The Human Genome Project's great potentials, therefore, must include discussion of related ethical, legal, and social concerns, such as issues of confidentiality, autonomy, fairness, stigmatization, and justice (Bowman, 1994: 165). The impetus to avoid the birth of people with "bad" genes, however, seems embedded in the genome project. Genetic testing seems to imply some kind of action on the part of the people tested. The genetic testing is not just for curiosity's sake. The screening programs, we are told, exist to provide important information that allows people to make informed reproductive decisions. The millions of taxpayer dollars spent on these programs, however, logically directs us to wonder if, in the words of James Bowman, "[s]creening for genetic disorders and genetically transmitted disease implicitly calls for a reduction in the number of affected children" (1994: 165).

An additional area where social forces are given short shrift in favor of genetic screening and "selective" abortions is with people with disabilities. Rather than spend the social capital to reduce the hardships and inconveniences of being different in this society and address the suffering caused by the prejudice against people with disabilities, we turn to a medical model to help eliminate the disabilities.

The "Gay Gene" Quest

Quests for the "gay gene" are also cause for concern, given the cultural biases against gay people. The ethics of research into sexual orientation has to be understood within the dominant culture's homophobia and the laws that do not protect gay citizens from discrimination or even abuse. Antigay voices charge that being a practicing homosexual is a "life-style choice" that does not qualify for civil rights protections. Some gay rights advocates counter that gay people are "born this way," much as other people are born into an ethnicity or gender they could not choose. Given the immutable and innate biological link to being gay, advocates for gay people maintain, homosexuals should be extended civil rights protections (the nature or nurture debate). Of course, whether being gay is genetic or not, many people favor extending civil rights protections to gay citizens.

Paradoxically, the advocates of the biological basis for being gay might have a difficult time justifying "gay science" that searches for the biological basis for homosexuality. I wonder why scientists are searching for this. Why is it interesting? Is this line of research truly neutral and disinterested? Why do they want to know? If a biological explanation is found for homosexuality, how will that information be used? How would being gay be framed after this knowledge is disseminated? Research on the "gay gene" deflects us from other quests to understand homosexuality (T. Murphy, 1997: 73). As Timothy Murphy observes, the research itself is not the problem (1997: 69). It is the way the research could be used that gives pause. "Just as genetic research need not be confined by its ancestry in eugenics," Murphy writes, "sexual orientation research need not be confined by its therapeutically driven and morally hostile history" (1997: 56). Many studies of sexual orientation have benefited gay people by showing them to be normal and by debunking antigay stereotypes (T. Murphy, 1997: 57–58). Murphy supports parents' options to utilize medical devices that might be developed as a result of "gay science": "Adults should be free from government oversight in regard to diagnostic tests, safe biomedical interventions, and abortion not only because the canons of biomedical ethics ordains that conclusion but also because gay children should not be forced on parents reluctant to have them" (1997: 135).

Yet an obligation of the research community is to consider the ethical ways and pace with which it proceeds with its research. Murphy contends, however, that "the existence of antigay prejudice should not be used as an outright bar to such research, for there is no society in which there is no antigay prejudice" (1997: 72). It is homophobia that must be redressed, not sexual orientation science, Murphy believes.

Homegrown eugenics, however, can affect the gay community. I am still concerned about the eugenic effect of the gay gene quest. One concern of mine is the selective abortion of "gay" fetuses within our homophobic society. Another worry is why scarce taxpayer health care dollars have been devoted to this quest. Only because being gay is controversial socially do we search for a gene to "cure" it. After all, being gay in an accepting society is not seen as a health problem requiring genetic research. The whole discussion, of course, begs the question of whether there is a "gay gene." Searching for it, however, is telling and

curious. Politically gay citizens might take refuge in a biological argument. We must remember, however, that refuge is sought only when
people are under attack. If not under social and political attack, gay citizens might not worry about whether being gay was biological. After all,
being gay is not a disease. Being gay does not kill you. It is prejudice that
makes gay citizens' lives difficult and might cause their deaths. The gay
gene quest also showcases a strong genetic determinism embedded within
the science itself.

Enhancements and Improvements

In abortion history, legal abortion was restricted to the very rare cases
for which medical doctors found compelling reasons. One reason was a
pregnant woman's exposure to German measles because of its association with birth defects. Abortion because of possible birth defect conjures
up concerns about diversity and ethics. In women's reproductive history, we must distinguish among the agents of decision making. When
governments or employers make reproductive decisions for people, individuals' human rights and dignity are violated. When concerned potential parents are making reproductive decisions, their rights and dignity
are enhanced. Families can take into account their capacities and values
and tacitly recognize a parental right to determine whether they could
care for a child born with congenital defects. These are inherently moral
questions that are inevitably hard and fraught with ambiguity and often
indecision. We must always remember the tremendous difference between a moral question that families address by incorporating their values and social context and the political question of who shall make reproductive decisions for people (Reagan, 1997: 204).

Control and access to genetic information are vital to everyone. When
newborn infants, for instance, are genetically tested, it must be only for
the clear benefit of the infant since the newborn cannot provide informed
consent. Newborn testing should include a backup system to confirm any
diagnosis and provide treatment and follow-up care (Andrews et al., 1994:
5, 47). Newborns and children who are candidates for adoption pose additional ethical issues because the genetic screening can be used to harm
them if the genetic test results decrease their chances of being adopted.
If genetic tests were used to help care properly for an adopted child, they
would benefit the child. The privacy rights of prospective adopting parents should also be protected, and any genetic testing should not be used
against them. One Institute of Medicine study of adoption and genetic
screening raised these conundrums and recommended more study on

appropriate use of genetic (and other medical) information in adoptions (Andrews et al., 1994: 297).

Future "enhancement" therapies are also of ethical concern. They could help create or make stronger certain traits, such as socially desirable height, weight, and perhaps even "intelligence." The availability of human growth hormone, for instance, has placed pressure on the medical community to redefine children of short stature as suffering a health problem worthy of the hormone treatment. Jeremy Rifkin, for instance, notes that redefining short-statured children as abnormal punishes victims of social prejudice for not measuring up to the social expectations of a majority. NIH funding for growth hormone research implicates the government as a party to these social prejudices. Rifkin contends that it also exposes "the new eugenics wind blowing over the land—a eugenics motivated by the push of the marketplace and the pull of consumer desire for better, more perfect children" (1998: 142). Genentech and Eli Lilly mounted an aggressive public relations and marketing campaign, with the help of family physicians, to redefine normal shortness as an "illness" that conscientious parents can now treat with growth hormones. The corporations thus helped create and ensure a market for the growth hormones (Rifkin: 1998: 141). It is not only pregnancy, then, that can be enterprised up.

I imagine that many of the children treated with human growth hormone are boys who are not "measuring up" to male standards of height. I also wonder what will happen in the future when the averages rise because of use of treatments like these; will the definition of those impaired by being below average also be adjusted?

The pressure to create "superior" human beings by the lights of prevailing social norms would be tremendous on potential parents. The fashion photographer offering model's eggs for sale, for instance, is tapping into cultural anxieties and expectations about which kinds of humans are more valuable. The egg broker here, Ron Harris, "said his offer is a reflection of American society, where beauty can be purchased by the highest bidder" ("Online Auction . . . ," 1999). The Web site describes the auction as "'Darwin's Natural Selection at its very best.' He [Harris] said society's obsession with appearance has made us stronger and healthier, and he pitches the egg auction as a chance for parents to give their children an advantage in society" ("Online Auction . . . ," 1999).

What is "defective" is also ethically troubling and noteworthy. Framing something as different or genetically diverse is more neutral than labeling it defective. However, there is a subtle shift occurring in biology that reflects these trends. Jeremy Rifkin writes, "It is within the context of this new language that molecular biologists first began to talk of genetic variation as 'errors' in the code rather than 'mutations.' The shift from the notion of genetic mutations in nature to genetic errors in codes represents a sea change in the way biologists approach their discipline, with profound implications for how we structure both our relationship to the natural world and our own human nature in the coming Biotech Century" (1998: 145).

In 1999, there were about five thousand egg donations in the United States, many brokered by the approximately two hundred private egg-donation agencies and clinics in the country (Mead, 1999: 58). The desired eggs are Caucasian and "intelligent" (defined by standardized test scores of the women, the "egg carriers"). One widely discussed ad for eggs, placed only in Ivy League college newspapers, specified desired height (at least five feet ten inches), athletic ability, and a donor with an SAT score of at least 1400 (Mead, 1999: 58). The Web site auction is a new twist on this business.

The Mixed Blessing of Knowing

Does knowing in advance about genetic probabilities make our lives better? We might think of a fetus differently if we knew its genetic endowment before we came to love the child and know it as a person instead of a genetic map. Today knowing ahead of time whether someone has a genetic probability of getting Alzheimer's disease or carries the "cancer gene" is useless information since there is virtually nothing a person can do about it. It is also important to remember that just because someone tests positive for the relevant gene marker, for instance for breast cancer, does not mean the person will develop the cancer. Yet the person's life and the lives of their loved ones will be altered by this knowledge. Conversely, if someone does not have the marker, it is no guarantee that the individual will not develop the malady.

The Family Impact of Misattributed Paternity

The family disruption from misattributed paternity experienced by some people participating in the sickle cell screening, as Annette Dula discussed, could be extended to many other families if genetic screening becomes the standard of care. As a result, one Institute of Medicine committee recommends that information on misattributed paternity be given to the mother of a child but not to the woman's partner (Andrews et al., 1994: 6; see also J. Edwards et al., 1993). Male partners or putative fathers, however, could figure out misattributed paternity from other genetic traits the child has that do not conform with the knowledge the man has of his genetic inheritance or family history.

Diseased Futures

In a moving, poignant memoir, Alice Wexler explains the impact Huntington's disease[2] has had on her family. Whether to be tested for it and then know part of their fate is one new choice and dilemma she and her sister, and similarly situated family members, now face (1995; see also N. Wexler, 1975 and 1979). She writes, "While my story shares some of the elements of the illness narratives written about cancer and AIDS, it is really less about an illness than about the possibility of an illness, less about the medical dilemma of living with disease than about the existential dilemma of living at risk" (A. Wexler, 1995: xxii). As Daniel Kevles and Leroy Hood point out, all genetic testing has a "wrenching ripple effect" throughout entire families (1992: 321).

One dilemma for people is whether they want to know ahead of time (maybe even decades before the initial possible onset of the disease) that they are likely to get it or will come down with it. With Huntington's disease, for example, identification of the genetic marker raised these issues and, as Alice Wexler points, "dramatized the distance between the power of scientists to predict diseases and their limited ability to cure or to treat them. It opened an abyss in all our lives, a vast space between prediction and prevention" (1995: 221). In this new scientific era, we have prediction outstripping prevention (N. Wexler, 1992: 223). Currently, there is nothing that can be done concerning most diseases or disabilities that can be diagnosed prenatally. "This means that," Ruth Cowan highlights, "for the foreseeable future, the ethical and social implications of the human genome project are going to be inextricable from the ethical and social implications of abortion" (1992: 246). In Venezuela, where the Huntington's disease search was launched in a huge extended family with a history of the disease, abortion is illegal. The dilemmas for researchers and family members in Venezuela, then, are acute. Alice Wexler writes, "The psychologist Schlomo Breznitz said that the moment when a predictive test becomes a real possibility marks a decisive emotional shift for the person at risk for Huntington's disease—and perhaps for any fatal, untreatable illness. At that moment the anticipation changes. And from that moment until the actual taking of the test is also a distinct time, quite unlike the period when one can fantasize about a test that does not yet exist" (1995: 224). Before people are tested, they need to be educated and fully informed about the procedure and the nature of the information that might be discovered not only vis-à-vis themselves but also other members of their family. Nancy Wexler (Alice Wexler's sister) comments, "You cannot crack open a person's very beneficial shell of denial too radically, and yet you also cannot allow someone to be tested without having some fundamental appreciation of the meaning of the results. It is difficult to shatter denial and shoal it up at the same time; denial is a critical component of coping and must be treated with respect. Information should be carefully titrated, and intensive counseling over time is essential" (1992: 230). What happens is that genetic testing replaces implacable fate with agonizing choices (Cook-Deegan, 1994: 236). Some characterizations of people who choose not to be genetically tested seem embedded within American and masculine social values (A. Wexler, 1995: 275). The imperative to test can rob people of hope if they are told they will come down with a disease for which there is no therapy or cure. Many people whose families have a history of Huntington's disease choose not to be tested. Their decision should not be seen as simple denial or avoidance. Optimism is preferable to pessimism for many people. There should be no governmental pressure to test, and there should be no social stigma attached to somebody's decision not to be genetically tested (Cantor, 1992: 105).

While genetic determinism can be dismissed as shallow, unwise, and untrue, as Walter Gilbert notes, "society will have to wrestle with the question of how much of our makeup is dictated by the environment, how much is dictated by our genetics, and how much is dictated by our own will and determination" (1992: 96–97). Gene studies thus far indicate that human beings are exactly the same in 99.9 percent of their genes. The connectedness of all life on earth might be incontrovertibly revealed by the genome map. "The data base of the human genome, coupled with our knowledge of the genetic makeup of model organisms, promises to reveal patterns of genes and to show us how we ourselves are embedded in the sweep of evolution that created our world," Gilbert declares (1992: 97). Humans have genes similar to those of mice; even the lowly nematode worm shares a third of its genes with humans. One "spin" of the genome mapping projects might be the one posited in a *National Geographic* article: "The last and most powerful secret revealed by our genes, in fact, is the indisputable unity of everything alive" (Shreeve, 1999: 75; see also Ridley, 1999: 21–22). Optimistically, then, illuminating our genetic maps could force us to see humans in a nonhierarchical way. Learning the genetic similarities between humans and all other creatures could also break down our anthropocentric tendencies and encourage us to see the ecological connectedness of all life. Considering human history, however, we usually manage to make monumental meanings out of tiny differences among us.

One similarity the Human Genome Project might frame is that everyone is susceptible to something and everyone carries some genetic risks. Visualizing this, through the power of the Human Genome Project maps, might bring pressure to bear for a national health insurance program in the United States, if all citizens' eyes opened to their expensive and troubling genetic endowments (Kevles and Hood, 1992: 325).

Reproduction, Parenting, and Abortion

Fetal testing can be confusing for even the most well-informed, highly educated person. Alice Wexler, for instance, during a time when she was trying to get pregnant, had to face the following choices if a "nondisclosing prenatal test" showed the fetus had inherited Wexler's mom's chromosomes:

> The fetus would be at 50% risk, since we wouldn't know which of Mom's chromosomes it carries. I'd have to decide at that point whether to go ahead and test the fetus for the marker; but if the fetus carries the marker for HD [Huntington's disease], that means I too must have the marker, and therefore the HD gene. I could abort the fetus at 50% risk, or go ahead and have the baby, not knowing its genetic status. It's an awful dilemma. Somehow it was not brought home to me that if you test the fetus in this way, you might be in a position of deciding on abortion without knowing the status of the fetus, or you might have to go through with the test yourself. (1995: 230)

The Russian roulette nature of these choices can paralyze people. When people do not know for certain what their genetic fate is, it permits them to keep on going with their lives even if denial is evident. "But," as Alice Wexler points out, "a positive test result removes that denial, or makes denial almost impossible to sustain" (1995: 232).

Media, doctors, and counselors sometimes subtly pressure people to take the genetic tests for Huntington's disease. Alice Wexler observes that people who take the test are portrayed as "somehow stronger, braver, more optimistic, more 'normal' than those of us who chose not to know. But isn't it also possible that those who opt not to know are more able to live with uncertainty and ambiguity?" (1995: 235). Finding the Huntington's gene in 1993 simplified presymptomatic testing for everyone (adopted people, those with small families, and those whose parents are dead, to name a few). Alice Wexler raises important questions about identifying the Huntington gene: "Will we ensure that the ability to test not be translated into the imperative to test? Will the decision not to take the test be respected as a legitimate choice and not represented as a failure of courage or a desire to 'remain ignorant,' as *Time* magazine wrote?" (1995: 260–61). The ability to test people genetically is so new that we need new and sensitive ways to describe and categorize the choices individuals make about these predictive tests. Alice Wexler aptly calls for

> new metaphors to talk about a deeply existential choice. For some, the decision to go through HD testing may indeed be a rational and realistic choice, as well as an emotionally compelling one. But for others the decision not to test is a rational and realistic choice. Certainly it is not a flight from truth and knowledge, a failure of courage, an avoidance of responsibility or a preference for "ignorance," as the popular media have sometimes suggested. It is not a sign of deficient "ego strength." (1995: 275)

For people who have tested positive for the Huntington's gene, its presence "creates a special atmosphere, a powerful aura, the haunted future we are trying to disrupt. How are people living with this 'toxic knowledge' as it has been called?" Alice Wexler asks (1995: 266). She notes it is important to remember that identifying these genes "does not immediately transform the medical landscape or translate into effective therapy. What has changed is the psychological landscape, the wider horizons of hope before us" (1995: 261).

From stories gathered about people who have tested for the Huntington's disease gene, we can make a number of observations. First, genetic testing involves families and has complex implications for family dynamics. Second, many people receive reassuring news that they are not likely to get a debilitating disease, thus freeing them of those worries. Third, more women than men have chosen to take the Huntington's disease predictive tests, an asymmetry that has received scant attention. Alice Wexler notes that this asymmetry "raises important questions about the gendered dimensions of predictive testing and the influence of women's childbearing on testing decisions which may or may not be directly related to reproduction" (1995: 268).[3] Fourth, more studies need to be done on the impact the predictive tests have on people who are told they are likely to manifest a disease. These studies need to incorporate the form of health care a community has (a national health care system or a pay-for-service one) and the impact of gender, race, culture, and social class on patients' reactions to the information (A. Wexler, 1995: 269). Fifth, studies that purport to document the responses of people to troubling genetic test results must address the sometimes high numbers of patients who do not participate in further studies or quickly drop out of an impact study (A. Wexler, 1995: 269–70). Sixth, discussions of the potential benefits and harms of these genetic studies must be broadened (A. Wexler, 1995: 271). Vague discussions of psychological benefits or increased ability to plan for the future based on genetic tests must remain cognizant that the information is absorbed into a social and political world in which pressures for presymptomatic testing are growing while insurance coverage diminishes (A. Wexler, 1995: 272).

Alice Wexler notes that today most people, doctors included, do not make distinctions "between *diagnostic testing* to confirm the nature of a disease when symptoms are already present, and where treatment may be called for, and *predictive testing* of a perfectly healthy person who is showing absolutely no signs of illness" (1995: 272). The dangers of coercing people to be genetically tested are evident because not just doctors but also insurers, employers, adoption agencies, and courts have asked for predictive genetic tests from people who did not seek them initially (A. Wexler, 1995: 273). The long-term consequences of genetic testing is unknown. Alice Wexler, reflecting on the experiences of people tested for Huntington's disease, noticed that the testing is never innocuous. The testing alone is a life-changing event. It alters families as well as the individual going through the test. Huntington's disease genetic testing should therefore never be routine or taken lightly (A. Wexler, 1995: 274).

One burden people with hereditary diseases or conditions bear in the United States is the heartless for-profit American medical system. Many family members document that the health problem in their family was often exacerbated by the unsupportive health care system in the United States. Lack of social and community supports also furthers the difficulties for families experiencing these health problems. Several task forces examining the condition of people with hereditary diseases in this country indict the American health care system and call for a system of universal health care (A. Wexler, 1995: 142). It is central to recall, however, that the Human Genome Project continues while American health care reform efforts have virtually stopped.

Impact on Mothers

Already, genetic screening and diagnostic fetal testing throughout pregnancy place responsibility and sometimes blame on mothers for having a "defective" baby. According to the scholar Gail Landsman, who is the mother of a child with a disability and has studied the experiences of mothering such children, the development of new reproductive technologies makes children embodiments of parental choices. Mothers of children with disabilities negotiate in a society that devalues their children. The mothers can feel the stigma that their motherhood "failed" to follow the culturally appropriate trajectory (1998: 77). When Landsman gathered the narratives of other mothers who had children with disabilities, she found that modern reproduction is publicly represented as subject to individual control. Mothers are held responsible, both through the obligation to undergo prenatal screening and selective abortion of defective fetuses and through women's presumed control of the uterine environment (1998: 80). Women's power or lack of power to affect the reception children with disabilities receive in our culture also shapes decisions made about continuing a particular pregnancy. Legal abortion puts women in a bind as presumed gatekeepers for the births of children with disabilities. At the same time, however, women have little power to shape the world into which their potentially disabled (or abled) children will come. It is a modern dilemma of motherhood that these choices are available without the means to shape the context in which the choices are presented (see also B. Rothman, 1998: 180).

With the amount of information given to women about their genetic chances of this or that, their prenatal tests for dozens of items can be incapacitating. These tests are transforming the experience of pregnancy for many women, making them tentative and rendering problematic many of the experiences of a wanted pregnancy. When prenatal testing is performed late in a pregnancy, the woman is racked with decisions about ending a wanted pregnancy. When the testing is earlier in a pregnancy and the results indicate "problems," women must face the decision to go on with the pregnancy knowing ahead of time that problems exist (B. Rothman, 1998: 192).

For prenatal, childhood, and adult screening and diagnosis, one Institute of Medicine committee report recommends that, given many of the ethical and social issues involved, the standard of care should be "*offering* the test, not actually providing it, and that no genetic test should be done without the consent of the persons being tested or, in the case of newborns, the consent of their parents" (Andrews et al., 1994: 51). Genetic testing should be "meticulously voluntary" and value sensitive (Andrews et al., 1994: 84). Overall, the Institute of Medicine "committee recommends that vigorous protection be given to *autonomy, privacy, confidentiality, and equity*" for everyone (Andrews et al., 1994: 21) and that disclosure of genetic information and genetic test taking not be mandated (Andrews et al., 1994: 280). Donna Haraway reminds us, "The corporatization of biology is not a conspiracy, and it is a mistake to assume all of its effects are necessarily dire. For example, I believe ease of technology transfer from academic research to other areas of social practice ought to be very important. I also insist that research priorities *and systems of research* must be shaped *from the start* by people and priorities from many areas of social practice, including, but not dominated by, profit-making industry" (1997: 93). Weaving social context and patient rights into these systems of research and medical practice, while essential for social justice, will be difficult.

Economic and Market Exchanges

The genetic probabilities and statistical chances notwithstanding, products for genetic testing will be developed and strongly marketed because many corporations have an economic stake in their dissemination. "Most scientists working in this area," Ruth Hubbard writes, "have links to industry" (1995: 50). She continues:

> For years they have promised more than the industry has delivered by way of useful therapies or cures. Once a genetic marker or gene is identified, the industry can make good on its financial promises by developing predictive tests for any condition that is supposedly associated with a specific piece of DNA. From an economic perspective, predictive tests are much more profitable than therapies since therapies are of use only to people who have the condition that the therapy is intended to improve or cure, whereas entire populations can be turned into consumers of predictive or screening tests" (1995: 50).

The profit motives here are tremendous. Tests that now are used on suspected "ill" people are sometimes touted by their corporate developers as future tests for the whole population, to detect those who carry a gene but manifest no symptoms. Although this could be excellent for particular businesses, the medical, educational, and social policy repercussions may be questionable. "To look at health and illness through the lens of genetics," Hubbard warns, "distorts our priorities by drawing attention away from the many biological, psychological, social, and economic factors that affect our health and play a part in generating disease or preventing its development" (1995: 51; see also Woliver, 1989a, 1989c, and 1995).

Ironically, we are preoccupied with preventing the birth of people with disabilities at the same time that we are doing less to prevent people from acquiring disabilities by adequately funding prenatal care and nutrition programs and enacting laws requiring motorcycle helmets and safety locks on guns, to name a few. Simply making a full-scale effort to eliminate lead poisoning from the environment of young children, for example, might do more to increase the health of poor children than the billions spent on mapping the human genome. The human genome industry and lobbying interests, however, have much more political clout than advocates for poor children. Moreover, genes can be patented, and testing can be routinized and highly profitable. Public health measures are embedded in community-based benefits and profits, not individualized, market-distributed profits.

One huge economic issue, a topic much too big and complex to be adequately covered in this chapter, is the issue of patenting and owning genetic markers, mapped genes, and other aspects of the research being done with mostly taxpayer money on the human genome. One group, trying to halt the patenting of genes, noted in a letter to interested parties that a company was trying to patent the gene "which causes breast cancer in women." The group points out, "Many scientists and researchers are opposed to the patenting of human genes, arguing that discoveries of nature were never meant to be classified as human inventions, owned and controlled by private companies" (Abzug et al., 1996: 1). If we mix and match genes as if living organisms were legitimate raw material for our manipulation and redesign, we violate the vital core of the natural integrity of those living things. When we oppose the production of transgenic organisms and object to the patents given to living things, which encourages private commercial exploitation of living creatures, we are appealing to, in Donna Haraway's words, "the integrity of all natural kinds" and "the natural *telos* or self-defining purpose of all life forms" (1997: 60). The continuing debate about patenting these discoveries from the publicly funded genome grants will profoundly shape people's access to this information, the marketing techniques and controls (or lack thereof) for the products, and the profits of the companies trying to patent and own genetic information. Market incentives, potential profits, and control through private patenting help push the research and its dissemination.

Human Diversity Genome Project: Save Genes, Not People

One aspect of the Human Genome Project is called the Human Genome Diversity Project. One of the foundational issues we should be asking about this, as with the quest for the gay gene, is why do people want to know this? How will it be utilized? Because the Human Genome Diversity Project is conducted in a world with profound power inequalities, these systems of genome classification will not be for purely historical and intellectual interest. Given our social fetish concerning race, for example, there are grave dangers in classifying categories of people (B. Rothman, 1998: 99). Usually our classifications are handy justifications for the inequalities we already have. The Human Genome Diversity Project, Barbara Rothman argues, is "very bad science and very bad politics" because "it is a science based on a presumption of difference that then shows difference" (1998: 102). Her methodological criticism of the Human Genome Diversity Project can be summed: "it treats human population diversity as if it were species diversity. Which is much the same criticism leveled at classic racism and racist science too. Humans are all one species. Birds are not" (B. Rothman, 1998: 103). In our world some people, as well as the plants and animals they live among, are genetic resources for other people.

Many of the genes that have been patented or where biomedical corporations will seek patents in the future derive from rare and exotic plants and animals discovered by gene diversity prospectors in third world and undeveloped countries. The rosy periwinkle, for instance, was found in the tropical rain forest of Madagascar and has made millions of dollars for Eli Lilly, the pharmaceutical company that developed a cancer-fighting drug from the plant, while the people of Madagascar have received nothing in compensation (Rifkin, 1998: 38). Similar stories abound. Some observers call this "biopiracy" or "biocolonialism" because the multinational corporations exploit and remove the resources of poor countries for the benefit of richer people with access to these technologies and medicines (Rifkin, 1998: 48–54).

Social Impact

Social circumstances affecting our health are not addressed when we focus only on our genes. In fact, this focus might make things worse, encouraging fatalism about our future health. We also will be creating a new class of "patients" seen as the asymptomatic or healthy ill. These people have no symptoms now but are predicted to develop them sometime in the future and should be treated accordingly (Hubbard, 1995: 52). Geneticization can debilitate people by increasing our dependence on the scientific and medical professions and by harming family relationships and our chances to obtain an education, employment, or health insurance (Hubbard, 1995: 52). Donna Haraway argues that controlling genes in a "regime of 'technobiopower' . . . drives venture capitalists, crafters of international treaties, makers of national science policies, bench scientists, and political activists alike. The control of genes means access both to naturally occurring diversity and to the material, social, and semiotic technology to recraft its riches to produce beings new to Earth" (1997: 57–58). The ethics and social pressure here can be acute. What kind of new beings will be created and why? Their creation and patenting will affect social justice, our economy, agriculture, medicine, labor, environment, and social structures. Parents will feel pressure to save scarce health care dollars by avoiding the birth of expensive disabled children. People who feel a child's life is not measurable in dollars might resist these admonitions. Studies show that families with disabled children tend not to seek genetic tests for subsequent children. This is partly because these families are familiar with the real impact of living with the disability. Cost-benefit justifications fall apart, however, when the cost of providing services to persons with disabilities is compared with the enormous resources devoted to testing for mostly rare genetic disorders (Saxton, 1998: 383). These concerns are intertwined with abortion politics. As Marsha Saxton puts it, "It is important to make the distinction between a pregnant woman who chooses to terminate the pregnancy because she *doesn't want to be pregnant* as opposed to a pregnant woman who *wanted to be pregnant* but rejects a particular fetus, a particular potential child. . . . Prenatal screening results can turn a 'wanted baby' into an 'unwanted fetus'" (1998: 384). Controlling the birth of "defective fetuses" and controlling women's bodies as vessels or producers of quality-controllable products merge together. To challenge the ways that new reproductive technologies can take control of reproduction away from women and place it in the commercial medical system, we have to address these motives for so-called perfect babies (Saxton, 1998: 385).

Often, however, the context of power and powerlessness within which women make their reproductive lives is slighted in favor of a "choice" and "freedom" frame. So, if we do not want "certain kinds" of people, individual parental choice can achieve social engineering for us (B. Rothman, 1998: 248–49). "Cars, violence, lead and other poisons in the air and water," Barbara Rothman admonishes us, and "all kinds of things are destroying our children, their bodies and their minds, at higher rates than our genes. A mother's zip code is still the best predictor of infant mortality" (1998: 248). Infant mortality and childhood illnesses, diseases, and deaths are often easily linked to poverty and socioeconomic disparities rather than to genetics the world over (Lerer, 1998: 240–41).

Edicts to examine our policy priorities, particularly given the enormous costs of the Human Genome Project, appear even in very accepting and favorable venues for the project. One Institute of Medicine report, for example, advises that large policy questions be asked, such as "Where do genetic services and genetic assessment fit into the broad picture of health care priorities? What is the appropriate relative priority for genetic services compared to alternative investments in prenatal care, childhood immunization, or prevention of child abuse, all of which have better-documented cost-effectiveness than genetic testing and screening now has" (Andrews et al., 1994: 305).

The differences among humans exist physically, but they matter socially. It is this social aspect that gets slighted in the new genetic focus. Dangerous segues from physical traits to determinism can result. The social outcomes of race, then, become justifications. This becomes politically very useful even though, as Barbara Rothman points out, "[t]here is too much genetic variation within populations, and too little between them, for 'race' to make sense" (1998: 92). Feminist scholars have made similar points about gender differences and gender determinism (Flammang, 1997; Epstein, 1988).

In our quest to uncover and map the human genome, we might still fail to understand human biology, human development, and environmental interactions. For instance, Barbara Rothman notes, "To diagnose, to predict Down syndrome is not to explain Down syndrome. And to predict the fact of Down syndrome is not to predict the experience of Down syndrome. One fetus so diagnosed is not strong enough to survive the pregnancy; another is born with grave physical and mental handicaps and dies very young; and another grows up well and strong and stars in a television show" (1998: 32). Informed observers of the Human Genome Project, such as Robert Cook-Deegan, do not forget that "[s]tudying the structure of DNA could not explain how Beethoven created his music or how Einstein thought about physics" (1994: 298). However, the force of the genome's paradigmatic shift is evident even among these careful and humble scholars. Cautioning against genetic determinism, gene scientists note that "the great lesson of modern molecular genetics is the profound complexity of both gene-gene interactions and gene-environment interactions in the determination of whether a specific trait or characteristic is expressed" (National Bioethics Advisory Commission, 1998: 39; see also Gould, 1998; and Ridley, 1999: 148). We would first utilize genome information in relation to human diseases. Within human diseases, we find great genetic diversity and variety. The central strategy is to approach biology from the genome (Cook-Deegan, 1994: 298). A genome starting point, however, can whittle away at our already fragile social cohesiveness (Hubbard, 1995: 63). Which illnesses will be defined as too expensive to take the risk that a fetus carrying the gene marker should be born and incur huge medical expenses?

In addition, simple links between genes and individual behavior (mental illnesses, criminal behaviors, homosexuality) are problematic. A marker for the possibility of developing schizophrenia later in life will shape a child's expectations for herself or himself and those of all the caregivers, teachers, doctors, and authorities who know the child and the predicted genetically based expectations.

One social impact might be discrimination in employment, insurance, adoption options for children, approval for adoption, and more. Instances of insurance discrimination based on genetic predispositions have already occurred (Gerstenzang, 2001). "Insurance companies claim they will go bankrupt if forced to insure people at risk for genetic diseases," the executive director of the Council for Responsible Genetics writes. "That claim is hard to take seriously, however, since such genetic diseases have *always* existed. It's only our ability to detect them that is new" (McGoodwin, 1996).

Breast Cancer Heartbreaks

Media coverage of genetic science can also be problematic, making people unnecessarily panic or unrealistically hopeful that "cures" have been found. Public discussion of the discovery of the "breast cancer gene" is illustrative. Media reports lead us to believe that *the* genetic marker for breast cancer had been discovered. In fact, it is much more limited than that. The BRAC1 gene associated with early-onset breast and ovarian cancer might be linked to only 5 percent of breast cancers (American Society of Human Genetics, 1994: 1). Such genetic tests as this can also identify presymptomatic people. This raises many ethical questions, including how young should a girl be screened for this gene? Lineage studies must be done to locate many of the pre-disease genetic markers, meaning that extended family members will be asked to participate in the laboratory work, regardless of whether they want to know their genetic "chances." When an extended family is studied, even the individuals who tell medical staff that they do not want to know the results will most likely figure them out from the behavior and reactions of the other members of their families who do know the results. The National Breast Cancer Coalition cautions, "A test that will tell a woman that she may have a substantially increased risk of developing a disease for which there is no known cure and which she cannot prevent, must be carefully considered. Safeguards must include legislation affording appropriate confidentiality and protection against discrimination in employment and in insurance coverage" (1995: 1).

People's health, including whether they will get a disease like breast cancer, is affected by all their genetic inheritance acting together and is shaped by their stress levels, nutrition, health practices, lifestyle, living conditions, socioeconomic status, gender, ethnicity, and experiences of discrimination and violence. Although many genetic scientists and counselors acknowledge this and warn about the limits to the genetic discoveries and the genetic "determinism" that seems to derive from it at times, the humbleness of a few in the Human Genome Project and its spin-off professions (such as genetic counseling) is often not evident in media accounts of the new genetic science, in cold-eyed insurance company decisions about coverage, or in the public policies that might result from politicians' seizing "objective, scientific" excuses not to "waste" money on social programs because maladies are in people's genes. The subtle nature of much of the responsible discourse in the genetic science community will most likely be lost on politicians not known for their subtle and nuanced approach to social policies.

Ownership and Patenting

What we have, according to Donna Haraway, is a "commodity fetishism" and an "obliquely related flavor of reification that transmutes material, contingent, human and nonhuman liveliness into maps of life itself and then mistakes the map and its reified entities for the bumptious, nonliteral world" (1997: 135). Strong objectivity is lost in the pseudo-objectivity of gene fetishism. Genetic determinism denies the work that it takes to nurture, sustain, and integrate "technoscientific material-semiotic bodies in the world" (Haraway, 1997: 142). Haraway, for one, is interested in the situated, contextual knowledge of the modest witness who might be able to see "the kinds of fetishism proper to worlds without tropes, to literal worlds, to genes as autotelic entities. Geographical maps are embodiments of multifaceted historical practices among specific humans and nonhumans" (1997: 135). The shifting terrains of reproductive power we are mapping with the genome echoes all our existing social structures and prejudices. These influences, however, are glossed over by the power of scientific, technical symbols, jargon, and discourses. When we map genes, Haraway argues, we are engaged in "a particular kind of spatialization of the body, perhaps better called 'corporealization,'" where we extend our capital accumulation, commodity fetishism to life itself (1997: 141). Objectification and measurement are not problematic per se. "But," she maintains, "the gene is fetishized when it seems to be itself the source of value, and those kinds of fetish-objects are the stuff of complex mistakes, denials, and disavowals" (Haraway, 1997: 143–44). A further complication is that many of the biotechnology scientists working on genome projects and policy-making also have industry affiliations, which in many other lines of work would cast doubt on their objectivity and raise questions of conflict of interest (Rifkin, 1998: 56).

The Human Genome Diversity Project, as well as the long history of colonization of indigenous plants and species for Western markets, brings up the ethics of exploitation, colonialism, and insensitivity (Hayden, 1998). For instance, instead of funding or creating conditions in which diverse pockets of humans can live and survive, the Human Genome Diversity Project is archiving these people's genes in case they might be useful in the future when the people themselves are extinct.[4] In the Human Genome Diversity Project, people become intellectual property (Rifkin, 1998: 56). Biotechnological practices, however, are resisted by indigenous people. The "commons" (what we as humans share) of the earth's diversity, ecology, and possible biological inheritance are appropriated as the private preserve of corporations if the diversity within the ecological system might be profitable in the future. Gene prospecting erodes indigenous peoples' self-determination, dignity, and sovereignty. If a region is designated as biodiverse and ripe for proprietary development, dire consequences can include negative repercussions on the environment and health; exportation of genetic determinism as scientific explanations; "intensified cruelty to and domination over animals; depletion of biodiversity; and the undermining of established practices of human and nonhuman life, culture, and production without engaging those most affected in democratic decision-making," according to Haraway (1997: 61). In 1994, a broad coalition of indigenous, environmental, consumer, and nongovernmental organizations working on issues of economic development called for eliminating the funding for the Human Genome Diversity Project. Haraway reports that their concerns included "the potential for commercialization, especially in the form of patents on human genes and proteins, without benefit to the sampled populations whose body parts would become museum specimens in an updated form" (1997: 252).

Genetic, Intentional, Enhanced Babies

Additional economic issues arise in the American market for eggs and sperm. "The United States," Rebecca Mead observes, "is the only country in the world in which the rules of the marketplace govern the trade in gametes and genes" (1999: 59). Egg "donation" has become thoroughly commercialized in the United States, with the only issue being the price. Legal fictions and the euphemistic parlance of the industry where egg "donations," not egg "sales," are sought mask the raw nature of this marketing in human eggs. An ideal egg donor embodies all sorts of paradoxes, however. The egg donor is compassionate toward an infertile stranger but feels no necessary "maternal" attachment to her own genetic kin (Mead, 1999: 60). Although men have always been able to biologically father a child they might never meet, this was almost impossible for women until egg donation. With egg donation, a woman can biologically create a child she may never meet. However, our language cannot completely adjust to this since "to father" and "to mother" still mean very different biological and emotional commitments. The egg donation market also creates great pressures among egg recipients/purchasers to genetically upgrade their potential children (Mead, 1999: 62). Yet genetic anxiety can also slip into egg donation arrangements, as Mead points out:

> Egg-donation specialists tend to tell their patients that they should not worry too much about behavioral genetics. Nonetheless, there is some speculation that paying donors high rates might have an effect on the character of the children produced. Robert Jansen, the Australian fertility doctor, told me, "As the price rises and becomes more and more of a motivating factor, and we also appreciate the genetics of personality and character, you start to ask, 'Do you really want to bring up a little girl whose biological mother was someone who decided to charge ten thousand dollars for eggs?'" (1999: 63)

One notorious case (*Buzzanca v. Buzzanca*) involved a leftover embryo from an unrelated IVF cycle from a donor egg and the IVF patient's husband's sperm, which was transferred to a hired gestational surrogate (the so-called complete surrogate). The contracting couple, the Buzzancas, separated and divorced after the surrogate's pregnancy began. Mr. Buzzanca claimed he did not have to pay child support because he was not genetically related to the child. Eventually a court ruled that it was the intent to be the parent, not the genetic connection, that was decisive. The baby lives with Ms. Buzzanca, and Mr. Buzzanca now pays child support. The *Buzzanca* case has far-reaching implications, as Mead indicates: "According to the Buzzanca ruling, parenthood is not a biological category but a conceptual one: its defining characteristic is that of intent. . . . This reasoning—the idea that intent trumps biology—makes for some remarkably slippery values" (1999: 64).

Women gestating an egg-donor child emphasize carrying and birthing the fetus as the central aspect of motherhood. Women who hire surrogates to carry their fertilized egg (full surrogates) assert that it is the genetic connection to the baby that makes them the mother. For full surrogate arrangements, the gestating and birthing is just a paid service. Genetically, biologically, an egg donor and a woman who hires a surrogate are in identical arrangements. However, egg donors are encouraged to emphasize that what makes a mother is the intent or wish to be a mother. In the infertility business, they are called the "social parent" and therefore the real parent (Mead, 1999: 64). In the genetic marketplace, Barbara Rothman writes, "the 'book of life' becomes a catalog" where we can place our orders. We map what we value, she continues but warns, "A map is a guide: it tells you what is there, but it also tells you how to get places. The genome map, as we have seen, may end up taking us places we don't want to go" (1998: 247).

ELSI: Ethics within the Project

At the beginning of the funding and organization of the Human Genome Project, Dr. James Watson and others (particularly a few vocal members of Congress) acknowledged the enormous ethical and social implications of the project they were about to undertake. For the first time in the history of government funding of scientific projects, these ethical and political ramifications of the research were institutionalized in the project itself through a line item in the funding to create a working committee within the Human Genome Project to study ethics, politics, and social impact. The committee is the Joint National Institutes of Health–Department of Energy Working Group on the Ethical, Legal, and Social Implications of Human Genome Research (ELSI), operating under the auspices of the Human Genome Project. James Watson's commitment of National Institutes of Health money to ethical debates regarding its research was unprecedented and shrewd. "His policy," Daniel Kevles contends, "undoubtedly helped defuse anxieties about the prospect of a genome project indifferent to or unrestrained by ethical considerations" (1992: 35). ELSI received a very small percent of the Human Genome Project funds (at first about 3 percent, later raised to approximately 5 percent) (Cook-Deegan, 1994; Kevles and Hood, 1992) and gives grants sparingly to groups engaged in scholarship on the social impact of the Human Genome Project.

Whether the recommendations of ELSI scholars are taken seriously is another question. One student of the Human Genome Project and ELSI participant comments, "But with all the power and the big money in the hands of the science, bioethics becomes a translator, sometimes an apologist, sometimes an enabler, of scientific 'progress'" (B. Rothman, 1998: 36). The proportional impact of the funding for the Human Genome Project, and derivatively for the ELSI grants, has perhaps also reshaped the field of bioethics. Robert Cook-Deegan writes, "One potentially adverse effect of the ELSI genome program was the concentration of resources in a relatively narrow field of biomedical research. As support for bioethics related to the genome project grew, and with few resources available for other lines of bioethical analysis, many bioethics programs developed modules on genetics. This may have helped achieve the goals of the genome office, but it also skewed concern with bioethics toward the genome research. Where cash went, ethics followed" (1994: 241).

On the one hand, ELSI is a step forward: scientists acknowledge that they do not work in a vacuum and that even the "purest" science coming from the lab can have serious and sometimes unanticipated consequences for society. On the other hand, some scholars wonder if ELSI serves as an institutionalized, in-house covering excuse for the human genome powerhouse labs and scientists who can claim that ELSI is responsible for the "ethics side" and will take care of all the sticky issues raised by the project during its lifespan.

ELSI should be used, some advocate, to educate the public about the Human Genome Project, to train genetic counselors, and to recruit more diverse genetic counselors (see, for example, Andrews et al., 1994: 16–17). Co-optation of ELSI in this manner should give us pause. ELSI would be a promotional, public relations tool for the Human Genome Project instead of a monitor. Much of what the Institute of Medicine study recommends (Andrews et al., 1994) regarding ELSI's role could lead to in-house shilling for the Human Genome Project and accepts the basic ineluctable, ubiquitous future for genetic testing.

The Women and Genetics in Contemporary Society Conference I went to was funded by ELSI/NIH, but it had plenty of dissent, doubt, and critique of the Human Genome Project (as well as many voices in support of the project or parts of it). Participants were concerned, however, that the hard work of the conference organizers and participants would likely be ignored by the powerful decision makers in the Human Genome Project, the National Institutes of Health, and the Department of Defense. Nevertheless, many troubling issues linked to mapping the human genome are being discussed and funded through the ELSI office, however inadequate the money is or however hard it is for independent scholars to be awarded the grants.

Gender, Power, and Bioethics

The 1996 Women and Genetics in Contemporary Society Conference I attended included a feminist ethics component, a unique and useful way of looking at the Human Genome Project. The feminist component expands the vision of bioethics because, as Susan Sherwin writes, "it demands that we consider the role of each action or practice with respect to the general structures of oppression in society. Thus medical and other health care practices should be reviewed not just with regard to their effects on the patients who are directly involved but also with respect to the patterns of discrimination, exploitation, and dominance that surround them" (1992: 5). The Human Genome Project should be examined within the context of people's lives, keeping the lives of women in the forefront.

For poor women, genetic counseling is often unavailable or inadequate. Once told of genetic "defects" in the fetuses they are carrying, they have few "choices" but many heartaches. First, their poverty and lack of adequate health care mean raising a child with a disability will be very difficult. Second, if poor women want to abort, they have no access to public funding for safe, legal abortions, except in the rarest circumstances. Public assistance reforms (welfare reform) might limit the number of children a mother's aid will cover, thus most likely forcing her reproductive "choices." African American and poor women, as James Bowman puts it, "are led to the brink and left on their own" (1994: 174). Further attention to the need for cultural, religious, and ethnic differences to be incorporated into genetic counseling is vital (see, for example, V. Wang, 1994).

Conclusion: The Ineluctable Human Genome Project and Fragile Reproductive Rights

"Paternalism, a denial of autonomy, and spurious justice mar today's genetic screening programs," Bowman argues (1994: 173). For the disability rights movement, the expanded knowledge potentially available from the Human Genome Project has troubling implications. Even now, with our limited DNA knowledge, one disability rights scholar writes, "The message at the heart of widespread selective abortion on the basis of prenatal diagnosis is the greatest insult: some of us are 'too flawed' at our very DNA to exist, we are unworthy of being born" (Saxton, 1998: 391). Mapping the human genome seems fraught with dangers that these social trends will be exaggerated and extended into new areas of human li (a genetic carrier, the presymptomatic ill). Moreover, conservative movements in the United States and elsewhere have made reproductive politics, particularly access to legal abortion, a "pivot" in their campaigns (Bashevkin, 1998: 50).

Designing genes also passes over the facts that all of us are dependent on one another to some degree, that the capacity for human flourishing is not exclusively in our genes, and that much of the work and nurturance expended to make families, raise children, and create communities are done by women and are often taken for granted. The so-called private world of women and home makes up the distaff side of life, one where the work, energy, and wisdom brought to bear to nurture and sustain families are often overlooked and belittled as "women's work." One mother of a profoundly disabled daughter notes that our rational choice, cost-benefit analysis framing of love, life, dependency, family, and community impoverishes us. She advocates a realistic, social solution (instead of genetic reductionism) to the joys and heartaches of human dependency work: "The principle of the social responsibility for care would read something like: *To each according to his or her need for care, from each according to his or her capacity for care, and such support from social institutions as to make available resources and opportunities to those providing care, so that all will be adequately attended in relations that are sustaining*" (Kittay, 1999a: 113). If our orientations were to work for such a world, our reproductive choices would be different.

The evolving frame of genetics as the cause of our behavior, life chances, and traits and the determining force in our lives is emerging in a culture where, in Barbara Rothman's words, the "mother-based tie is the growing of children, the carrying and bearing and raising; the patriarchal tie is based on genetics, the seed connection" (1998: 16). Matriarchal societies see persons as what women grow; patriarchal ones see persons as products of the male seed. Genetics is rooted in a traditional, father-based worldview. The genes are an updated version of male seed power, sperm on a blank background (B. Rothman, 1998: 18). This patriarchal standpoint interprets how societies describe women's labor in childbirth. Rothman explains otherwise: "We begin as part of our mothers' bodies. Our bodies grow out of the bodies that surround us. We don't, as our language would have us believe, 'enter the world,' or 'arrive.' From where? Women who give birth, I have often pointed out, don't feel babies *arrive*. We feel them *leave*" (1998: 17). The metonym of the "arrival" of new babies into the world speaks volumes about the social and

aphy of women's bodies. What occurred in our bodies for
nths and how we labored to birth our babies are not evi-
ymbolic "arrival" from nowhere of men's new babies.
xamination of the politics of the Human Genome Project
ore the inequitable health care system into which the project
w.. oduced, the specter of past scientific and medical misuses of
power, the potentials for genetic discrimination, and the changes, both
good and bad, it will bring to reproductive decisions. Too often our ethical debates about a new reproductive dilemma are post hoc and respond
to faits accomplis. The diminution of women's true choices, our sense
of human community, and human worth occurs, however, ineluctably
and thoughtlessly. This chapter is just a beginning examination of some
of these social and political issues.

Notes

I thank Dr. Rebecca B. Holmes for organizing and securing funding from the
National Institutes of Health for the stimulating and important ELSI Wom-
en and Genetics in Contemporary Society Conference, May 16–19, 1996, in
Zanesville, Ohio, and for including me as a participant. Much of the literature utilized and ideas explored in this chapter derive from that conference
and the supporting materials Dr. Holmes and her staff sent to all the participants. Ideas expressed in this chapter are revisions from a number of convention papers of mine ("Terrains of Reproductive Power," American Political Science Association Annual Meeting, 1999c; "The Politics of the Human
Genome Project," Southern Political Science Association Annual Meeting,
1996d; and "Designer Genes: Cultural Shifting on Reproductive Values and
the Impact on Gender, Race, Class and Sexualities," Southern Political Science Association Annual Meeting, 1999b [awarded the 2000 Marion Irish
Award for the Best Paper in Women and Politics at the 1999 Southern Political Science Association Annual Meeting]). Participants on those panels
helped me clarify my thoughts on this subject and expand my reading. For
this, I thank them.

1. Barbara Rothman maintains that "all the inherited breast cancers together still leave 93 to 95 percent of breast cancers unexplained" (1998: 150; see
also Eisenstein, 2001). This seems shockingly at odds with the media's reports and the genetic hype about finding the breast cancer "gene."
2. Also known as Huntington's chorea, it is a rare inherited disease of the
central nervous system characterized by involuntary movements and progressive dementia.
3. Matt Ridley quips about this phenomenon: "Curiously, but perhaps
understandably, men are three times as likely to choose ignorance as wom-

en. Men are more concerned with themselves rather than their progeny"
(1999: 63).

4. Programs to save the genes and perhaps one day clone such endangered species as the giant panda are already in full operation. Another program uses other species as surrogate moms to produce more of the endangered animals (Begley, 2000). Although I admire these efforts, it saddens me to read in these stories the resignation that many species will soon be extinct and that we therefore need a "Plan B": surrogates, genetic storage, and cloning. We must also remember that cloning can go awry.

4 *Abortion Politics:*
Discourses on Lives

> In its ability to embody the union of science and nature,
> the embryo might be described as a cyborg kinship entity.
> —Sarah Franklin, "Making Representations"

> In many domains in contemporary European and U.S.
> cultures, the fetus functions as a kind of metonym, seed
> crystal, or icon for configurations of person, family, na-
> tion, origin, choice, life, and future. . . . The fetus as
> sacrum is the repository of heterogeneous people's sto-
> ries, hopes, and imprecations.
> —Donna Haraway, *Modest-Witness@Second-*
> *Millennium.FemaleMan© Meets OncoMouse™*

Abortion's nitroglycerine political controversy has affected birth control, family planning, and women's health politics deeply. Abortion's public political emergence in the 1960s, as Donald Critchlow puts it, "transformed the politics of population and family planning policy" (1999: 113). Fetuses as metonyms take on powerful symbolic forms in our culture. The status of the fetus stands in for the problems independent, demanding, sexually active women allegedly cause in our society. They want "abortion on demand," for instance, while not accepting responsibility for becoming pregnant in the first place. Legal abortion distills many perceived social problems onto misbehaving women.

One dimension of abortion politics that sets the scene for policy recommendations and rhetoric on rights is the framing of the topic as if it were simply a forty-week time frame focusing on whether to terminate a pregnancy (Sprague and Greer, 1998: 59). According to Joey Sprague and Margaret Greer, this is partly explained by the "contemporary discourse on abortion" that revolves around four themes: "(1) a narrow construction of reproduction as an issue; (2) a reliance on logical dichotomy and decontextualized abstraction in talking about the issue; (3) a tendency to construct justifications using an individualistic language of rights; and (4) an orientation that is confrontative and dominating" (1998: 58–59). Central in abortion politics is the agency of women to construct their own reproductive lives and choose their own forms of sexual activity. Instead, the gender issues at the heart of abortion politics are often masked politically. If we honestly discussed abortion within the territory of gender politics and women's rights and health instead of centering on fetal life, we would have to answer questions about how abortion is singled out for special regulations that presume incompetent, selfish, misinformed female decision making instead of simply regulating abortion with the same health and safety provisions for other medical procedures (see also Jaggar, 1998: 351). Debates on which women might be "worthy" of a legal, safe abortion since they are innocently pregnant (i.e., through no fault of their own) highlight this position. Exceptions for victims of rape or incest from restrictive abortion efforts are based on an idea that all the other unwanted pregnancies are the "sexual fault" of the women (Siegel, 1992: 361). Anti-abortion adherents, Catharine MacKinnon observes, "make *exceptions* for those special occasions during which they presume women did *not* control sex," which assumes that women significantly do control sex (1987: 94). A study of women's abortion reasonings and decision making found that the views of anti-abortion women depended on the circumstances of the situation, including the motives and intentions of aborting women. The researcher found the difference between "pro- and anti-choice women's abortion morality . . . was their different perspective on the trustworthiness of women" (Cannold, 2000: 95).

Genetic counseling, prenatal diagnosis, and genetic testing are all intertwined with the politics of abortion. Aborting defective, disabled, genetically troublesome fetuses is problematic to many, as discussed in the previous chapter. However, as Ruth Cowan reports, feminist ethicists who have studied the decision making of women choosing abortion find little to fear "as long as individual women are left in control of their own reproduction. For when left free to decide, most women decide to abort for reasons that have to do with their sense of good nurturance: for example, when they feel either that this is not a time when they can nurture a child properly or this is not the fetus that will grow into a child whom they can nurture properly. Why fear a future in which ever more children will be ever more wanted by their mothers?" (1992: 262). Women make ethical, rational decisions regarding the continuation of their pregnancies and, out of an ethic of care, decide what would be best for them and their families (Cannold, 2000). Governmental control over reproductive decisions is fearsome. "If nothing else," Cowan warns, "the history of the twentieth century ought to have taught us that individuals can sometimes behave badly, but they can never behave as badly, or as destructively, as governments can" (1992: 263).

Most nations have abortion laws that public opinion polls indicate most of their citizens want (Simon, 1998: 107). Particular cultural and political histories, practices, and contexts shape community views of the status of a fetus and even, in some countries, the personhood of newborns (Picone, 1998; Morgan. 1998). Women worldwide negotiate their reproductive lives as best they can given their religious beliefs, relative power within the family, age, marital status, education levels, and social class. One comparative study of women's reproductive lives reminds us, "Whilst women in all countries surely seek safe, effective methods of contraception and abortion, they also want healthy conditions for childbearing, sexuality free from violence and disease, food security, skills and incomes of their own, and dignity and respect as service recipients and human beings" (Petchesky, 1998b: 2). The restrictive abortion laws of many countries, however, are correlated with high maternal deathrates from illegal and dangerous clandestine abortions.

Revealed History and Political Action

Part of the context of abortion politics is the history of what women did when abortion was a crime. Studies of abortion show that the demand for abortion is highly inelastic (women will seek abortions if necessary, no matter how high the cost). Policymakers need to be realistic about abortion and accept that, in Deborah McFarlane and Kenneth Meier's words, "[o]utlawing abortion would not change its price elasticity; it would only change the price" (2001: 163). One change in the price would be women's safety and maternal mortality. The history of illegal abortion also shows that making it a crime means criminal syndicates can set up shop, as they did on the U.S. West Coast from 1934 to 1935. That syndicate eventually organized all abortion business up and down the West Coast and threatened doctors and abortionists who did not cooperate (Solinger, 1994: 55–85). The history of illegal abortion in the United States demonstrates women's continuous demand for abortion "regardless of law" (Reagan, 1997: 1; see also Joffe, 1995; Solinger, 1994; Hertz,

1991: 70–73; Hern, 1984b: 21; and Gorney, 1998: 15–36). Moreover, as Leslie Reagan points out, history reveals a relationship between attacks on abortion and women's claims for political power and independence:

> In the nineteenth century, abortion came under attack at a moment when women were claiming political power; in the twentieth century, it came under attack when they claimed sexual freedom. Abortion, like contraception, means that women can separate sex and procreation—still a controversial notion. Antiabortion campaigns developed when women asserted sexual independence, as during the Progressive Era and since the 1970s. When abortion was most firmly linked to the needs of family rather than the freedoms of women, as during the Depression, it was most ignored by those who would suppress it. Periods of antiabortion activity mark moments of hostility to female independence. (1997: 14)

Dr. Mary Calderone, the medical director of the Planned Parenthood Federation of America, helped highlight the public health issues of illegal abortions when she organized a national convention on abortion research and practice in 1955 (Gorney, 1998: 23). Rachel DuPlessis and Ann Snitow describe an early and dramatic confrontation over the usual treatment of abortion in a male-dominated setting: "In February 1969, after a New York hearing about abortion laws where the experts were fourteen men and one nun, women set up a counter-hearing. Twelve gave evidence about their (illegal) abortion, claiming that as women they were the true experts on unwanted pregnancies. (This formulation, 'unwanted' pregnancies, was a radical break with female compliance at the time and has, in the 1990s, once again become taboo)" (1998: 12–13).

The idea that women are experts on their own experiences has typically been dismissed. Reagan recounts how the antiabortion movement of the nineteenth century, for instance, disempowered women's accounts of quickening: "As physicians targeted quickening, they discredited women's experiences of pregnancy and claimed pregnancy as medical terrain. 'Quickening,' as Storer described it, 'is in fact but a sensation.' A sensation that had emotional, social, and legal meaning was thus denigrated. Quickening was based on women's own bodily sensations—not on medical diagnosis. It made physicians, and obstetricians in particular, dependent on female self-diagnosis and judgment" (1997: 12). The demise of quickening as a reliable, accepted piece of information about a woman's pregnancy antedates the development of ultrasound machines, but the new machines and technologies hastened the displacement of the woman as a source of knowledge about her own pregnancy and body.

Numerous memoirs, biographies, histories, and ethnographies establish the traumatic experiences girls and women endured to obtain abortions before *Roe v. Wade.* The experiences often politicized the women involved. One woman recalls, "What I learned from that experience was that women with connections could always get abortions, but even middle-class women had to go through humiliating and painful rituals to exercise control over their bodies and choices" (Winslow, 1998: 229; see also Stewart and Gold-Steinberg, 1996).

The same woman recounts how in 1969 her feminist abortion reform committee in Seattle was influenced by a visit and speech by Fannie Lou Hamer. Hamer, who was opposed to abortion, told the committee about how she was sterilized without her consent. Because of this testimony, Barbara Winslow relates, "our abortion committee always recognized the issue of forced sterilization" within the domain of women's reproductive freedoms and choices (1998: 243). Similarly, Alice Wolfson recounts how in the District of Columbia, a city with a large African American population, her feminist group "could not address abortion in isolation from the issues of sterilization abuse and population control," thus always linking race and gender issues in health and reproductive politics (1998: 269; see also Tobias, 1997: 91). Wolfson's leadership in the National Women's Health Network, especially in response to the Hyde Amendment that prohibited the use of Medicaid funds for abortions, solidified her concerns about the gender, race, and *class* biases within the whole gamut of reproductive rights and choices (Wolfson, 1998: 279–80). Other feminists responded in kind to the Hyde Amendment and data on sterilization abuse, starting multiracial coalitions, such as the Committee to End Sterilization Abuse and the Committee for Abortion Rights and against Sterilization Abuse (Tax, 1998: 319–20). Meredith Tax recalls, "Together we began to develop an analysis of reproductive rights that has now become so strong that few people care to remember how different the prevailing ideas were just fifteen years ago" (1998: 319–20).

These histories also counter the anti-abortion story that *Roe v. Wade* was created whole cloth from rampant judicial activism in our politics. In fact, many citizens, groups, and state legislatures were working to liberalize restrictive abortion laws before 1973. These include in 1969 and 1970 the American Public Health Association, Planned Parenthood, the trustees of the American Medical Association, and the board of managers of Church Women United (L. Kaplan, 1995: 117). Moderate groups, such as the American Association of University Women (AAUW), took early and consistent stances in favor of women's access to safe and affordable birth control and abortion. In 1935, the AAUW began its official support of reproductive rights by urging legalizing contraceptive distribution by physicians (Levy, 1998: 25). At its 1971 annual convention, Katherine Levy recounts, the AAUW "delegates passed a resolution stating that 'AAUW encourages its members and state divisions to work for repeal of restrictive laws on abortion, making abortion legal for those who wish it after medical consultation'" (1998: 25).

Scholars have also reexamined the history of religious views on abortion. Although the Catholic church's history on abortion has been used politically and ideologically to maintain a story of a consistent and total ban on abortion, careful scholarship has revealed that such major Catholic thinkers as Augustine and Thomas Aquinas relied on sentiency as a condition to being a moral patient and viewed early developing fetuses as akin to vegetation. "To put the matter in Augustinian or Thomistic terms," Daniel Dombrowski and Robert Deltete write, "fetal development consists in the transition from a vegetative state to a sentient one, *after which* (!) it is possible for human ensoulment (or personhood) to occur" (2000: 16). The position of many Catholic authorities that the fetus is a moral person from the moment of conception, then, is a more recent view for the Catholic church.

Subversive Behaviors

Women's "demand for abortions, generally hidden from public view and rarely spoken of in public, transformed medical practice and law over the course of the twentieth century," according to Reagan (1997: 1). During the era of illegal abortion, female patients exercised their powers to influence and change medical practice, while many physicians listened to their needs and demands (Reagan, 1997: 4). As women asserted their need for abortion, Reagan points out, they "implicitly asserted their sense of having a right to control their own reproduction," (1997: 6), but the era of illegal abortions "was devastating for women. A dual system of abortion, divided by race and class, developed" (1997: 15; see also Reagan, 2000; Schoen, 2000; Graber, 1996; Kesselman, 1998; and Gorney, 1998: 15–36).

Women's demands for abortion, however, eventually altered medical thinking and reshaped public policy. Women's abortion history resonated with the slogans "breaking the silence" and "silent no more," emboldening women to speak out in new ways. "In the late 1960s," Reagan writes, "an important tactic of the movement to legalize abortion was getting women to tell of their abortions at 'speakouts' and thus discover their shared experiences and shared oppression" (1997: 20). Reagan's research leads her to emphasize that the silence metaphor is apt for specific public and political forums that traditionally excluded women's speech. However, the metaphor has limitations, as Reagan points out:

> Emphasizing the "silence" surrounding abortion inaccurately represents the history of abortion and ignores what women did say in other arenas; women talked about abortion often. We need a more nuanced understanding of the ability of women to voice their concerns and of the limits on women's speech. They did not proclaim their abortions in open, political forums, but they did speak of their abortions among themselves and within smaller, more intimate spaces. Women talked about abortion in "private" spaces, at home, and in the semiprivate, semipublic spaces of medicine such as drug stores, doctors' and midwives' offices, hospitals, and birth control clinics. Discussion of abortion, like other female experiences of reproduction, was part of female life and conversation. (1997: 21)

Scholarship on Jane, the underground abortion service operating in Chicago before *Roe v. Wade*, reveals the lengths to which women would go to end unwanted pregnancies and how a sense of sisterhood and care developed among the women (and men) who kept the clandestine organization going for ideological rather than financial reasons (L. Kaplan, 1995; Gorney, 1998: 214). In time, the women in Jane boldly started to perform the abortions themselves. Ultimately, seven of the women abortionists were arrested (L. Kaplan, 1995: 219). After the *Roe* decision, the charges were dropped against the seven. During the four-year life of Jane, more than a hundred women were members of the secret group, and an estimated 11,000 abortions were performed through Jane (L. Kaplan, 1995: 280).

One thread within women's self-help activities involving women's health and abortion was to demystify them as "medical procedures" and remove them from the control of the mostly male medical profession (Gorney, 1998: 211–13). These self-help groups and the Jane network were audacious and subversive of the powers that be.

Telling Women's Stories

Women's stories were important political narratives in the pressure campaigns to reform criminal abortion laws. "Statistics," Celeste Condit writes, "delineated the scale of the problem, but narratives conveyed the nature of the human suffering and its moral status" (1990: 24). Compelling narratives of women's suffering under criminal abortion laws often centered on an "innocent" or "good" girl victim of these restrictive laws and policies. One example of this is Sherri Finkbine. Her case became a cause célèbre in 1962. A mother of four, Finkbine had taken thalidomide for nausea while she was pregnant with her fifth child. Thalidomide had recently been linked to birth defects. Finkbine's attempts to obtain a therapeutic abortion in her home state of Arizona were denied. She ultimately had the procedure in Sweden. The case highlighted problems with abortion laws and the class disparities for people not able to travel abroad for an abortion. For challenges to succeed, Condit contends, "rhetorical narratives must produce personal involvement and emotional arousal of a large audience. For a broad public to feel sorry for the agent and angry with the forces that bring her suffering, the character depicted must be 'good,' or, at the least, unable to control her own destiny" (1990: 25). Sympathetic women had to appear proper in the sense of being married and needing therapeutic abortions for reasons beyond their control. If women requested abortions because they were raped, they also had to be proper and sympathetic. Rape victims had to fit into the narrow script of what society sees as a "real rape" (Estrich, 1987). The abortion narratives, according to Condit, "avoided challenging the key values held by the public at the time, generally by portraying the woman as a helpless victim. She was making a choice not *against* motherhood but against situations which themselves violated the idealized image of motherhood" (1990: 26).

Condit's research suggests that the 1960–61 narratives of women who had had illegal abortions "generated the 'physicians' story,' most prominent in 1964–65" (1990: 189). The physicians told of maternal deaths, the damages from illegal abortions they had to deal with in emergency rooms around the country, and their inability to cope with individual women's health issues when restrictive statutes prohibited abortions unless the woman's life was in danger.

Rickie Solinger maintains that the physicians also participated in another angle to the story:

> An important strategy of many doctors in this era [1950–70] was to draw on the vulnerability of pregnant women to construct a definition of pregnancy that effaced the personhood of the individual pregnant woman. This definition created a safe place for the fetus and also for the doctor forced by law to adjudicate the extremely personal decisions of women, many of whom were resisting effacement. The subordination of the pregnant woman to the fetus revitalized medical participation in the abortion decision because the doctor was now required to make sure that the woman stayed moral, that is, *served her fetus correctly.* These postwar ideas are powerful demonstrations of the prevailing relationship then between scientific advances and ideological positions on women, pregnancy, and fetuses. (1998: 26, emphasis added)

In the abortion narratives testifying to the dangers girls and women faced when abortion was criminal, detailed and graphic descriptions of "back alley" abortions, the underworld and clandestine nature of the arrangements and their concomitant dangers and fears for the girls and women, stomach-turning images of the blood, guts, pain, and results of these illegal abortions helped make the case for reforms.

The history of illegal abortion also reveals how male authorities "punished" women who sought out illegal abortionists, suffered health consequences, and came into contact with police. For women who violated sexual norms, subtle methods of gendered discipline occurred. "The penalties imposed upon women for having illegal abortions," Reagan notes, "were not fines or jail sentences, but humiliating interrogation about sexual matters by male officials—often while women were on their death beds—and public exposure of their abortions" (1997: 114). Reagan contends that prosecutors, needing testimony from the patients themselves against illegal abortion providers, "understood the dangers of public exposure to women and used it for their own purposes" (1997: 168).

Articulating what girls and women went through when abortion was illegal is central to the pro-choice movements' message today to keep abortion "safe and legal." Solinger concludes from her study of the history of illegal abortion that political power and a prurient interest in sex are also evident. Abortion trials became occasions for male doctors, lawyers, judges, police, and jury members to publicly affirm their right to govern women's bodies, to punish and shame defiant women, and to enforce female vulnerability. In the name of sexual purity, these sex drenched trials were, in Solinger's words, actually "titillating dramas that pitted one woman against another—the alleged abortionist (cast most often as a perverse and mercenary harridan) against her putative client (the slut)" (1998: 18). The trials became cryptoporn displays ostensibly in the name of law, order, and public morality as "men invoked women's naked bodies, their sexuality, and their vulnerability in a style that was both contemptuous and erotic" (Solinger, 1998: 19). After World War II, in particular, many men felt threatened by the new roles women were assuming, and they reasserted their power over women's bodies. Abortion trial scripts called for women to be degraded, humiliated, exposed, and pitted against one another. Private and intimate aspects of their lives were exposed. The dramaturgy showcased male authority figures reaffirming their prerogatives over women's bodies, lives, and rights (Solinger, 1998: 19). The court spectacles, Solinger writes, "announced the danger and the just desserts for any woman associated with abortion" (1998: 20). These political trials also affirmed the state's willingness to place women in danger by upholding criminal abortion laws. Many women, however, resisted these definitions of themselves and their agency. Solinger points out it is important to remember "that it was *the law*, not illegal abortionists, that created, even mandated, danger for all women before *Roe v. Wade*" (Solinger, 1998: 28).

It was not until the *Thornburgh* case in 1986 that women's direct voices were presented to the Court by the National Abortion Rights Action League's amicus brief. These voices from the women who would be directly affected by abortion jurisprudence presented to the judges the cultural context, or the political meaning of abortion, a viewpoint that added to the legal conventions involving constitutional rights (Behuniak, 1999: 144).

The 1989 *Webster v. Reproductive Health Services* case displayed another remarkable effort by pro-choice adherents to make visible and tangible the lives of real women negotiating their reproductive lives and sometimes needing a legal, safe abortion (Woliver, 1992b and 1993b; see also Colker, 1990; and Gorney, 1998: 402–6). In one amicus brief, nicknamed "the voices brief," the National Abortion Rights Action League (NARAL) compiled letters from 2,887 women who had had abortions (those illegal before *Roe* and legal ones after *Roe*) and 627 friends of women and girls who had had both illegal and legal abortions (Brief for the Amici Curiae Women Who Have Had Abortions in *Webster*, 1989). The NARAL brief's message complemented its advertising campaign at the time entitled "Silent No More," which was directed at making public the hidden history of abortion.

Similarly, the amicus brief called "the women of color" brief in *Webster* sought to add the dimensions of race and social class to girls' and women's reproductive lives (Amicus Brief of the National Council of Negro Women et al., in *Webster v. Reproductive Services*, 1989). Later cases, in particular the *Casey* (1992) decision, included feminist data and analysis on the lives of women (for example, the extent of domestic violence in relationships) in the majority opinion.

Spotlighting the lack of women's voices in abortion politics, one amicus brief asserts, "Every restrictive abortion law has been passed by a legislature in which men constitute a numerical majority. And every restrictive abortion law, by definition, contains an unwritten clause exempting all men from its strictures" ("Amicus Brief of 274 Organizations in Support of *Roe v. Wade* in *Turnock v. Ragsdale* [1994]," 2001: 561). These feminist lawyers thus stress the need for "strict scrutiny standards"[1] of equal protection law under the Fourteenth Amendment to the U.S. Constitution (based not on privacy but on equality) in abortion cases: "That is particularly so where, as here, the women most likely to be affected are those whom the political process protects least well. A world without *Roe* will not be a world without abortion, but a world in which abortion is accessible according to one's constitutional caste" ("Amicus Brief of 274 Organizations in Support of *Roe v. Wade* in *Turnock v. Ragsdale* [1994]," 2001: 561).

Telling Fetuses' Stories

Ironically, narratives and images of the process and results of abortions are also used by those against legal abortion for the same effect. Abortion is unique among political issues because the event itself can be symbolized with blood, body parts, "gross" and "indecent" depictions of women's genitals, and reproductive organs. In a culture where the details of innocuous female physical occurrences, such as menstruation, are kept hidden and private, the public display of the physical details of abortions is sure to evoke repugnance in an audience. In fact, any surgery, if filmed, photographed, blown up, detailed, backgrounded, or highlighted, would be shocking for many people. The anti-abortion movement has also projected the "voice" of the fetus, as Reagan points out, "to compete with and discredit the voices of real, live women, a group that only recently spoke of its experiences in public, political arenas. The fetus has been used to shift the debate away from women and their narratives about the crimes of illegal abortion. Silencing the political voice of women, however, is only one aspect of a far-reaching project" (1997: 248).

The power of narrative is also evoked by anti-abortion adherents. One narrative links fetuses who stand outside the law by U.S. Supreme Court decision and African Americans who also stood outside the law by the Supreme Court's *Dred Scott* decision in 1857 and Jews whose persecution was justified by Nazi laws. As Condit observes, the "pro-life heritage tale" seeks to invoke and retell the story of our past "in order to reinvigorate the heritage, giving it enough force to combat the new tales" (1990: 43). American slavery, the Nazi Holocaust, other horrific acts of human cruelty, and legal abortion are all presented as strands of evil in history that Americans overcome through a series of trials and tribulations. "Because the meaning of history arises from the intertwining of theme and event, and because the dimension of evil is a powerful magnifier," Condit contends, these are forceful techniques (1990: 49).

One rhetorical devise seen in abortion politics is "over-weighing." "The rhetorical tactic of over-weighing," Condit explains, "is a basic comparison strategy. With it, rhetors attempt to show that the values and interests on their side carry more weight than those of the opposition" (1990: 159). Pro-life activists might concede, for instance, that a woman has a right to privacy and to control her body, but those rights are not more powerful than the right of the fetus to live; the woman does not have the right to murder her potential child in the name of the lesser rights of privacy and bodily integrity. Over-weighing is a dominant discursive force in the late 1970s and the 1980s as anti-abortion forces were unable to recriminalize abortion. Over-weighing, however, has dangerous potentials, as Condit makes clear:

> Those who choose to over-weigh rather than to seek compromise write off any competing claims and move into a uni-dimensional understanding of the world unbounded by other restraining principles, terms, and factors. Once a set of activists decides that the opposition's values are outweighed by its own, *and can therefore be totally ignored,* they can easily depict opponents as devil figures and supporters as saints. One's own grounds become the sole values; therefore, any means are justified to secure those ends. The dominance of the over-weighing strategy was thus the necessary rhetorical component which led pro-Life activists away from the sanctioned American method of persuasion and toward coercion, law-breaking, and violence. (1990: 160)

While many pro-life organizations and activists are intertwined with churches and religious movements, this connection is a touchy subject for some in American politics. In the late 1980s and throughout the 1990s, religious activists often remarked that those who critiqued their positions on religious grounds were engaged in "Christian bashing" or were anti-religious altogether. Many people defended the religiously based nature of political activism, comparing anti-abortion links to religious institutions with those of the American civil rights movement. Anti-choice activists argued that religious beliefs have a place in American political discourse and that the mere connection to a religious principle does not refute the message of an activist. Sometimes, however, the religion and political entanglements imbroglio meant that activists minimized the religious roots of their convictions regarding abortion.[2]

The plausibility of the linkage to the civil rights movement provides political mileage for the anti-choice cause, but as Condit points out, "its argument contained gaps serious enough to leave it stalemated against the reform narrative" and revealed women's history, which forced its retelling (1990: 43).

Roe's Progress and Limitations

In the landmark abortion case *Roe v. Wade* (1973), however, the complexities of women's lives are strikingly absent. Much abortion jurisprudence is a story about doctors and fetuses instead of women's lives, because the court often reasons about reproductive policies in physiological paradigms, framing regulation as state action concerning women's bodies rather than women's rights. This is despite the historical context for the regulation and criminalization of abortion, which was to control women's social roles and lives (Siegel, 1992: 261). *Roe v. Wade*, as Susan Behuniak writes, "is without a doubt a case intimately connected with women—their rights, their status, and their lives—it is also a case in which women's knowledge was eclipsed by medical knowledge, and women's interests were obscured by physicians' interests" (1999: 31).

Behuniak argues that the twenty-four abortion cases decided after *Roe v. Wade* display a pattern "dependent not so much on patients' rights but on whether the restriction impinges on the discretion of physicians to practice. The impact of the Court's reliance on medical knowledge, then, reaches beyond the issue of what is heard to affect as well what is decided and how" (1999: 32). Given these legal norms, Behuniak writes, "some types of knowledge were amplified while other forms were muted" (1999: 33). Examining the amicus, plaintiff, and appellant briefs for the landmark *Roe v. Wade* case, Behuniak found that patients' stories were in the dissonant notes of the amicus briefs. Even then, however, "the sound has been dubbed: when patients' concerns and experiences are presented, they are told by others and not by patients themselves. There are no first-person accounts of what abortion means (for better or for worse) for the women who have experienced it, no stories, no telling of the horror of what it was like to undergo an illegal abortion or how it felt to lack reliable information about the procedure" (Behuniak, 1999: 38–39). As a collection, the amicus briefs did not directly challenge the dominant theme that abortion is a *medical* issue (Behuniak, 1999: 38–39). Because of the legal norms, the concrete, emotional, and experiential nature of patients' knowledge rendered them virtually voiceless in *Roe v. Wade* (Behuniak, 1999: 40). However, these same legal norms amplified the voice of medical knowledge, thus dictating that the terms of the discussion would fit the medico-legal template. "By defining abortion as a medical issue," Behuniak observes, "physicians moved to the center of the case whether they had official standing or not" (1999: 40–41). "In essence," Behuniak writes, "*Roe* holds that while the state may not interfere with the woman's decision during the first trimester, the physician, a lack of physicians, or a lack of money may" (1999: 51). Physicians become required participants in the abortion decision, and *Roe*'s use of negative privacy rights protects physicians' use of their own medical discretion. Physicians' discretion, not women's rights, triumph in *Roe v.*

Wade (Behuniak, 1999: 51). One consequence of shaping abortion jurisprudence in *Roe* "as a medical decision is that it forces women to fit their
experiences into the medical model and themselves into a decision making partnership with doctors, whether the abortion decision is based on
health needs or not" (Behuniak, 1999: 52).

Female patient knowledge about abortion contradicted medical and
legal givens in two ways. First, women told of the relationships at stake
in movements for legal abortion rights. Second, women were willing to
be the judges on whether state regulations and restrictions on abortion
were "undue burdens" on women's decision-making abilities (Behuniak,
1999: 145). Patients knowledge, for instance, meant that "[w]hile physicians asked for protection as they worked within the doctor-patient relationship, women asked the Court to give them clear access to abortion
services so that they could protect relationships of emotional significance.
The *Roe* decision respected the concerns of the physicians while ignoring those of the pregnant women," according to Behuniak (1999: 146).

Behuniak's careful study of the twenty-four abortion cases after *Roe*
echoes the same power of medical authorities over women's experiences.
Behuniak's study displays the contrasting powerlessness of women patients: "[S]tate measures that second-guess the decision, that attempt to
dissuade women from the abortion decision, that allow parents, the state,
and physicians to exert influence, and that delay the abortion procedure
demonstrate that patients' judgments can be challenged in a way that
physicians' judgments cannot" (1999: 60). Harm done to patients is un-
addressed. Because the cost of "objectivity" in these legal decisions is a
lack of care, physicians win more than women patients in the abortion
decisions. "In the name of justice, medical knowledge was given a legal
forum while patients were denied recognition as knowers," Behuniak
concluded (1999: 63).

Abortion, Women's Praxis of the Ethic of Care

Including the voices of women who have chosen abortions would also
reveal that for the most part these women make ethical decisions embedded in an ethic of care, cognizant of their own contexts and situations,
and aware of the nurturing needs of prospective and existing children and
themselves. Carol Gilligan's book *In a Different Voice* is partly based on
interviews with women who decided to have abortions. Gilligan and
other scholars, including Rosalind Petchesky, Rayna Rapp, Barbara Katz
Rothman, and Kristin Luker, converge in their findings that women (and
couples) who choose abortions do so with a nurturing ethic in mind, one

based on relationships and a fully fleshed out assessment of their own capabilities and needs. The ethical principle threaded throughout these abortion narratives, interviews, and social science studies is that *"nurturance matters"* (Cowan, 1992: 257). Feminist ethicists understand from their experiences as wives, parents, nurses, and social workers that you must balance caring for others with proper care of yourself. Women should not be expected to take care of others at the expense of themselves. "Indeed," Ruth Cowan asserts, "those who call the decision to abort when the mother is pregnant with an afflicted fetus 'selfish' are responding in the context of an ethical system in which both nurturers and nurturance have never been accorded primacy and in which the sacrifice of individual to group goals has always been favored—precisely the ethical system which feminist ethicists are hoping to supersede" (Cowan, 1992: 258). Gail Landsman and Eva Kittay know the centrality of human dependency on community and nurturing from their lives raising children with disabilities and doing much of the nurturing work for dependent loved ones, including the disabled. The work of care is important, overlooked, and undervalued, yet it is an essential aspect of human communities. Because mostly women do this dependency work, however, it is written out of much social theory or discussions on reproductive politics.

Nurturance (which can be folded into and validated within an ethic of care) is a liberal, feminist, ethical principle. "An abortion policy constructed in accordance with the principle that *nurturance matters* is clearly one in which the decision to abort should rest entirely in the hands of the woman who is pregnant," Cowan insists (1992: 258).

An alternative jurisprudence of justice and care would enable the courts to hear the knowledge of patients. A caring jurisprudence would integrate an ethic of justice and an ethic of care by recognizing the knowledge that patients have to offer, whereas willful blindness to patients' knowledge results in uncaring jurisprudence (Behuniak, 1999: 103–32). Behuniak's point in her admonitions for a caring jurisprudence "is that patients' knowledge, though particular, involved, and emotional, is still knowledge and is still of value to the Court" (1999: 163).

Abortion Politics in Local Communities

Whether a woman can choose a legal abortion depends on access. Since the physical facilities where women go to have abortions are most often in cities, highly contentious conflicts concerning abortion often get fought out within the regulatory jurisdictions and powers of local governments, ineluctably pulling city officials into "the eye of a firestorm"

(Sharp, 1996: 738; Tatalovich and Daynes, 1988). The uncompromising nature of abortion politics guarantees its role as fodder in urban culture wars. As Elaine Sharp points out, "In the case of culture wars, ideas—and in particular the cultural ideals and moralistic stakes that are at the root of culture war controversies—are also raw materials for political entrepreneurs and constraints upon political repressors" (1998: 261).

The U.S. Supreme Court decision in *Webster v. Reproductive Health Services, Inc.* (1989) permitted state restrictions on abortion services, heightening the potential political power of grass-roots mobilizing over state and local abortion legislation. Some assert that *Webster* "refederalized" abortion politics by returning the primary focus of abortion policy-making to the states (Segers and Byrnes, 1995: 5–12). Abortion has become an important issue in state elections (Cook, Jelen, and Wilcox, 1994: 198). Anti-abortion groups have succeeded in targeting state legislatures for restrictions on abortion providers, services, and procedures (O'Connor, 1996: 62–65; Halva-Neubauer, 1993). State and local policies, cultures, and practices will therefore be very important for future access to legal abortions.

Mobilizing grass-roots activists to pressure the national government is also a time-honored and powerful tactic (see, for example, Garrow, 1978; Woliver, 1996b, 1998a, and 1998c; and Gimpel, 1998). How city officials handle aspects of modern political culture wars will shape abortion access tremendously. Culture wars involve people with opposing worldviews about the role of the state in dictating personal morality and private behavior. Such issues as gay rights, legal abortion, sex education for children, single motherhood, and divorce invoke heated battles in our culture wars. Communication, pressure tactics and results, and political resources flow from national social movements (anti-choice, pro-choice, feminist, antifeminist) to state and local abortion interest groups. A reverse flow from local activists to state and national movements is also evident in abortion politics.

Social Movements, Abortion, and Culture Wars

Grass-roots mobilizing is facilitated by fluid social movements and preexisting networks, coalitions, and organizations that reshape themselves to incorporate the new local issue. As Debra Friedman and Doug McAdam explain, "Successful movements usually do not create attractive collective identities from scratch; rather, they redefine existing roles within established organizations as the basis of an emerging activist identity" (1992: 162). Local abortion politics displays this as religious, conservative, progressive, and liberal groups and networks reorient their goals and attentions and overlap in their involvements with abortion issues.

My examination of abortion in South Carolina is informed by dozens of interviews conducted since 1991 with lobbyists, amicus brief writers, interest group leaders, and spokespeople in both pro-life and pro-choice camps at the national level and in South Carolina. In Columbia and Greenville, South Carolina, additional interviews were conducted with retired and active city, police, and court officials. Correspondence, personal interviews, and direct observations of both pro-life and pro-choice speakers, protests, church gatherings, court proceedings, and legislative hearings over the years in South Carolina are also woven into this analysis. The hope is to explore the way large, fluid social movements impact abortion activists at the state and local levels, fueling local culture wars that affect access to legal abortion and thus shift the terrain of reproductive powers.

As Kristin Luker found, pro-life and pro-choice abortion activists have opposing worldviews, in which the moral status of the embryo is an implicit statement about the role of children and women in modern American society (1984; see also Rhode and Lawson, 1993: 4; and N. Press and Cole, 1999). Abortion activists manifest the link between status movements and identity issues. Hank Johnston, Enrique Larana, and Joseph Gusfield explain: "Here the grievances are actuated by perceived threats to how one defines oneself, such as the way that the popularization of abortion threatens, for some women, traditional conceptions of motherhood. Status movements take action about 'other people's business' because that business often poses a threat to how the mobilizing group defines itself" (1994: 23). These identity issues about status, worth, and rights can become mobilizing factors for new social movements whose adherents bring their culture wars to cities.

The Context for Urban Abortion Battles: The State

South Carolina is a very conservative state, tending to be strongly Republican in both national and state elections (Barone and Ujifusa, 1998: 1266–90). Republican party leaders nationwide have increasingly taken staunch pro-life positions (G. Adams, 1997). South Carolina Republican party leaders are similarly anti-abortion. At the same time, South Carolina has a number of clinics that openly provide abortion services and a fairly healthy and well-supported Planned Parenthood affiliate that offers a range of health care options for women, including abortion. However, the number of clinics providing abortion service in South Carolina has dwindled from eighteen in 1992 to five in 2001 (Woliver and Ledford, 2001).

A sample of county-level party activists in the South found women and men divided on women's equality issues; 55 percent of the females and only 29 percent of the men strongly favored women's equality with men (Day and Hadley, 1997: 684). South Carolina ranks near the bottom of the fifty states in many indicators of women's political integration, including the percentage of women elected to public office (Woliver and Ledford, 2001; Darcy, Welsch, and Clark, 1987; see also C. Graham and Moore, 1994: 122–23; and Keyserling, 1998). The proportion of women in state legislatures is one indicator for the shape of abortion politics in that state; low female representation means a greater likelihood that restrictive abortion laws will pass (Byrnes, 1995: 260–63).

South Carolina has many politically active churches. The power and activism of conservative churches and religiously based organizations, law firms, and think tanks have played an important role in abortion politics nationally and at the local level (J. Green, Rozell, and Wilcox, 2000; Guth, 1995; Ivers, 1998; J. Green, Guth, Smidt, and Kellstedt, 1996; Smith, 1997). The anti-abortion movement has been able to tap into deeply felt religious beliefs and disgust with mainstream modern American society, politics, and values (Aho, 1996; Blanchard, 1994; R. Williams and Blackburn, 1996; Simonds, 1996; Himmelstein, 1990).

One dominant cultural theme in recent South Carolina politics is aggressive courting of economic development prospects. Political Action Committee contributions to South Carolina politicians reflect a dominant pro-business presence and an almost invisible union effort (Botsch, 1992; see also M. Schneider and Teske, 1993). Even traditionally hallowed, religiously based laws, such as the "blue laws" that restricted commerce and liquor sales on Sundays, have recently been reformed in the face of strong business interests concerned with tourism and industrial and resort development. In 1996, the Greenville County Council passed an anti-gay ordinance that resulted in the Olympic Torch's being shrouded as it passed through Greenville County on the way to Atlanta (the torch was uncovered in the city of Greenville itself). The bad publicity this caused for Greenville was universally lamented by interviewees and was linked in their assessments to local anti-abortion activism (interviews; see also Wyman, 1996a and 1996b). City officials worried that publicity over anti-gay county ordinances or strident and conflictual showdowns at such places as the women's clinics would harm the area's pro-business prospects.

Current abortion politics reflects outrage when practices and behaviors long known to have occurred clandestinely, with governmental knowledge if not protection, are brought out into the open. As Dallas Blanchard puts it, "Their [anti-abortion activists'] primary concern is not the *occurrence* of abortion but its *legalization,* which gives it the stamp of legal and, more important, moral approval" (1994: 107). As many scholars have documented, abortions have always occurred, with selective enforcement of the police powers to stop them in states that officially outlawed the procedure (Graber, 1996; J. Mohr, 1978). South Carolina's history and practices are no different (interviews).

Greenville and Columbia, South Carolina: Clinics in the Opposition's Backyard

Greenville is more conservative than Columbia. Greenville is home to the conservative Bob Jones University, for one thing.[3] While the Bob Jones University community seems to set a tone in the city, it has only indirect influence in the abortion wars. However, the influence of Bob Jones University faculty, staff, students, and alumni is widely acknowledged in Greenville politics. Columbia, as the state capital and the site of the University of South Carolina,[4] is not as conservative as the rest of the area or many other parts of the state. Richland County, where Columbia is located, for instance, is a Democratic county. Columbia is also more racially diverse than Greenville.

Both cities have experienced rapid population growth in the last fifteen years. The Greenville-Spartanburg area, in particular, has had a boom in growth and economic development (the BMW automobile manufacturing plant and many others have located to the area). This rapid and dramatic growth, one Greenville official postulated, helped cause some of the political friction in the area as the old guard, which had handled everything quietly, is now challenged by new people with new ideas and lifestyles, who do not as a matter of course accept the ruling hand of that old guard.

Greenville has had more anti-abortion activity than any other place in the state. Columbia, with similar numbers of clinics, has had fewer confrontations and arrests. Operation Rescue, an anti-abortion organization, targeted Greenville in 1989, resulting in many arrests.

The Grass-Roots Issue Context

A 1990 study classified South Carolina as an "acquiescer state," noting a propensity to avoid discussing abortion in the aftermath of *Roe v. Wade.* South Carolina was one of only fifteen states to enact a therapeutic abortion law before *Roe v. Wade* (Halva-Neubauer, Tatalovich, and Daynes, 1993: 17). The complexity of the general public's attitudes toward abortion and the increasingly partisan distinctions on the issue (K. Dugger, 1991; G. Adams, 1997; Conway, Steuernagel, and Ahern, 1997; N. Press and Cole, 1999) are echoed in South Carolina.

National social movement influences are evident at the state level regarding abortion politics in South Carolina. Many of the groups active in abortion issues at the local level are "repeat players," with all the advantages of experience, connections, networks, and seasoned staff that entails (Galanter, 1974; see also Staggenborg, 1991 and 1996; and O'Connor, 1996 and 1998: 282). Pro-choice interests are connected to national offices of pro-choice groups, have commitments and coalitions that are feminist, and are staffed by activists who are feminist (interviews). Both Greenville and Columbia have chapters of the National Organization for Women (NOW). In Greenville, the local NOW chapter is instrumental in organizing clinic escorts when needed, and chapter leaders are frequently relied on by the local press for statements on abortion disputes. The pro-life activists are also tied to national groups that lobby for the pro-life point of view. Pro-life interests in South Carolina can tap into another network as well: conservative church groups, which provide an easily mobilizable, co-optable network of participants.

Niche positioning, where interest groups specialize in certain tactics, political behavior, and positions, is evident in South Carolina abortion politics. The state Planned Parenthood affiliate, for instance, monitors legislation that would inhibit the ability of abortion clinics to conduct business. The state American Civil Liberties Union argues the bigger, more politically based points regarding privacy rights, First Amendment freedoms, and women's rights more broadly (interviews).

Pro-life groups also have niches. Columbia Sidewalk Counseling and Greenville's Pastors for Life engage in face-to-face debates with clinic staff, patients, and supporters on more than a weekly basis, while South Carolina Citizens for Life (the state National Right to Life affiliate) does more traditional lobbying and grass-roots organizing (interviews). Overlayed is the lobbying by conservative Christian groups concerned with "family values," "morality," and "parental rights" (as in parental consent to a teenager's abortion).

Radical groups play an important role in abortion politics, particularly among pro-life activists. Pro-life spokespersons consistently denounce pro-life activists who engage in civil disobedience and destructive acts, including the killing of abortion clinic personnel (interviews). Yet the outrageousness of those people makes the behavior of more "reasoned," seemingly less radical pro-life groups seem moderate and under-standable. This "radical flank effect" redounds to the benefit of other, perhaps more reasonable groups in a larger movement (McAdam, McCar-thy, and Zald, 1996: 14) and plays a role in the fluid nature of social movements.

In 1995–96, an important battle was waged over licensing regulations being written by the South Carolina Department of Health and Environ-mental Control (DHEC) for any clinic where five or more abortions are performed per month (Woliver and Ledford, 2001). Proposed regulations included disclosure of the names of doctors, patients, and patient's hus-bands to DHEC, detailed requirements about the physical plant and equipment, and mandatory reporting rules. Pro-choice groups saw these as increasing the financial costs for clinics and patients and raising the psychic cost to patients who feared their names could slip into public records (Scoppe, 1996; Planned Parenthood of Central South Carolina and Planned Parenthood of the Low Country, 1996). Pro-life forces saw these regulations as protecting the health and safety of the women seeking abortions and any potentially viable fetus that survives the procedure. Pro-life forces saw the clinic regulations as a small, incremental victory in their long march to close all abortion clinics and stop all the provid-ers (interviews). The regulations passed and have withstood pro-choice legal challenges. Pro-choice activists in South Carolina believe the regu-lations are forcing some clinics to close.

One related development in South Carolina was a recent South Caro-lina Supreme Court decision upholding the prosecution and conviction of a substance-abusing woman for taking illegal drugs in the days before her baby was born. She was prosecuted and convicted of child abuse for providing an illegal drug to a child. The South Carolina Supreme Court decision (*Whitner v. State of South Carolina*, No. 24468, July 15, 1996) held that a viable fetus is a person for certain purposes under South Caro-lina law, including being protected by criminal child abuse statutes. The holding and language in this majority opinion (there was one dissenter) are very encouraging and important for pro-life groups in South Carolina.

Partial-Birth, Late-Term Abortion Ban

The strength of pro-life interests in South Carolina is seen in the recent quick passage of a state ban on late-term abortions. Terminology here is important. As Katha Pollitt notes, "It isn't often that the insur-gents define the language of the debate" (1997: 9). With late-term abortions, however, they do. The media utilize the insurgent, anti-choice language of "partial-birth abortion," a much more loaded term than the medical term "intact dilation and extraction." The media were able to do this because the pro-abortion adherents lacked a similarly catchy, succinct phrase to describe this rare and complicated procedure. The debate about these procedures is therefore framed in the insurgent's symbolic language by both media outlets and anti-choice politicians and lobbyists. At the same time, the disputes over banning late-term abortions deflect discussion from the poverty, ignorance, fear, youth, and lack of access to health care that might have caused girls and women to be in situations where they would be seeking these more dangerous and traumatic medical procedures.

After President Clinton's 1996 veto of the "partial-birth abortion" ban, the National Right to Life Committee (NRLC) sent copies of the federal bill to their state affiliates. The South Carolina affiliate quickly handed a copy of the federal bill to an ally in the South Carolina legislature. The slightly amended bill passed the South Carolina assembly (the house) by a vote of 105 to 4, with no amendments. In the South Carolina senate, the bill moved through in a record nine days and was passed without amendment and without opposition. The senate had a voice vote on the bill, and no nays were heard (interviews; see also Scoppe, 1997a and 1997b). The only exception to the ban is if it is documented that the abortion is the *only* way the mother's life can be saved. South Carolina's Governor David Beasley happily signed the bill.

National and local pro-life activists have stated that these bans are just the start of their piece-by-piece efforts to scare doctors away from offering abortions and to establish precedents where state authorities protect the fetus as human life (Pollitt, 1997: 9). The *Whitner* decision in South Carolina goes hand in glove with these local victories. These state legislative and judicial victories illustrate the relative power of groups and activists concerned about abortion policy in South Carolina. This climate is well understood by city officials when abortion issues are raised in their jurisdictions.

A National Conflagration Negotiated Locally One Day at a Time

On January 24, 1994, the U.S. Supreme Court in the *National Organization for Women v. Scheidler* upheld the use of the Racketeer Influenced and Corrupt Organization Act (RICO) against abortion clinic protesters. In 1994, the Freedom of Access to Clinic Entrances Act (FACE) made violence at abortion clinics a federal offense and provided for stiff jail sentences and fines and potentially (depending on a president's abortion stance and directions to the attorney general) strong enforcement through the huge resources of the Department of Justice. Potential use of both RICO and FACE, with their stiff fines, jail terms, and Department of Justice involvement, along with a further U.S. Supreme Court ruling (*Madsen v. Women's Health Center,* 1994) that a thirty-six-foot buffer zone between protesters and clinic entrances and driveways was not a violation of the First Amendment rights to free speech and assembly, has hampered some of the aggressive local anti-abortion protest (interviews; see also Kelly, 1995: 207; and Risen and Thomas, 1998: 339–71). Officials in Columbia and Greenville (no matter what their views might be on abortion) expressed gratitude for the relief federal court orders and FACE provided in trying to negotiate and contain clinic confrontations. In abortion conflicts at the local level, procedures that diminished a repression potential by local officials were from federal court cases, injunctions, and legislation. These procedures provided local officials with authority to regulate the free speech rights of the protesters and the free access rights for the clinics. At the same time, city officials could avoid the wrath of local activists by claiming they were merely implementing federal laws and orders.

Although criticized as "the feds mandate," RICO and FACE actually help structure the local officials' responses and deflect criticism from city authorities trying to negotiate some kind of coexistence day by day. In almost every interview I conducted, city officials stated some version of the position that *Roe v. Wade* was the law of the land and that their role was simply to keep the peace and not make abortion policy. Well known, however, to South Carolina politicians at all levels is the steady tightening down of state laws on abortion regulations and the tremendous Republican party victories in the state. One evasive maneuver by local officials in the culture wars involving abortion is to invoke their powerlessness in policy-making and to direct outraged citizens to state and federal authorities.

Another theme the interviews revealed is how vulnerable local officials feel about whether one city or another becomes a locus for another "Wichita" (a reference to the prolonged period of civil disobedience, clinic blockades, protests, and arrests in Wichita, Kansas, staged by Operation Rescue). Although interviewees expressed faith that their own home-grown demonstrators (on both sides of the issue), with whom they have

been routinely dealing for years, would not resort to violence, many officials recounted their fears of "an outside nut case" coming through. The
safety of the doctors at the clinics was particularly of concern to them.
The specter of outside groups deciding that your city would be a good
target for a sustained, highly media-genic protest or the nightmares caused
by a "single nut case," as one official put it, driving to your town with
his loaded guns makes these officials face the randomness and "simply
fate" nature of how such an issue as abortion could play out locally.

One derivative of the conservative political climate in South Carolina is an intolerance of vociferous dissent and a steely law-and-order
orientation. In both Greenville and Columbia, the willingness of law
enforcement to arrest abortion protesters and prosecute them was well
publicized before announced or rumored blockades, and, for the most part,
their admonishments were implemented (interviews; see also Halva-
Neubauer, Tatalovich, and Daynes, 1993: 20).

What city officials did have in the 1990s, however, which they did
not have in the 1980s, were the federal court injunctions, the RICO threat,
and FACE. These they credit with a recent downturn in arrests and vio-
lently disruptive confrontations at the clinics (see also Segers, 1995: 237).

The anti-abortionists' focus at the Greenville city level has shifted
to constantly questioning city officials about zoning ordinances, public
health requirements, and traffic safety, to name a few. These complaints
take an inordinate amount of local officials' time. In Greenville, this
minute monitoring (to some people "harassing") of whether clinics have
violated any ordinance, code, or health policy was made easier when
Pastors for Life purchased the building adjacent to one of the main Greenville clinics. The two buildings "share" a driveway. Disputes concerning the driveway and much else (the tall fence, zoning ordinance violations, the traffic in and out) have continuously been brought to city
officials. "One side always wants the other side to be whipped into shape
by the City," one experienced hand reported, continuing, "So our involvement [the City of Greenville's] doesn't relate to the critical issue of whether a woman should be able to choose freely to carry a fetus or whether
this is a human being who should be protected, this is the concern of those
advocates. But, they articulate their issue within the city administrative
framework of zoning, safety, and having the police enforce a city's court
injunction" (interviews). Often clinic personnel, anti-abortion protesters,
and police officers develop standard routines surrounding their efforts
(interviews; see also Simonds, 1996; and Hertz, 1991).

City officials assert these are not really what city workers, police, and elected local officials are trained and hired or elected to do. As one high-ranking official sighed, "What you need is a good kindergarten teacher" (interview).

Evaluations of grass-roots successes and failures need to be judged within a community context. Pro-choice and pro-life groups have battled for years in South Carolina over parental consent laws, licensing requirements, "right to know" legislation, the "human life" amendment, "rescue" operations, and much more. Given the politics of South Carolina, what is very interesting is how steady the support has been for Planned Parenthood in South Carolina and how consistently the public opinion polls in South Carolina indicate basic citizen support for legal abortion. The rate of abortions in South Carolina is similar to that of other states. Yet, at the same time, pro-life forces have made steady inroads. Moreover, the pro-abortion forces in South Carolina have a difficult time mobilizing their adherents. The 1997 abortion clinic regulations are expected to close some clinics down or at least raise their expenses, which will have to be passed on to patients. A future fear for pro-choice activists, and a future dream for pro-life, is the inability to find doctors and medical staff for the clinics currently operating. State and local restriction on abortion access has been severe (Schroedel, 2000; Pertman, 2001).

The easy victory of the pro-life forces in 1997 in the South Carolina "partial-birth abortion" ban indicates the growing strength of the pro-life coalition to dominate debates in a state like South Carolina. Interviewees revealed that pro-life forces see the 1997 ban as a first step in a long process "to take Supreme Court decisions to their limits" and push hard to decrease access, physician involvement, and public support for abortion. Local anti-abortion activists try to bring to bear city ordinances, zoning issues, and heightened public awareness of the locations and business of the abortion clinics to keep the pressure up at the local level, while anti-abortion interests further clamp down on the clinics through state legislation. Pro-choice interests counter with the imprimatur of *Roe v. Wade*, RICO, FACE, and related court decisions to make city officials keep the peace at their clinics and permit them to conduct their business without undue hindrances. Many of the objectives of local pro-life activists are thus achieved in the state legislature and courts. For pro-choice people, a steady whittling away of options and choices affects the future operations of the clinics. Pro-choice activists hope that eventual diffusion of new choices, such as RU-486, the abortion "pill," will decenter the clinics as foci of struggles and place pregnancy-termination decisions and policy-making more within the private realm of doctors and their female patients making individualized health care decisions. Local diffusion of RU-486, however, has been hampered and restricted (Woliver and Ledford, 2001).

Interest Group Representations of Reproductive Politics

Interest groups representing doctors have been partly responsible for the marginalization and stigmatization of abortion (Joffe, 1995: 27–52). Curiously, a lengthy history of the American Medical Association (AMA) since 1940, authorized by the AMA and written by a longtime employee of the association, does not discuss reproductive politics. In the entire 603–page volume, there are two lines on abortion. One is a mention of the Student American Medical Association's 1967 statement supporting liberalization of abortion laws (Campion, 1984: 300). The second line is on the next page and refers to the incoming AMA president's intent to "liberalize the A.M.A.'s traditional and strongly conservative stand on abortion" (Campion, 1984: 301). Several themes of the book strike me as appropriate to medical doctors' involvement in abortion politics. The study documents how doctors want to be independent, autonomous professionals. The AMA has a time-honored opposition to government control of medicine and vociferously attempts to keep politics out of the practice of medicine. The doctors want to be able to do what is best for each individual patient as determined by the doctor's professional judgment and scientific training. Even in defeat (Medicare, Medicaid), the AMA has consistently fought against perceived encroachments of government control on medical care.

In 1967, the American Medical Association's house of delegates endorsed a reform proposal called the ALI (American Law Institute) model legislation, a liberal reform of abortion laws. At the same time, a poll taken for *Modern Medicine* magazine showed 86.9 percent of the forty thousand surveyed doctors in favor of liberalized abortion laws (Risen and Thomas, 1998, 14). Ironically, decades earlier, the medical profession was largely responsible for instituting the criminal abortion statutes that the doctors now believe need liberal reform (Joffe, 1995: 27–52).

Perhaps if this history of the AMA were updated, it would include more about reproductive politics. The AMA, for instance, took a controversial stand when it did not oppose the latest "partial-birth abortion" ban in the Congress (interviews). After all, state legislatures and the U.S. Congress now debate and define when life begins, what a "partial-birth abortion" is, and how doctors must proceed to care for patients regarding reproductive decisions and options. The AMA and many other medical associations were thus pulled into reproductive politics, partly as a defensive maneuver.

Groups representing the medical profession are drawn into abortion politics, not necessarily out of a concern about the rights of women but because the outcome of the abortion wars will profoundly affect medicine. The abortion wars are currently affecting biomedical research directly, as can be seen in the disputes over stem cell research.

In a previous study, I examined the way medical groups represented their interests in four U.S. Supreme Court abortion cases (*Webster v. Reproductive Health Services* [1989], *Rust v. Sullivan* [1991], *Planned Parenthood of Southeastern Pennsylvania v. Casey* [1992], and *Bray v. Alexandria Women's Health Clinic* [1993]) (Woliver, 1993).[5] Associations of hospitals, doctors, nurses, public health officials, bioethicists, and medical school faculty have argued to the court the medical nature of abortion, government's intrusion in the doctor-patient relationship, and the ethical obligations of medical professionals in reproductive health.

The medical representation in current abortion cases is partly a result of the medical emphasis in the *Roe* majority opinion. The medical arguments, though, might unnecessarily highlight the science and technology of abortion procedures, with the perhaps unintentional result of overshadowing the social context in which women make their abortion decisions and reifying science as one of the arbiters of abortion jurisprudence. Women's reproductive decisions, however, are much more complex than simply medical or technological choices. The entire context in which women negotiate their reproduction should be included in abortion politics (see also Colker, 1992; and Luker, 1975). Scientific and medical discussions of abortion politics tend to increase what Rosalind Petchesky calls "the mystification of molecular biology" (1990: 363n33), at the expense of women's moral autonomy.

A few abortion providers have publicly and dramatically described their practices and claimed abortion as a medical, health care issue. One of these doctors is Warren M. Hern, the director of the Boulder (Colorado) Abortion Clinic. All abortions, he maintains, are therapeutic. Distinctions drawn in the past, particularly between nontherapeutic and therapeutic abortion, are false (interview; Hern, 1984a: 47). On the basis of his decades of practice, he frames abortion thus: "Abortion is safe; it is legal; it ought to stay that way; people who think otherwise are interfering with your private business and trying to run your life. . . . Abortion is not a moral or religious issue with regard to public policy; it is no longer even a medical issue. It is a question of power: Who is going to run your life, you or the government?" (1984a: 324). Hern asks the media and other audiences to consider the consequences of actually prohibiting legal abortion (1984a: 325). Such doctors as Hern, however, are feeling more isolated and targeted within the politics of abortion (interviews).

Abortion Politics: New Frames

If abortion were discussed and debated within the context of gender politics directly, the rhetorical frames would change. For one thing, questions would have to be answered about why half of all U.S. pregnancies are aborted when most American women want at least one child (Jaggar, 1998: 351). Where is the disconnect occurring between women's desire for one child and the difficulties they have managing their sexual encounters and subsequent pregnancies to fit their own reproductive desires? As one medical doctor puts it, "Nobody has avoided an abortion by saying, 'I don't believe in abortion.' Knowing what does cause abortion helps. Sperm cause abortion. Women's self-perceived weakness and related unhealthy behaviors cause abortion. My job as a doctor is to help my patients change unhealthy behaviors" (Karlin, 1998: 274). The gendered nature of abortion is clearly stated by this doctor: "Abortion is an integral part of the woman's condition, and the woman's condition only. Men don't have them" (Karlin, 1998: 275). She reports that many of her patients despise themselves partly because "[a]bortion is so often cast as a more offensive sexual act than the intercourse that led to it. And unfortunately, women's sexuality is fair game for degradation and derision" (Karlin, 1998: 275). If we could talk honestly about abortion, we could also discuss women and sex. "When we concentrate on what caused the abortion, what kind of sex, when, and with whom, then we can prevent unhealthy sexual sequelae," she declares (Karlin, 1998: 276). To make sex safer and healthier for women, we would have to accept female sexuality in all its diversity. Then we could rationally discuss the dynamics of how women come to abort or continue a pregnancy.

Mark Graber's (1996) research showing that criminalized abortion laws in the past were selectively enforced, with great freedom given private doctors to provide safe abortions to their private patients, leads him to construct a new frame for abortion choice: an equal protection argument. The private patients quietly taken care of were overwhelmingly middle-class or upper-class white women. Poorer women, young women with no connections to private doctors, and women of color, however, could not avail themselves of these safe options. The criminal statutes applied to them.

Grounding her study in the actual geography of pregnancy (in other words, where pregnancies take place), Eileen McDonagh draws a new vision of abortion issues. McDonagh bases her pro-choice argument on a morally based examination of "women's true consent to be pregnant." McDonagh's nuanced construction of a potentially transformative vision of abortion also shows how to restore government abortion funding. She grants pro-life movement arguments on the possible humanity of fetuses and shows that nonetheless no person (even a fetus) has the right to intrude into another's body without explicit consent. As McDonagh puts it, "[T]o the extent that the law protects the fetus as human life, the law must hold the fetus accountable for what it does" (1996: 7). The existence of the fetus causes a pregnancy, McDonagh argues. The pregnancy has a profound impact on women's bodies; therefore, women should have the right to choose to resist an unconsented to intrusion by a fetus and ask the state to help stop the pregnancy (1996: 138). McDonagh's study "breaks the deadlock over abortion rights created by the clash of absolutes over the personhood of the fetus by recentering the abortion issue on a premise of self-defense, which is the common ground that can unite pro-life and pro-choice forces alike" (1996: 11).

A new emerging frame in abortion politics is one I call "the context of women's reproductive situations" or, in the vernacular, "how women get pregnant to begin with." Some of the new discourse is about what men and boys do or don't do to prevent unwanted pregnancies (use of effective and safe birth control by males, for instance, or discussions on whether girls and women are really consenting to sexual intercourse). Another dimension to this debate is the context in which girls and women make their reproductive decisions and whether governments are providing care and social services to help girls and women make healthy choices. One rubric in anti-choice rhetoric is their pro-family, pro-child posturing. Recent empirical research by Jean Reith.Schroedel, however, shows the opposite: states with the fewest programs for children, babies, and women have the strictest abortion laws. States with more liberal abortion policies and programs also have social services in place to help babies, children, women, and families (Schroedel, 2000; see also Pollitt, 1999).

"Anti-abortion states do not consistently value fetal life. They are far more concerned with drug use by pregnant women than with the battering and killing of pregnant women—the main way men harm fetuses. . . . In six of the most stringent anti-choice states, it is not even a crime for a third party to kill a fetus—but drug users can be prosecuted for murder if the pregnancy goes awry," Katha Pollitt observes in her discussion of Schroedel's study (1999: 10). The lower women's status in each state (measured by education levels, ratio of female to male earnings, percentage of women in poverty, percentage of female legislators, and state mandates that insurers cover minimum hospital stays for child-birth), the stricter and more anti-choice the abortion laws. Anti-choice states also spend less money per child on services, from adoption of special needs children to foster care to welfare to education. Schroedel found "virtually no support" for the anti-choice position that opposition to legal abortion is based on caring about babies and children (quoted in Pollitt, 1999: 10).

Discussions of women's agency and bodily integrity sometimes use an analogy that the woman is in charge of her body since it is her property. However, these links to property might not be the best way to defend and discuss women's abortion rights. If bodily ownership or property is invoked as the frame for discussion, problems occur when the mind-body connections are not acknowledged. Abortion politics is about not just the body of the woman but also the woman herself because policies about reproduction affect women's bodies and minds, not simply their material bodies (Roy, 1999; see also Bowers, 1994). As a minimum condition of individualization, girls and women must be able to imagine their lives and their futures where they themselves are the agents of their own bodies. In this imaginary domain, women must be able to envision their futures where their bodily, cognitive, spiritual, and psychic individuation is integrated. Without bodily coherence, woman are subjected to being, in Drucilla Cornell's words, "dismembered selves and wandering wombs" (1995: 31). "Simply put," Cornell writes, "once we understand abortion as a right of bodily integrity, we can begin to understand both how devastating it is for a woman to be denied that right and, correspondingly, how essential its protection is if women are to achieve minimum conditions of individuation" (1995: 37). Women's selfhood cannot be severed from our future projections of our selves within our whole bodies. An unwanted pregnancy can threaten that concept of selfhood, even theoretically. The laws on abortion limit our definitions of our selfhood, imposing someone else's vision of our futures onto our bodies. If laws deny women the right to a legal abortion, we are reduced to other people's definitions of our futures entrapped in our bodies. These "restrictive symbolizations deny a woman her imaginary domain," Cornell contends (1995: 52). Laws can make our bodies not really ours. It reduces us to our sex, our wombs, our maternal reproductive and productive functions. Under these terms, we better produce well.

Conclusion: Lives and Agencies

The history of abortion, whether legal or illegal, documents that, in Leslie Reagan's words, "legalization of abortion was a positive development for all women, not just those who seek abortions" (1997: 253). To be pro-life is actually to be pro-choice because humans require reproductive discretion for some of our babies to survive and flourish. Since infants require extensive care, Sarah Hrdy contends, "the single most important source of variation in female reproductive success is not how many young are born; what matters is how many survive and grow up to reproduce themselves" (1999: 90). Abortion's import includes women's ability to avoid motherhood. "Legal abortion," as Reagan points out, "helps create new meanings for motherhood and fatherhood as chosen and desirable life experiences" (1997: 253). Restrictions or reversals of abortion rights impart the opposite: "women cannot be trusted to make moral decisions about children and family, but must be overseen and regulated by men; procreation is a state mandate not a choice; women's lives, sexuality, and bodies are not their own" (Reagan, 1997: 253). Women cannot have their own imaginary domain when they cannot control their own bodies.

Legal abortion was achieved by women's work and the willingness of some doctors to listen to women and speak out about the dire effects of illegal abortion. Some women secured abortions while it was officially illegal through private arrangements with a few physicians and the support of networks of friends, relatives, and others. These behaviors protected women from public exposure and shame. But keeping these practices private and hidden also helped sustain the stigmatized and illegal status of abortion. Public debate, speak-outs, narratives of women's experiences of illegal abortions, political organizing, coalition building, and sustained collective political actions made abortion legal (Reagan, 1997: 254). The concept of women's reproductive privacy rights regarding sexuality and procreation was a hard-fought key concept that now permits us to begin to imagine for ourselves our reproductive futures.

Uncovering and acknowledging the history of illegal abortion and its class and racial dimensions can help protect legal abortion now. Abortion's history shows that even when illegal, it was an "open secret." The law, church, shame, and taboos could not stop women's need and desire for abortion. Although these women did not invoke the rhetoric of civil rights, their behavior indicated that they simply assumed the decision to control their reproduction (through either birth control or abortion) belonged to them. "In their conversations and behavior, women expressed their sense that abortion was morally acceptable, and through their actions they asserted a 'right' to make moral decisions about reproduction and to use abortion," Reagan notes (1997: 44).

Abortion history also reveals that courts during the illegal period were very concerned with who performed the abortion. A medical doctor could say it was necessary for the life or health of the mother. Before high-tech monitoring of pregnancy, doctors and court officials were also dependent on the woman's information for how far along she was. Early pregnancies (before quickening or outward showing) could be classified by doctors as a medical D&C to correct a menstrual blockage. They would not have to characterize the procedure as an abortion. The courts believed male medical doctors about the need for medicinal abortions but often punished others for performing illegal abortions (Solinger, 1994: 198). An equal protection argument could therefore be mounted to support legal abortion. "Equal justice under law" would strongly defend legal abortion since it is a deeply valued principle in American law. If *Roe v. Wade* is ever overturned, the flip side of this decision would likely be that abortion would be quickly relegalized if law enforcement uniformly applied the criminal abortion laws to all women (white, rich, poor, women of color). One weakness in the pro-choice movement now, Mark Graber explains, is that, considering the history of abortion before *Roe v. Wade*, many people of privilege do not believe they or their daughters would actually lose the choice of abortion if abortion were recriminalized or severely restricted. I would add that abortion rights might be restored if people of privilege were faced with enforcement of paternal support payments for the men and boys who contributed to the unwanted and unaborted pregnancies of women and girls.

The right to abortion is therefore not simply a right to choose but, borrowing Cornell's words, "a fundamental condition of one's ability to imagine—and to project into the future—one's bodily integrity" (1995: 67). Such a feminist vision of justice is an ongoing process, project, struggle, not simply an endpoint. As Ursula Le Guin says about feminism, it is "an archeology of the future" (Le Guin quoted by Cornell, 1995: 237), requiring much digging work, uncovering, deducting, and openness about ways humans (including women) create their diverse, ever-changing families.

Notes

An earlier version of the section "Abortion Politics in Local Communities" appeared in Sharp, 1999: 21–42.

1. "Strict scrutiny" is a heightened standard for cases alleging discrimination by such categories as race. Women's advocates have found the usual court standard of "rational basis" for gender discrimination defenses permits too many instances of gender inequality. Many feminists therefore advocate that gender be treated like race, with a strict scrutiny test.

2. Use of the Internet to inform girls and women about birth control, abortion, and the morning-after pill (also called emergency contraceptive) is increasing (Stoller, 1999). Such technologies might get around restrictive local or state gag rules, advertising bans, or public education rules and regulations, thus helping girls and women who are savvy enough to conduct a Web search and learn more about their options. However, many of the blocking devices parents and schools use to keep children and teenagers away from pornography or other harmful Internet sites also block sites with information about breast cancer or birth control because the phrases include such words such as *breast* or *birth* or *human reproduction*. Providing girls with honest and accurate information on abortions can therefore be stymied by these Internet-blocking devices.

3. However, Furman University is also in Greenville.

4. Columbia has five other colleges as well. Four are private: Columbia College, Benedict College, Allen University, and the Lutheran Theological Southern Seminary; and one is public: Midlands Technical College.

5. There were eighteen amicus briefs filed in *Bray*, a clinic blockade case brought by Operation Rescue. Interestingly, no briefs were filed by the AMA or any other mainstream medical association. Perhaps this reflects the isolation of abortion clinic operators in the medical profession and the unwillingness of the AMA to defend them. Future research will have to look into this curiosity. Perhaps after the murders of clinic workers and doctors, the AMA will be more active in protecting the rights of member doctors who perform abortions or have clinics that do. Also interesting in *Bray* is that no amicus briefs were filed by the coalition of pro-life doctors, ob-gyns, and nurses that were filed in the other cases. Perhaps clinic blockades and the obstruction of doctors' places of business through civil disobedience are too much for the pro-life medical groups to support.

5 Adoption and Surrogacy: Children as Commodities, Wombs for Rent

> When money is as central to a human service as it is in
> adoption practice, money not only drives the process,
> but it shapes the results.
> —Anne Babb, *Ethics in American Adoption*

There is an amazing, glaring silence in the politics of motherhood: the voices of birthmothers are absent from policy-making, news coverage, and legal disputes. Whenever I mention the race, class, and nationalistic privileges and injustices on which modern adoption practices are based, I am sure to offend some people. Feminists rarely discuss adoption (Cornell, 1998: 96–99 and 1999; Solinger, 1992: 240, 246). We have published a lot about surrogacy, abortion, single mothers, and family law, but we seem to leave out adoption. I think this is because it hits too close to home. Many academic feminists have adopted children themselves or have relatives who have. Academic feminists, despite our somewhat precarious position in the academy, are middle-class, articulate, and able to utilize social services, lawyers, and networks to get what we want. Our children are rarely, I would venture, "given up" for adoption. Drucilla Cornell writes "that it is a form of class elitism to think that yearnings of the heart are available only to the middle class and the wealthy" (1998: xii). I appropriate her point for my examination of adoption and surrogacy.

Adoption Markets

The few times we hear from birthmothers involved in our closed, hierarchical, patriarchal, and male-normed adoption system, we learn that their grief and sorrow is often lifelong (Robbins, 2001; Cannold, 2000: 108–10; Crary, 2000; Babb, 1999: 178; McKay, 1998; Saltzman, 1998; Sullivan, 2001a and 2001b; Solinger, 1992). Allowing women to contract out their wombs, as well as holding them to these contracts, also indicates, in Carole Pateman's words, "a transformation of modern patriarchy." "Father-right," she observes, "is reappearing in a new, contractual form" (1988: 209). As Anne Babb points out, many professionals involved in the adoption business fail "to serve birth parents ethically or even competently" (1999: 90; see also Freundlich, 2000). Only in a legal system so embedded in patriarchy could a birthmother be erased, her human rights denied, in the name of the sanctity of contracts and the need to protect patriarchal family forms (Cornell, 1998: 102–10). Adopted children also feel cut off from their heritages and histories and have to battle heartless rules and laws erected to erase the birthmothers and bar the children from locating them (Lifton, 1994 and 1998).

Sometimes adoption is glibly thrown out as the alternative to abortion. What both abortion and adoption must be, many feminist observers maintain, is a personal choice. Natalie Angier, a *New York Times* science writer puts it this way:

> For all the reasons that I remain a staunch supporter of abortion rights, for all the reasons that a woman is entitled to her full sexuality regardless of the unreliability of birth control and of the human heart, here is another one. It is vicious to force a woman to bear a baby she doesn't want, to prod her vengefully through the compound priming of pregnancy and force her to be imprinted through every physiological contrivance at evolution's disposal with an infant she can't keep, an infant that will remain forever stuck in her blood, an antigen to the attachment response, try as she will to shed her sad past. The "adoption option" is fine if a young woman chooses it and is at peace with it. But option it must remain, for the body is a creature of habit, and the longer it has been exposed to the chemistry of bondage, the more prone it becomes to emotional flashbacks, to recurrent neuroendocrine nightmares. . . . (1999: 349–50)

American adoption practices are rife with potential and real conflicts of interest, the taint of money and baby-selling, and the illusions that adoption is easy and painless. As one scholar points out, adoption does not only "build families" but also tears them apart by severing the birth families from their children (Babb, 1999). Professionals involved in the adoption business often have conflicts of interest vis-à-vis the birthmothers because their adoption agencies depend on babies being placed for adoption. Adoptive parents are sometimes harmed by these conflicts of interest if they are not told the full story of an adopted child's past, medical history, or life experiences. Often the lawyers who conduct the adoption represent both the agency and the birthmother, a clear conflict of interest. The professionals and agencies involved in adoption also do not have alternatives to offer the girls and women, such as money to live on if they decide to keep their babies, places to live or access to good health care during pregnancy, childbirth, and recovery, and health care for their babies after birth. The needs of the child for the next eighteen to twenty years must also be addressed. For some girls and women, especially in the past, they felt they had no choice except to give the baby up to the adoption officials. Those who wanted to keep their babies were often considered neurotic and selfish (Solinger, 1992).

In adoption, people with money usually get what they want (Babb, 1999: 169–71; Solinger, 1998: 389–90).[1] Interviews with adopting couples indicate that many of them turn to private adoption rather than public or regular adoption agencies to avoid problems and a waiting period. Christine Gailey's study found that "[r]ace was a submerged motive for most of the couples" using private adoption (2000: 44). The same study also found that couples concerned about legal problems with birth parents in the future saw private adoptions as a way to establish secure legal rights to the intended infant and to minimize any subsequent claims by birth parents (2000: 45, 50; see also D'Amato, 1999).

The adoption industry appears often to treat children as chattel. "Although adoption agencies claim to provide superior services and better outcomes for their clients," Anne Babb writes, "as long as agencies operate through fees and donations based on completed adoptions, any promise of unbiased professionalism can only be self-serving. Indeed, the private, licensed adoption agency and independent adoption facilitator are both supported by fees paid by prospective adopters . . ." (1999: 168). It is no accident, then, that the flow of adopted children is in one direction: from the less affluent to the more affluent groups within any society, from less affluent countries to the middle and upper classes in more affluent countries, and from minority groups to majority groups in the United States (Babb, 1999: 169; Simon and Altstein, 2000: 145). Periodically, an adoption scandal will appear in the media highlighting some of the problems of gray markets, brokers, bribes, kickbacks, and other unethical practices. The government of Romania, for instance, has been accused of basically "selling" its children ("Romania Suspends International Adoptions," 2001; see also Greene, 2000).

The social value placed on gender in different countries is also echoed in adoptions wherein more girls than boys are exported as intercountry adoptees (Simon and Altstein, 2000: 145). The children are discussed and bargained for like commodities—those less in demand, those more in demand, those where there is a surplus—and the price is adjusted accordingly. Commercial norms are insinuated into these parental arrangements (Babb, 1999: 169; Freundlich, 2000; Duryea, 1996). Almost everyone suffers in this system: the adopted children, the birth parents, and the adoptive parents, as Babb points out:

> Although agencies and professionals may say that no discrimination exists in practice, and that single adoptive parents are welcome to adopt America's waiting children, the truth is that oftentimes married couples are preferred and single adopters passed over for consideration of the most easily placed children. Single parents are then offered the children who are most difficult to place and raise—older children, children with severe handicaps, children with emotional problems—even though single parents usually have fewer emotional and financial resources than their married counterparts upon which to draw. In a field so often driven by commerce rather than caring, it seems that the least "valuable" children are reserved for the least moneyed prospective adopters to the possible detriment of both. (1999: 169)

Only recently has there been much research on what adoptions are like for the birthmothers involved. Rickie Solinger's *Wake up Little Susie: Single Pregnancy and Race before Roe v. Wade* is one such study. In a later publication, Solinger sums up what she found and how different these experiences were for white and black girls. Solinger explains what it was like for white girls:

> Briefly, after World War II tens of thousands of white girls and women who became pregnant outside of marriage each year were unable to determine either the course of their pregnancies or the conditions of their maternity. They were, in astonishing numbers, deeply shamed by their families, removed from school, diagnosed as psychologically disturbed, and defined as not-mothers without husbands. They were pressed, even coerced, into giving up their "valuable" white babies for adoption to infertile, white, married couples prescreened and judged by social workers to be eager and proper parents. (1998: 27)

Black girls and women, in contrast, kept their children, often with the help of extended families. Yet they were harshly blamed by white politicians and commentators for causing dysfunction in the black community (Solinger, 1998: 27; Rhode, 1993; Luker, 1996).

Disapproving of teenage mothers and blaming them for various social ills are cottage industries in many countries. One article otherwise sympathetic to the lives and choices of women and girls mentions that the United States has the highest teenage birthrate of any industrialized nation and states, "This is bad news" (Zwingle, 1998: 50). The mixed message in American culture, which sexualizes teenage girls yet condemns them for their sexual activity, is admirably fleshed out in the article. However, abortion as a choice is negatively portrayed when the author reports, "Many girls do not have the support or the determination that Mandy [a sixteen-year-old mother] did. Fifty percent of abortions in the U.S. are sought by women younger than 25" (Zwingle, 1998: 54). The author does not consider the possibility that some teenage girls who do have a lot of support and determination choose abortion in the United States. The only completely positive result coming from all the teenage mothers portrayed in the article is that one teenage father testifies that being involved in his son's life has kept him out of juvenile hall since the baby changed him for the better (Zwingle, 1998: 55). Positive changes for the girls are not explored. This essay exemplifies what Kristen Luker has noticed in many popular media and political uses of statistics regarding teenage mothers. The teenage mother is sixteen; however, the data cited on U.S. abortion rates are for the age group twenty-five and younger. What we cannot tell is what the abortion rate is for the teenage mother (Mandy) the author is discussing.

Knowing the history and context of girls' and women's reproductive lives offers some glimmer of hope that increased agency for women and girls has helped our communities. Solinger notes:

> The lessons of mid[twentieth]century reproductive politics are not, however, all cautionary and grim. For example, it is instructive to know that in the late 1950s, among broadly middle-class white girls and women who got pregnant while unmarried, over 95 percent gave their babies up for adoption. Today the rate for all such girls and women is 3 percent. This is a startling change and suggests that with *Roe v. Wade*, women won more than the right to decide whether to stay pregnant. They also won the overlapping but distinct right to decide whether to become a mother. With the dramatic decline of coerced adoptions and the advent of legal abortion, many women in the United States have rights and choices that were virtually unimaginable in the recent past and certainly unobtainable. Social change is possible and, in the case of reproductive politics, was realized largely during the resurgence of the feminist movement from 1965 to 1980. (1998: 29)

Ironically, single adopting mothers in one study realized the commonalities between themselves and their adopted child's birthmothers. One single adoptive mother told a researcher, "I can't help but realize that if this country had decent social supports, my kid probably could have grown up with her birth mother" (quoted in Gailey, 2000: 51; see also Bartholet, 1993: xvi).

Surrogacy: Wombs for Rent, Power, Class, and Control

Hiring women to have babies and then give those babies up to the purchasing parties has troubling implications for how society views women and children. Illustrative of the fading vision of the women involved is the practice of surrogate motherhood, which highlights fetuses as distinct legal entities, the primacy of father rights, and the commodification of children. Some arguments based on women's rights to "choose" these arrangements gloss over the economic pressures many women might face that restrict their freedom to choose. Allowing surrogacy contracts is an aspect of libertarianism, not liberalism. After all, liberalism allows the state to step in to protect individuals from harming themselves and society (for example, prohibitions against suicide). Falling back on market justifications for creating families through commercial surrogacy increases the commodification of life and damages human dignity.

Surrogacy is a very old practice. There is reference to it in the biblical story of Abraham. His wife, Sarah, was said to be barren. Sarah and Abraham agreed that he would father a child with Sarah's slave-girl, Hagar. Hagar was made to serve as a surrogate. Although this is an old story, some elements of it are still relevant today: we do not know how Hagar felt about this, but we do know that she probably had few real "choices" in the arrangement (see, for instance, Minow, 1999). New to surrogacy arrangements now are how they are being formalized into contract laws (instead of informal agreements between Abraham and Sarah to use Hagar). In addition, surrogacy can be very complicated today because of the different iterations possible with artificial insemination, egg donation, embryo transfer, and the like.

The expression "surrogate mother" is actually misleading and insensitive because the so-called surrogate is usually the biological, genetic mother, and the contracting or adopting wife of the genetic father is the actual surrogate mother. Now we have "traditional surrogates" (those simply artificially inseminated by the contracting man's sperm and with a genetic connection to the child) and "full surrogates" (women who gestate and birth a child genetically unrelated to them). The terms reveal the power of money, status, and privilege to define and redefine who the actual mothers and surrogates are.

Surrogate mothers are embroiled in a relatively new controversy that challenges legal standards on what is illegal baby-selling or legal adoption. Surrogacy also raises disturbing questions about the status of women in society and the tendency to commodify and thus justify the exchange of even children (Ragone, 1999; E. Roberts, 1998; Radin, 1987).

George Annas, a professor of health law, takes the position that surrogacy contracts should be void because they treat children as commodities and women as slaves. He is also concerned about the dehumanization of women evident in the original contracts. For example, many contracts gave the biological father the exclusive right to demand abortion: "They transform the surrogate into a container, a nonhuman box for gestating a fetus. The box is supposed to do whatever the sperm donor tells it to" ("Surrogate Parenthood," 1987: 38).

We could face conundrums as in the following fictional scenario. A woman is explaining to her husband why she is considering becoming an egg donor after previously serving as a surrogate mother. Her husband queries, "'Let me get this straight. You'll be selling your eggs to be used by a woman who's unable to produce her own eggs but who is able to carry a pregnancy. And the baby will be hers. That's just the opposite of what happened with that Roberts lady [a surrogacy dispute], right? Her eggs were okay, but she couldn't carry a pregnancy, and that's why she hired a surrogate. And the baby was hers. I don't get it. How can a baby belong to the woman whose egg it comes from in one case but belong to the woman who carries and gives birth to it in another?'" (Macklin, 1994: 179). In this scenario and others, the determination seems to derive from the intention of the people arranging the pregnancy and birth. Legal parenthood can thus be different in different situations.

Fragile Power of Mothers: The Baby M Case

The Baby M trial (Superior Court of New Jersey, 1987) was a well-publicized dispute that drew attention to some of the issues raised by new reproductive arrangements. The *Baby M* case illustrates that women's experiences of maternity are belittled even in the least technologically dependent situation of surrogacy (Bassin, Honey, and Kaplan, 1994: 19; Ketchum, 1987; M. Harrison, 1987; Pollitt, 1987; B. Rothman, 1989; Woliver, 1989a: 27–33).

As agreed to in a surrogacy contract, Mary Beth Whitehead was artificially inseminated with Richard Stern's sperm. She was to relinquish the child to Stern and his wife, Elizabeth, for a $10,000 fee. When the baby girl was born, Whitehead refused to give her up to the Sterns. After a lengthy trial, complete with expert witnesses, intense media coverage, and public commentary, Judge Harvey R. Sorkow upheld the surrogacy contract, severed Whitehead's parental rights, and presided over Elizabeth Stern's adoption of Baby M. A year later, the New Jersey Supreme Court reestablished Whitehead's parental rights, ruled surrogacy for hire illegal because it resembled baby-selling, and made Richard Stern the primary custodial parent. Whitehead was granted visitation rights.[2]

The *Baby M* case was like a political trial, spotlighting troubling issues about shifting modern-day meanings and rights of parents and warning troublesome birthmothers what they might have to endure if they rebelled against the terms of contracts.

The experience of Mary Beth Whitehead reveals ominous forces that might align against women in these situations (Woliver, 1989a and 1989c; Coles, 1988; Eisenstein, 1988: 191–94). Evident in Whitehead's custody battle, for example, are class and gender biases in experts' evaluations of good parenting potentials. The testimony of mental health experts was completely biased. "It was as if—once prejudged—Mary Beth Whitehead could do no right," Michelle Harrison observes (1987: 301). "When Mary Beth Whitehead did poorly on a test," for example, "it was considered a sign of psychopathology; when the Sterns did poorly it was considered either irrelevant or a sign of anxiety" (M. Harrison, 1987: 304). Whitehead's coping strategies and her self-evaluation as a "survivor" were strikes against her. The Sterns' respect for and willingness to use mental health professionals, though, put them in a favorable light. As Katha Pollitt points out, a double standard was evident when "Mrs. Whitehead was portrayed as mercenary for agreeing to sell, but not Mr. Stern for proposing to buy" (1987: 682). The context of Whitehead's life and her constrained choices were devalued by these experts. "The mental health experts in this case attempted to turn life experience and human coping mechanisms into pathology," Harrison concludes (1987: 308).

The trial judge's initial decision in the *Baby M* case, where he terminated Mary Beth Whitehead's parental rights (*In the Matter of Baby M*, 1987: 120), foreshadows the possibility of similar injustices. What this case discounted is the experience of a mother. The lifelong impact on a woman's body from the birth of a child, even the most healthy and wanted pregnancy and birth, is belittled (McDonagh, 1996). Women's services are not merely rented in surrogacy; a part of the woman is taken away, and she is forever after a woman whose body and mind have carried and bore that one additional child. The sense of loss and anxiety even willing birth-mothers who put their babies up for adoption experience is one indica-tion of how deeply pregnancy and birth affects most women.

Barbara Rothman provides an insightful example of how pregnancy and motherhood are continuously described from a male perspective. Many women who are planning to place their babies up for adoption at birth are advised not to "hold" the baby when it is born, least they be-come attached to it and suffer more heartache when it is taken away. Think about those terms, Rothman asks us (1989: 126). The observer is saying that the birthmother will "first" hold the child after it is born, af-ter it is outside her body. Of course, the woman has really been holding that child for the nine months of her pregnancy and feeling its every move-ment, kick, roll, and hiccup. To say that women first hold their babies after they are born is to say that the nine-month experience of pregnancy was nothing. One reason pregnancy does not "count" here is because men cannot experience it. As an exclusively female experience, pregnancy is often discounted and belittled in powerful men's discussions about babies.

Not only are pregnancy, birth, holding, seeing, and motherhood en-visioned from a male perspective, but so is healthy ego development for a newborn baby. The infant's ego, dominant psychological theory asserts, needs to grow *out of* the intense, dependent relationship with a caregiv-er (usually a mother). An alternative view of a healthy personality is when the child can grow *into* a more active, sovereign relationship with the mother (Benjamin, 1988: 18). Envisioning the healthy personality this new way incorporates the experience of a baby not simply "arriving in the world" but leaving the mother's body, an orientation counter to the male perspective.

The birthmothers in surrogacy are treated as reproductive machines. The language sometimes used to describe the birthmothers objectifies them: "rented wombs," "incubators," "vessel for the man's seed," "re-ceptacles," "a kind of hatchery," "gestators," or "a surrogate uterus" (Corea, 1985b: 222; Ince, 1984). One law review author referred to the birthmother in surrogacy as a "uterine hostess" (Hollinger, 1985: 901, 903).

It is fascinating to see how the lawyers and agencies brokering con-tracts between surrogates and purchasers utilize language to paint them-selves as advocates for the surrogate's freedom and liberation. In one law review article, for instance, Noel P. Kean, who made a fortune arranging surrogacy contracts before the controversial Baby M arrangement prob-lematized these practices, was called an "attorney advocate for surrogate mothers' rights" (Sly, 1982–83: 550n52).

Whitehead's gestation, birthing, and genetic connection to her baby were belittled, while the sanctity of the contract and the privileges of paternity were upheld (Woliver, 1989a and 1989c; B. Rothman 1989: 47). As the Baby M controversy reminds us, motherhood is too complicated and unpredictable an experience for a woman to simply sign it away in an advanced contract and later coldly be told to abide by the contract. "When Mary Beth Whitehead signed her contract," Katha Pollitt wrote, "she was promising something it is not in anyone's power to promise: not to fall in love with her baby" (1987: 685–86). Adoption laws recognize this in the waiting periods birthmothers are allowed, where they can change their minds and keep their babies. "As the surrogacy case demonstrated," Jean Elshtain writes, "women's attachment to their own children is a problem" to those hoping to codify surrogacy and otherwise regulate reproduction (1989: 23; see also B. Rothman, 1989: 54). Motherhood, many scholars assert, should be beyond the bounds of contract laws.

Full Surrogacy

Although surrogacy does not require technology, policy on surrogacy is intertwined with much more technologically dependent reproductive options. New technologies, such as in vitro fertilization and embryo transfers, further complicate surrogacy issues by enabling women to gestate fetuses genetically unrelated to them. The surrogate mother not genetically linked to the baby might open up a "market" for poorer women, third world women, and minority women to carry the embryos of the rich and middle class (Ragone, 2000; Corea, 1985b: 213, 243).

"Full surrogacy," or gestational surrogacy, permits white contracting couples to hire women of color to gestate and birth their white babies (Ragone, 2000). Recent court decisions also make gestational surrogacy more secure for the contracting couples. Courts have ruled that a person who does not contribute an ovum or egg to a child, even if she gestates and births the child, has little to no claim on the child after birth. In addition, courts have held that it is the intent to parent that brings with it legal obligations for child support, even in a case where a divorce occurred before the gestational surrogate gave birth (Ragone, 2000; Dalton, 2000: 214–29).

Underemphasized are the risks to embryo donors. These include infection, spontaneous abortion or the need for an abortion if things go wrong, the effects of experimental hormone drugs, surgery for ectopic pregnancy, the impairment or loss of fertility, and, if complications arise, even death (Corea, 1985: 89). These factors, among others, make embryo donation and transfer much different from simple sperm donation. In addition, embryo transfer offers the potential for diagnosing the genetic makeup and potential health problems of embryos before they are implanted into the gestating woman. Even for women not using a surrogate, embryo evaluation could replace amniocentesis and become routine prenatal care.

Robert Blank warns:

> Caution must be exercised to explicate second-order consequences of each option under consideration because often disparate applications of a single innovation will have sequential effects. For instance, although the technique of *in vitro* fertilization is distinct from its potential employment in surrogate motherhood, human cloning, or eugenic programs, it is a means by which these applications might be conducted. In other words, the achievement of one technology might serve as the means through which other, perhaps less desirable and unanticipated, developments occur. Priority setting must take into consideration these interconnections between technologies to the maximum extent possible and must be based on attempts to anticipate second- and third-order consequences of each application. Each of these decisions will require hard choices by policymakers, but they can be aided significantly by adequate formulation of the alternatives. (1984b: 202)

Another publicized surrogacy dispute echoes many of the issues from the Baby M situation and foreshadows the permutations of surrogacy possible with new reproductive technologies. Anna M. Johnson contracted to gestate and birth a child conceived from the ovum and sperm of a contracting couple. When Johnson sued in a California court to have her contract invalidated, the court upheld the contract. Johnson appealed to the California Supreme Court, which upheld the contract and awarded custody of the child to the genetic (and contracting) parents (*Johnson v. Calvert*, 1993). Johnson had no claim to the child, the court said, in part because she had no genetic link. At the time the contract was signed, Johnson was a single mother, and the contracting, genetic parents were middle class (Schwartz, 1994: 240). Again, social class helps shape who the surrogate is and who the contracting, purchasing woman is.

In surrogate disputes, like adoption lawsuits, control, single clear title, and ownership and patriarchal norms dominate and limit the possible outcomes. There was no discussion in the courts that the *Baby M* or *Anna Johnson* cases could be resolved by the children's having more than one mother (see also Schwartz, 1994: 244; and Grayson, 1998). Instead, as in most market, capitalist transactions, the title and control had to be clear. Both the birthgivers and the baby become objects or property

(McEwen, 1999; Sandel, 1997; Ruddick, 1994: 37; see also Goslinga-Roy, 2000; and Lopez, 1998). Complex cultural overlays of gift-giving rituals also influence surrogate arrangements. Women without genetic ties to the children they gestate and birth sometimes see themselves as less connected to the child, whereas those surrogates who also are genetically related to the child often frame their act as a "gift" to the contracting couple (Ragone, 1999). The patina of gift giving diminishes the market, monetary taint in many of these arrangements.

Many feminist scholars, after studying the Baby M trial and other testimonials of surrogate mothers, oppose these arrangements. A legal system based on male standards as the norm rationalizes surrogacy contracts as fair and impartial arrangements. Logically, this means that, to borrow Carole Pateman's words, "sexual difference becomes irrelevant to physical reproduction," as the "former status of 'mother' and 'father' is . . . rendered inoperative by contract and must be replaced by the (ostensibly sex-neutral) 'parent'" (1988: 216). But this can be dangerous to women because in classic patriarchy the father is the only parent. Male seeds within the empty vessel of the modern "surrogate" mother make males once again the only parent. Through the medium of modern contract law, today's males appropriate physical genesis, continuing a time-honored tradition of denying significance to women's reproductive powers, while appropriating those very same powers and transmuting it as a masculine feat. In this way, surrogacy contracts repeat patriarchal patterns in a new guise or, in Pateman's words, "The creative force of the male seed turns the empty property contracted out by an 'individual' into new human life" (1988: 216–17).

Drucilla Cornell maintains, "Mothering takes on the significance it does only within the patriarchal order that would deny the maternal body and its disruptive force" (1999a: 42). Disruptive powers are the connectedness evident throughout a wanted pregnancy, labor, and birth and in the mother-child relationship often experienced during lactation. Such connected intimacy decenters male-normed autonomy and isolated individualism. This insight applies to surrogacy contracts as well. Surrogacy contracts repeat aspects of slavery, as Mary Shanley explains: "In both contract pregnancy and consensual slavery, fulfilling the agreement, even if it appears to be freely undertaken, violates the ongoing freedom of the individual in a way that does not simply restrict future options (such as whether I may leave my employer) but does violence to the self (my understanding of who I am)" (1993: 629; see also P. Williams, 1988 and 1991: 224–26).

It is unclear what impact these arrangements will have on the purchased children in their futures. Another issue is what impact surrogacy arrangements might have on any children witnessing it. If mommy has a baby and gives it up for money, even under the happiest circumstances, what must the other children in the family go through? Will they wonder if they might be sold, too? Will they worry that the next baby will be sold, too? Will they harden their hearts and become rational market maximizers and badger mommy to have a new baby to sell so that the family can go on a vacation, buy a house, send them to college, or have enough to eat? As these questions highlight, bartering even a few children like this is not good for all children.

Surrogacy Policy Recommendations

Feminist scholars take diverse positions on this reproductive arrangement. For example, Lori Andrews favors enforceable surrogacy contracts (1989b). Martha Field advocates a middle position between banning the contracts and a laissez-faire, free-market approach (1988). Barbara Rothman sees surrogacy as unnecessarily commodifying life yet permissible if nurturing instead of genetics alone determined parenthood (1989). Surrogacy, if framed as a contract for reproductive services instead of baby-selling, can empower women, Carmel Shalev asserts: "The idea of personal agency in contracting to become a parent seeks to empower women to reclaim the power of their wombs and to wield it responsibly with due respect for the biological vulnerability of men who must be able to trust and depend on women if they are to become fathers (1989: 17).

Field advocates that surrogacy contracts made before the baby's birth should be unenforceable, as they are in current adoption laws. In addition, a mother who withdraws from a surrogacy contract should be entitled to retain custody of her child without having to prove to a court that she would be a better parent than the biological father. Otherwise, affluent contracting couples will be favored in custody contests with less affluent surrogates (Field, 1988: 131–32). Field explains, "Rules prohibiting surrogacy *are* protectionist toward women, but they also accord best with the kind of society we want to live in" (1988: 26).

Barbara Rothman presents another point of view on surrogate motherhood—indeed, on all the new reproductive technologies. She asks us to abandon genetic connections to children in determining parental rights and substitute a nurturing standard (1989). There is already precedent for Rothman's proposal in existing artificial insemination legislation, where

the genetic father (the sperm donor) is not granted paternal rights or as-
signed paternal responsibilities to any offspring resulting from artificial
insemination by his sperm.

Dominick Vetri found as early as 1988 that the twenty-nine states
that adopted legislation on artificial insemination use the preconception
intent of the parties as the basis for determining fatherhood, namely the
intent of the husband to be the responsible father and the donor's intention not to be. These states have rejected genetics as the necessary link
for fatherhood, relying instead on preconception intent. A focus on intent might be significant in future policies about the use of in vitro fertilization with a surrogate mother (Vetri, 1988: 512).

Similarly, the intention to nurture a child is more important than
genetics for Barbara Rothman (1989: 18). Included in her concept of nurturing is the nine-month relationship a birthmother has with a fetus
during a pregnancy. This position considers the role of a "full surrogate"
birthmother, albeit genetically unconnected to a child she gestated and
bore from donated eggs and sperm (B. Rothman, 1989: 235–36). Rothman
advocates a national policy establishing that gestational mothers are
mothers of the children they bear regardless of the source of the egg and
sperm; the purchase of any baby is illegal baby-selling; and the acceptance
of a baby as a gift from a mother, regardless of the source of the egg and
sperm, is a variety of adoption (1989: 239). She emphasizes relationships
based on intentions to nurture and respect for the role of nurturing fathers, birthmothers, and adopted and blended families, while not deval-
uing the unique experience of pregnancy.

Surrogacy debates must be informed by what motherhood means to
women and the socioeconomic conditions that pressure women into
"choosing" these arrangements. We should not dismiss the economic
pressures that force women's choices in signing these contracts. Many
surrogate mothers' stories reveal that rich couples are purchasing this
service from women who need the money. Birthmothers who challenge
contracts in court face an expensive and insensitive legal system with a
legacy of favoring the desires of the upper and middle classes (Coles, 1988).
Gross inequalities related to gender are masked, though, by the language
of individual market choice.

Margaret Radin argues for some exchanges to be "market-inalien-
able," because they are "grounded in noncommodification of things important to personhood" (1987: 1903). Radin points out that in our nonideal world, market-inalienability must be judged against a background
of unequal power. Keeping unequal powers in mind means that "it may
sometimes be better to commodify incompletely than not to commodi-

fy at all. Market-inalienability may be ideally justified in light of an appropriate conception of human flourishing, and yet sometimes be unjustifiable because of our nonideal circumstances" (1987: 1903). In our culture, rhetoric and presumptions in favor of commodification lead us into an unreflective use of markets as fair comparisons for almost everything people value, Radin points out. Such raw market mechanisms, however, propel us toward inferior conceptions of our personhood (Radin, 1987: 1936). In paid surrogacy arrangements, for example, "the role of paid breeder is incompatible with a society in which individuals are valued for themselves and are aided in achieving a full sense of human well-being and potentiality" (Capron and Radin, 1988: 62).

Discussions of surrogacy often emphasize the sanctity of contracts ("She was a competent adult when she freely chose to sign this contract . . .") and analogies to wet nurses, babysitters, and sperm donors. Structuring discussions in these terms ignores gestation and birth, exclusively female experiences. The gestalt of maternity—women's psychological as well as physical experiences—is compartmentalized and devalued by defining childbirth in discontinuous terms (a "rented womb") rather than as the woman's linear experience of maternity (O'Brien, 1981; B. Rothman, 1986 and 1989).

Equating the male experience of genetic parenthood with the woman's or comparing men's abilities to separate out their sperm from their bodies, sell it (as in artificial insemination and sperm labs), or pass it on to a surrogate mother, with women's "equal opportunity" to do the same through surrogacy, imposes male experience as the universal. But, as Pateman notes, "women's equal standing must be accepted as an expression of the freedom of women *as women*, and not treated as an indication that women can be just like men" (1988: 231; see also Woliver, 1988). Similarly, Eisenstein argues, "because law is engendered, that is, *structured through the multiple oppositional layerings embedded in the dualism of man/woman*, it is not able to move beyond the male referent as the standard for sex equality" (1988: 42). Law values certainty, not ambiguity, and looks for either-or situations, not both. Law often cannot incorporate female experiences into decision making because these experiences are not male, so they are problematized as particularistic, biased, and unique.

Although scholars reach different policy recommendations for the future of surrogacy, they all recognize the challenges of surrogacy and its interdependence with new reproductive technologies and what these issues pose for family law and the future of motherhood. These new reproductive technologies are introduced into societies having emotional commitments and political and cultural investments in older norms of paternity and maternity. The Baby M and Anna Johnson trials show that disputes about reproductive arrangements also involve complicated issues of class, race, and gender.

The Patriarchal, Nuclear Family Paradigm

Adoption laws and practices assume that all families should look like a patriarchal, nuclear family: one dad, one mom, siblings perhaps, with visits from aunts, uncles, and grandparents. The paradigm means that judges cannot imagine a family with two moms (the birth mom and adoptive mom sharing the child; or two women parenting as partners; or the surrogate and the contracting couple) or two dads with no mom. African American families extend themselves to encompass "all our kin" instead of shutting members out (Stack, 1974). The need to choose and sanction only one "real" mother, then, is not present (Bryant, 1996; Cornell, 1998: 99–100; Ragone, 1996). But, as Drucilla Cornell points out, adoption "law in most states pits the two mothers against one another while the media dramatizes the purportedly hostile relationship between the two" (1998: 96).

Judges often have to pick the "real" mother in adoption and surrogacy disputes. Cornell explains:

> The woman who is picked by law as the "real" mother is the one privileged by class and race. The politics of imperialist domination and the struggle of post-colonial nations to constitute themselves as independent nations are inevitably implicated in international adoption. Hence, it is not surprising that one of the first steps in the constitution of nationhood is an end to international adoptions. Adoption is fraught with issues of race, class, and imperialist domination that have persistently caused divisions in the second wave of feminism. (1998: 97)

We have a fear of the return of the birthmother that is based on class, race, nationalism, and the need for control and clear and free-title ownership. These dominant family structures are, according to Kathryn Bryant, "ineffective eurocentric male-centered traditional standards" that hinder the construction of diverse, beneficial family formations in adoption (1996: 5). Current adoption practices are aimed at, in her words, the "social control of unwed mothers and the reproduction of an accepted model of family based on an abstract eurocentric male standard" (1996: 5–6). Cornell places these fears within the large paradigm of our exclusive nuclear family thinking: "We cannot lose our children because they are not ours to have. That children are not property is recognized by their inclusion in the moral community of persons from birth. Obviously, this idea of custodial responsibility and children's rights demands that we stretch our imaginations. It demands that we struggle to free ourselves from the picture of the family as 'Mommy and Daddy and baby makes three'" (1998: 127). It is not obvious a priori that single mothers are destructive to society. "Instead," Bryant argues, single mothers as pariahs are "an ideologically constructed controlling image that reflects the changing needs of the dominant male-centered hierarchical power structure to control women's reproduction" (1996: 10). These stereotypes are obvious when comparisons are made between African American and white women's participation in adoption, as well as these two groups' diverse practices as mothers, family members, and adoption participants (Bryant, 1996: 10).

In addition to embracing the glib "Adoption, Not Abortion" slogan, some "family values" activists, such as the Christian Coalition and the National Council for Adoption, lobby against birthmothers who seek their children or desire open records. It is as if birthmothers are "good girls" only if they stay erased; they will be demonized if they "resurface" and ask for contact with (or custody of) their children. Opponents of open records, open adoptions, and recontact with birthmothers claim these reforms will push pregnant women toward abortions rather than adoptions. Actually, data show that many pregnant women will abort rather than give their baby up to a *closed* adoption system. Alternatively, birthmothers keep their babies, even when being a single, poor mother will be hard, rather than give them up to a closed adoption system (Cannold, 2000: 108–10). The adoption reform movement in the West is "pushing to restructure adoption practices and policy (and thus single motherhood's social meaning) into a less punitive and more matricentric form," according to Bryant (1996: 18; see also Bryant, forthcoming; Modell, 1999; Carp, 1998; and Bartholet, 1999).

The market nature of many modern adoption arrangements raises questions about the ethics of opposing other practices, such as commercial surrogacy. "Can anyone really argue that the use of a surrogate by a woman born without a uterus," one French scholar asks, "is worse than engaging in the kind of traffic in children now common in international adoption circles?" (Costa-Lascoux, 1994: 583).

When considering adoption practices, it is important not to essentialize women's biology and to recognize that adoption is freely chosen by some birthmothers. A belief that women are all the same, that their biology is their destiny, and that they are buffeted by their innate maternal instincts makes them essentially the same as their wombs. Primate behavior, however, is not so simple; mothers' natures are very complex and contextualized (Hrdy, 1999). Choices need to be truly freely chosen, though, not just imagined by adopting parents. There is widespread abuse and exploitation of vulnerable birthmothers within the adoption market that must be recognized and addressed. Social structures need to be in place that permit poor and vulnerable girls and women to keep the children that they love and want. Sharing of children, instead of a mandate for clear titles, should be a worldwide possibility (not just in Western countries). In the future, a birth-respecting, nonexploitative, less traumatic form of adoption, then, might be possible (see also Ruddick, 1994: 38; and Baker, 1996).

Voices Silenced

Much of the adoption and surrogacy debates focuses on what wealthy people want, not on what heartaches working-class and poor women must endure. Using surrogacy as a solution for the demand for babies by some people distracts society from asking very important questions about the sources of the surrogacy market. Infertility prevention and healthy environments should be discussed when surrogacy is offered as the solution. The social and political conditions of women's lives also need to be seriously addressed. The possibility of surrogacy or use of reproductive technologies is offered to women to ease their concern about whether they will be able to have a baby. Women's delay of motherhood or the unhealthy conditions of their lives is also used to justify the "demand" for surrogacy, adoption, and new reproductive technologies. Society is deflected from structural changes that might make it easier to be a pregnant employee or working mother (Woliver, 1989a). To employers, the women in many jobs are just fine, as long as they act like men (that is, do not get pregnant or become mothers).

Missing from the debates on adoption and surrogacy are the experiences of the birthmothers themselves. In a poignant memoir, Elizabeth Kane, a surrogate mother and one-time media darling for the pro-surrogacy, happily-ever-after story on surrogacy, confesses her heartaches and lifelong pains from being a surrogate. Kane now believes surrogacy should be banned: "I now believe that surrogate motherhood is nothing more than the transference of pain from one woman to another" (1988: 275).

Careful reading of adoption and surrogate stories reveals the lifelong heartaches many of these birthmothers endure (Lifton, 1994 and 1998; Carp, 1998; Chesler, 1987; Coles, 1988; Ketchum, 1987: 5–6; Pollitt, 1987;

B. Rothman, 1989; Field, 1988; Lasker and Borg, 1987: 77–91) and the sexist and classist nature of the arrangements. Of course, women's practice of selling their physical abilities is not new. Wet nurses and nannies have been with us for a long time. People with financial resources have often hired more financially vulnerable girls and women to care for their babies and raise their children. Adoption and surrogacy are therefore framed as just an extension of this hiring of poor women. For example, in an interview at the height of the Baby M controversy, the law professor John Robertson observed, "The bottom line is—even if there is a class bias here, it is no different than the class biases that run throughout society. If it's all right to hire poor women to be nannies and to do childrearing, why is it not all right to hire them as surrogates?" (quoted in "Surrogate Parenthood," 1987: 39). We are expected, George Annas points out, "not to look behind the resulting children to see their lower-middle-class and lower-class mothers. But the core reality of surrogate motherhood is that it is both classist and sexist: a method to obtain children genetically related to white males by exploiting poor women" (1988: 43).

Perhaps some things should not be bartered on the open market because of potential abuse of vulnerable people and damage to human dignity. Today, for example, you may not sell your second kidney or other "excess" organs, skin, bone marrow, and other body parts on the open market. There are people desperate for these "products," who might die without them. They would be happy to pay a fair market price, and you would provide a humanitarian service in the bargain. Voluntary donation programs (akin to our voluntary adoption system) have not met the demand for these products. Nevertheless, government has determined that human body parts (with the exceptions of sperm, eggs,[3] and blood) cannot be sold. Marketing these "products" (like marketing babies in some surrogacy and adoption arrangements) is banned by the state because the ends do not justify the means. Although some people would benefit from being able to purchase these desired body parts or bodily services, the market exchanges damage communal values of human dignity and worth.

Conclusion: All Our Kin and Kinder

Feminist concern about adoption and surrogacy arrangements is grounded in what Gayle Binion calls "progressive feminism," which argues for the inclusion of women's values and experiences in our legal system (1991). Women's experiences of pregnancy would therefore "trump" prior agreements in a contractual pregnancy because, as Mary Shanley points out, "enforcement of a pregnancy contract against the gestational mother's wishes would constitute a legal refusal to recognize the reality of the woman and fetus as beings-in-relationship, which the law should protect as it does many other personal relationships" (1993: 632).

There are diverse opinions among feminist scholars as well as others on whether and how to regulate these new reproductive arrangements. One common theme in feminist analysis of these issues, however, is the need for policies that are sensitive to the realities of women's lives. Surrogacy could shift the cultural meaning of "to mother," making it more biological, discontinuous, and distant. Currently, "to mother" means, among other things, to nurture, a long-term emotional commitment. The ethic of nurturing is very gendered in our culture. "To father," in contrast, means the biological connection of sperm. Surrogacy and justifications voiced in its favor cloud the contemporary meanings of these terms and might limit "mothering" to mere genetic connection, comparable to "fathering" (recall the amazingly carefree market in human sperm[4]). The long-term impact will shift the terrain of reproduction by altering our cultural beliefs about these reproductive roles, rights, and markets.

Surrogate mother arrangements involving monetary compensation (as opposed to good samaritan or philanthropic surrogacy, as between female relatives) engender debates about the buying and selling of women's bodies and resulting babies. To ensure human flourishing in an ideal world (not the present situation full of gender inequalities and double binds for women), core aspects of personhood, such as sexuality, should not be for sale. Margaret Radin explains that because "our ideal of personhood includes the ideal of sexual interaction as equal nonmonetized sharing," such market arrangements as prostitution, surrogacy, and the sale of babies should not be legal because they are "inconsistent with the equal sharing of sex required for human flourishing" (1987: 1849, 1921). Radin's position explains the ethical and moral ripple effects feared from such practices as commercial surrogacy or prostitution. She contends that "the argument for noncommodification of sexuality based on the domino effect, in its strongest form, is that we do not wish to unleash market forces onto the shaping of our discourse regarding sexuality and hence onto our very conception of sexuality and our sexual feelings" (1987: 1922). Governments have a legitimate role to play in determining the permissibility of these arrangements partly because of the effect on all people. Adoption and surrogacy challenge us to assert fundamental principles regarding human dignity. "What is probably most remarkable about the debate over surrogate motherhood," Alexander Capron and Radin point out, "is that it has necessitated defending a claim that was previously taken as self-evident: namely, that society has an interest in people being regarded as intrinsically valuable, not as monetized units in a marketplace" (1988: 63; see also Holder, 1988).

Unintended consequences might result from outlawing private and international adoptions and commercial surrogacy. These practices might just be driven underground to illegal and completely unregulated markets, where the potential for exploiting girls and women is great. Open, noncommercial, altruistic acts of adoption and surrogacy, however, might be justifiable. The demands of adoption and surrogacy brokers and the desires of a very few privileged customers for adoption and surrogacy, however, should not determine our policies. What closed adoptions and commercial surrogacy do to the status of women, the commodification of children, the primacy of father rights, and the degradation of human dignity makes it worth the struggle to figure out how to regulate these arrangements for the least harm.

Notes

Portions of this chapter evolve from my earlier works (see Woliver, 1989a, 1990c, 1991a, and 1995). Earlier versions of this chapter were delivered at the Law and Society Convention, Madison, Wisconsin, June 8–11, 1989, and the American Political Science Association Convention, Atlanta, Georgia, August 31–September 3, 1989. I thank Patricia McRae for her research assistance on this portion of my project.

1. Prices and costs can be obtained at the National Abortion Information Clearinghouse Web site: <http://www/calib.com/naic>. Internet searches are also a growing part of the adoption business (Wetzstein, 1998).

2. For Whitehead's version of events, see Whitehead, 1989. For a scathing critique of Whitehead's book, see Roiphe, 1989.

3. Technically, human eggs are not "sold" but are donated for a fee. The verbal legerdemain here is akin to fees paid/donated in many adoption arrangements.

4. Recent studies, however, indicate that even being a sperm donor is complicated. Some sperm donors wonder if they have children in the world they do not know about and often would not mind contact with them. Sperm donations are frequently used for male infertility and bump up against male cultural norms of potency. Often the female in the couple covers up the need for fertility interventions as her "fault" to spare her male partner the stigma (K. Daniels and Haimes, 1998).

6 Social Controls and Reproductive Politics: Punitive Monitoring of Pregnant Women

> Motherhood has always been, and continues to be, a colonized concept—an event physically practiced and experienced by women but occupied, defined, and given content and value by the core concepts of patriarchal ideology.
>
> —Martha Fineman, "Images of Mothers in Poverty Discourse"

The female body is easily deconstructed into its culturally significant parts and pieces, particularly when the womb is a metonym for the whole female body. The objectification of the pregnant body, as Anne Balsamo points out, "also supports the naturalization of the scientific management of fertilization, implantation, and pregnancy more broadly" (1996: 81). Colonized geographical areas, whether encompassing terrains of the earth or the terrain of a woman's body, place decision making and control in the hands of outsiders. Colonized people do not control their own resources; their indigenous resources are extracted, exported, and expropriated for the benefit of the colonizers. Controlled from outside, the space of human reproduction has been overlapped with the space of public interest. Thus, as Nathan Stormer argues, "regulation of abortion and the biomedical knowledge that has been used to specify such regulation has liquidated boundaries between the family, the state, and the bodies of women" (2000: 111).

State manipulations of women's reproductive choices are important issues in politics and feminist scholarship. Individual rights, women's legal rights and responsibilities compared with men's, and the power of state interference or restrictions in such intimate and private areas as reproduction should trigger concern by scholars and policymakers monitoring reproductive rights and the roles of an increasingly intrusive and often punitive state.

Framing: Fetus as Patient

Modern women are often surveilled during their now public pregnancies. Our "magical thinking" about reproduction results in the following, according to Balsamo:

> (1) a pregnant woman is divested of ownership of her body, as if to reassert in some primitive way her functional service to the species—she ceases to be an individual defined through recourse to rights of privacy, and becomes a biological spectacle. In many cases she also becomes an eroticized spectacle, the visual emblem of the sexual woman; (2) the entity growing in her, off of her, through her (referred to variously as a pre-embryo, embryo, fetus, baby, or child), has some sort of ascendant right (to produce pain, to be nourished properly, to be born) that the maternal body is beholden to; (3) that the state of being pregnant is so "wondrous"—or, variously, thrilling, fulfilling, and soulfully satisfying— for a woman that she would endure any discomfort, humiliation, or hardship to experience this "blessed event." (1996: 80)

With the increased medicalization of pregnancy, the contentious politics in this country concerning abortion, and the now visible fetus, often pictured as separate from the woman within which it exists, social control of pregnant women is apt to increase (Woliver, 1989a, 1989c, 1990c, 1998a, and 1998c). One legal scholar noted that as early as 1986, the law "conferred rights upon the fetus qua fetus" (Johnsen, 1986: 599). Anti-smoking discourse aimed at pregnant women, for example, makes fetuses everyone's business and frames the issues in terms of not women's health but their obligation to fetuses (Oaks, 2000). Pitting the fetus against the woman in so-called cocaine-baby situations is an example of the punitive means with which the "pregnancy police" drive wedges between women, their bodies, and pregnancies. Often these women's health is so poor, from their poverty, homelessness, violent partner situations, the illegal drugs they are taking, their use of alcohol and tobacco, or all of these in combination, that they menstruate irregularly, if at all. Many of them believe they are infertile. When they discover they are pregnant, they are often "very far along," and it is a big surprise to them (S. Murphy and Rosenbaum, 1999: 52–53).

The lack of prenatal care for all poor women is well documented in this country. For poor pregnant women who also need drug or alcohol treatment and who might also be HIV positive, homeless, or in an abusive or chaotic relationship, treatment facilities are usually not available (Chavkin, 1992: 197). Many drug treatment facilities categorically exclude pregnant drug abusers. Waiting lists, lack of child care, and prohibitive transportation problems, among many other issues, make treatment for these women a bitter and cruel "catch-22." They need treatment, but none is available. When they do not get treatment, they can be punished.

The actions of the state have a disproportionate impact on poor women of color. As Dorothy Roberts has written, "Poor Black women bear the brunt of prosecutors' punitive approach. These women are the primary targets of prosecutors, not because they are more likely to be guilty of fetal abuse, but because they are Black and poor" (1991: 1432; see also Ikemoto, 1992). Police and prosecutors focus on crack cocaine use and increasingly file charges against pregnant crack cocaine users for endangering their fetuses. As Roberts points out, "When a drug-addicted woman becomes pregnant, she has only one realistic avenue to escape criminal charges: abortion," adding that ultimately "she is penalized for choosing to have the baby rather than having an abortion" (1991: 1445). Roberts adds one further point: "The history of overwhelming state neglect of Black children casts further doubt on its professed concern for the welfare of the fetus" (1991: 1446).

Skepticism about the sincerity of the state in protecting children through policing pregnant women is rampant. As one law school textbook asks, "Does the state have any obligations to the fetus of a drug addicted mother? If so, is there any inconsistency with *DeShaney v. Winnebago County Dep't of Social Services* . . . (1989) (holding that the state has no obligation to intervene to protect a child from abuse, even abuse of which it is aware)? If the state has no obligation under *DeShaney* even *after* the child is born, why are we willing to impose so much on the mother even before the child is born?" (M. Becker, Bowman, and Torrey, 1994: 428)

Jurisprudence on prenatal abuse reached its height in the South Carolina Supreme Court case *Whitner v. State of South Carolina* (1997), where a pregnant woman was charged with child abuse and jailed for using illegal drugs. The pregnancy police are also evident when states permit

coerced medical treatment of pregnant women and direct injunctive regulation of such women's actions (Johnsen, 1986: 603; Jos, Marshall, and
Perlmutter, 1995). State intervention dismembers the nature of the relationship between the fetus and the pregnant woman and is insensitive
to the harm inflicted on women by these interventionist policies. Moreover, state control of women's actions in the name of fetal rights, as Dawn
Johnsen points out, frames the fetus as separate from the pregnant women
and denies the true geography of pregnancy (Johnsen, 1986). It bodes ill
for every woman when these punitive state controls are in place. Paradoxically, such state controls and punitive monitoring place fetal health
as well as maternal health in jeopardy if women begin avoiding medical
care (Chavkin, 1992: 199). Dominant controlling images of these bad
mothers is one facet of a cultural drive to monitor and regulate intensively
all mothers. But, as Deborah Connolly points out, the "population most
affected by such regulatory trends are women who are already marginalized, those who are already suspect because their poverty, their lack of
education, and their immersion in pain render them unable to act out the
middle-class ideal" (2000: 274).

The state thus creates an adversarial relationship between the woman
and the fetus. One dire result is that the state is likely to exaggerate in
legal procedures the potential risks to the fetus while undervaluing the
loss of autonomy suffered by women (Johnsen, 1986). If a woman does
not exercise her right to an abortion, she is likely to care about the child
she will have. State regulation of all women or a "suspect" few is not
rational and has dire unintended consequences. The pregnant woman
herself is the best judge of what is best for her, given her life circumstances
(Johnsen 1986).

A presumption against drug-addicted mothers raises many ethical
considerations. We should ask whether users of illegal substances are
inherently incapable of adequate parenting. Automatically depriving
women of custody for using illegal substances is tantamount to punishing women based on culturally loaded predictions and stereotypes regarding their future conduct as mothers (Maher, 1992: 182–83). Given our
abysmal foster care system, the phenomenon of "boarder babies" in many
urban hospitals, and the stress placed on children and babies removed
from their biological mothers, these policies do not seem oriented to the
true "best interests of the child." One observer of medical ethics and
women's rights under this surveillance regime found "the material ap-
plications of new technologies are implicated in, and in part productive
of, a new *discourse* on maternal identity, parental responsibilities, and
the authority of science. At the heart of this discursive formation of re-

production are evocative cultural narratives about motherhood, the family, the role of techno-science, and the medicalized citizen" (Balsamo, 1996: 82–83). Visualization technologies, such as ultrasound, laparoscopy, and fetal monitoring, introduce new agents to help monitor female behavior if needed. The "war on drugs" in the United States, echoed in media coverage, public policy initiatives, and "get tough" policies of mandatory sentences, three/two/or one strike and you're "out" proposals by campaigning politicians, overlays the new medical technologies to spotlight and scapegoat the least powerful pregnant women for control, surveillance, and punishment (Woliver, 1996c; Glantz, 1991; McGinnis, 1990; Paltrow, 1999a and 1999b; S. Murphy and Rosenbaum, 1999; Jos, Marshall, and Perlmutter, 1995). Anne Balsamo contends, "This articulation of instruments, professional histories, and mediated discourses has created cultural conditions in which new reproductive technologies are used to discipline material, female bodies as if they were all potentially maternal bodies, and maternal bodies as if they were all potentially criminal," thus, creating "public pregnancies" with extensive surveillance (1996: 83). Prenatal genetic testing, for instance, makes pregnancies public. As Abby Lippman points out, "That the birth of certain babies should be avoided is announced merely by making testing available" (1994a: 24). Women feel that they must explain and defend themselves if certain problematic pregnancies continue. Women addicted to illegal drugs are punished for not ending their pregnancies.

Legal and Illegal Drugs and Pregnant Women

The media-enhanced spectacle of the "cocaine mother" horror story (Fineman, 1983; Edelman, 1977; Gomez, 1997) erases the complex context of these women's lives. When the women involved in these cases are African American, racial stereotypes, evocative tropes, and "controlling images" of pathological and dangerous black mothers are conjured up (P. Collins, 1991: 67–90), making it easier to scapegoat and target them. "When people believe the hand that rocks the cradle would rather be smoking rocks," Sheigla Murphy and Marsha Rosenbaum write, "diverse constituencies unite in moral outrage and condemnation" (1999: 1).

The majority of women prosecuted and monitored by the government are poor and African American. Government targeting of pregnant women is particularly targeted toward poor women of color. "They are," Dorothy Roberts notes, "the least likely to obtain adequate prenatal care, the most vulnerable to government monitoring, and the least able to conform to the white, middle-class standard of motherhood" (1998: 125). The punitive response by government, she contends, "perpetuates the historical devaluation of Black women as mothers" (1998: 126). Roberts argues "that punishing drug addicts who choose to carry their pregnancies to term burdens the constitutional right to autonomy over reproductive decisions," helping to perpetuate a racist hierarchy in our society (1998: 127). Rights to privacy must include consideration of racial inequality and the damage done to all women when predominately black women are punished for having babies, instead of being given adequate drug treatment options. Rather than punitive controls, "a commitment to guaranteeing these fundamental rights of poor women of color . . . is the true solution to the problem of unhealthy babies," Roberts insists (1998: 150).

If government were genuinely concerned about the health and safety of pregnant women and fetuses, it would have to embrace policies to prevent violence to pregnant women, including domestic violence. However, this aspect of women's lives and health is suspiciously missing in the government's surveillance of pregnant women. Many studies on violence experienced by women in the year before they give birth focus on the characteristics of the women themselves, instead of the perpetrators. "It was clear," Balsamo writes, "that the issue of maternal health and physical violence was not conceptualized through a 'maternalist' logic that would see the issue of violence against pregnant women as a social and systemic problem, tied closely to the characteristics of violent men, rather than an individual problem somehow tied to characteristics of the woman herself" (1996: 104–5). What goes unstudied and unmonitored by state surveillance is also very important and telling.

Lack of treatment facilities for pregnant women is also a barrier to true assistance for pregnant women using illegal drugs (Paltrow, 1999a and 1999b; S. Murphy and Rosenbaum, 1999; Jos, Marshall, and Perlmutter, 1995). Additionally, Balsamo argues, "if we look at the issue of cocaine use among pregnant women and at the documented effects of cocaine ingestion on the developing fetus, we find that the medical and scientific findings do not warrant the kind of surveillance that interferes with a pregnant woman's search for treatment" (1996: 106; see also McGinnis, 1990; Gustavsson and MacEachron, 1997; Goldsmith, 1990; De Ville and Kopelman, 1999; and American Medical Association, 1990). When women learn from one another about the punitive nature of the police involvement they will bring down on themselves if they test positive for illegal drugs during routine prenatal visits, they will keep away from prenatal care out of self-protection.

Media and political interest in "cocaine baby" scandals could even be influencing the acceptance rate of medical research articles for publication: 58 percent of articles reporting adverse effects of cocaine use for fetuses and babies were accepted, one study found, while only 11 percent of abstracts that showed no ill effects were accepted (Balsamo, 1996: 106). Publication bias against the null hypothesis (when studies display no differences between genders, races, or similar categories), combined with the confusion of sorting out the effects of polydrug use (including such legal drugs as alcohol and nicotine) on fetuses, further problematizes the state's rush to monitor pregnant drug users (Humphries et al., 1992: 207). The published research, then, represents a certain political ideology. "Not only is this reproductive research focused exclusively on only one party (the female), but studies that report minimal or no negative consequences of drug use have little visibility in the professional literature," Nora Gustavsson and Ann MacEachron report (1997: 676). A dominant narrative of maternal excess and fetal victimization is therefore created by the pernicious culture of journalistic sensationalism and public health rhetoric (Balsamo, 1996: 107; Gomez, 1997). Balsamo writes:

> These events and discussions establish the fact that a foundation has been set in place to de-individualize the notion of pregnancy and to make women's reproductive health a matter of *public* health policy. Mass-mediated narratives establish the pregnant woman as the agent of a new public health crisis: the pregnant woman is both disempowered and held responsible at the same time. As the guilty culprit, she requires additional surveillance in order to protect her babies and society from her criminal excesses. (1996: 110)

Echoing themes in abortion politics (see chapter 5), Balsamo observes, "we witness the process whereby women are interpolated into a very convoluted narrative that defines wombs as unruly, childbirth as inherently pathological, and women of childbearing age as unreliably duplicitous and possibly dangerous" (1996: 110).

The social context of anyone's drug use (not just pregnant women's) is overlooked here. Balsamo presents another vision, "one that does not inadvertently delimit women's agency by reifying their identity as victims, and also does not bestow upon them exaggerated powers of contamination and infection. Seeing this issue through a 'maternalist' logic would suggest the investigation of the social forces that influence women's drug use, the conditions under which drug *use* becomes abusive to self and other, and the institutional arrangements that support women's stigmatized identity as public health offenders" (1996: 110–11). Instead, the blame is placed solely on the individual who needs fixing or punishing. From a larger social perspective, the behavior of mothers who might harm their children, in Connolly's words, "suggests certain patterns that, rather than creating public hysteria and a backlash that seeks to stigmatize and regulate women, could instead result in social measures that would support and protect families" (2000: 281).

Framing/Reframing: Criminal or Medical Problem?

Doctors and medical associations have been very concerned about punitive treatment and criminalization of pregnant women who use illegal substances. Many of the women involved already lack adequate prenatal health care. Doctors fear an erosion of already fragile doctor-patient relationships if pregnant women are earmarked for close surveillance. Medical professionals want to treat these people, not inform on them (Gomez, 1997: 49). Prosecutors, Laura Gomez's study of California showed, are influenced by the media's sensationalistic portrayal of the problem and by experts in the field. Teachers serve as proxies for other experts. Experts such as teachers have an influence on policymakers and prosecutors, even though longitudinal studies of drug-exposed children do not bear out their observations. However, California law enforcement officials' rhetoric constitutes claims-making, a frame from which to define the problem and shape possible responses, as Gomez notes: "From their typical use of the 'crack baby' terminology to their linking of the problem with other issues long associated with racial minorities and the inner city, their rhetoric laid a foundation for recognition of the issue as one falling within the ambit of regulation by the criminal justice system" (1997: 74).

Gomez's study of California's response to substance-abusing pregnant women found that policy elites and experts in the field (medical doctors, social workers, and such groups as California Advocates for Pregnant Women) formed a coalition with two goals: "to prevent criminalization of pregnant women's drug use and to increase health care, drug treatment, and other services for pregnant substance abusers and their children. Within the context of the legislature as a site for institutionalization, they waged a war for the portrayal and ultimate ownership of the social problem as medical rather than as criminal" (1997: 50–51). Eventually, Gomez reports, "initial moves to frame pregnant women's drug use as criminal failed. . . . Instead, second-round claims-makers succeeded (including some lawmakers and prosecutors) in casting the social problem as essentially a medical problem that should be addressed by existing public health, social welfare, and other service agencies" (1997: 119). Particularly doctors (as secondary claims makers) worked to frame the problem as theirs, better suited to treatment than to punishment (Gomez, 1997: 120–21). Moreover, Gomez relates, "women's and particularly feminist organizations reshaped efforts to criminalize drug use by pregnant women as a broader attack on women's autonomy and, especially, their reproductive rights" (1997: 121). The feminist coalition in California linked the prosecution of pregnant women to abortion rights and reproductive freedom jurisprudence. It also "had to recast the social problem as affecting *all* women, rather than the subset of drug-addicted women (or poor women of color presumed to be candidates for drug addiction)" (Gomez, 1997: 122). In California, Gomez concludes, "[f]eminist claims-makers (with allies in the medical profession) chose to downplay racial and class specificity and, alternatively, to emphasize threats to all women's reproductive autonomy. . . . the feminist coalition succeeded in shifting the discourse from one about bad women who need to be punished to one about sick women who needed help by focusing on drug-using women in general" (1997: 122–23). As a result, prosecutors, lawmakers, and social elites (doctors) "overwhelmingly defined pregnant drug users as victims rather than villains" (Gomez, 1997: 123). This required monumental efforts, however, to overcome and reframe the initial media and political "monster" stories of these women and their pregnancies.

Criminalizing Prenatal Care: Whitner v. State of South Carolina

In South Carolina, this effort produced different results. The complexities of women's lives has been lost in the rhetoric and grandstanding by highly placed South Carolina government officials to get tough on these crack babies' mothers. Gomez characterizes the response in South Carolina as "moderately punitive" or "hard diversion" (1997: 79).

Cornelia Whitner's story is complex, multilayered, sad, and tragic. As a poor, African American single mother, she tried to raise her children in an environment of poverty, violence, stress, racism, and sexism. When her youngest son was born, she tested positive for illegal drugs. A crusading pro-life prosecutor charged her with child abuse for delivering cocaine to a minor through her umbilical cord. She was convicted though released from prison while awaiting her appeal, during which time she was drug free, working, and raising her children as best her circumstances would allow. Her youngest son seemed normal and without dire health effects from any exposure to illegal drugs in utero. Nonetheless, the South Carolina Supreme Court upheld her conviction and ruled that child abuse statutes could include such situations. When the court's decision was handed down, Whitner was rounded up, her children placed with relatives, and she was reimprisoned (interviews; see also Paltrow, 1999a and 1999b; and Dubler, 1996).

In June of 2001, the South Carolina Supreme Court heard oral arguments in a case requesting the overturning of the *Whitner* decision (*State of South Carolina v. Brenda Kay Peppers*). Again, interest groups from around the country involved in women's rights, drug treatment, public health, and medicine submitted amicus briefs in the case (see, for example, American Public Health Association et al., 2001). The brief writers documented the counterproductive nature of the punitive monitoring and punishing of these pregnant women and emphasized the need to have accessible and affordable drug treatment programs and health services available to make the women healthy. They argued that when women are healthy, the fetuses will be, too. The case is still pending.

With precedents like *Whitner*, women will be punished for telling medical staff the truth about their drug use and for seeking prenatal care, and they will have to "battle the baby snatchers" from state social service agencies, who will remove their other children as well as the new baby (see S. Murphy and Rosenbaum, 1999: 109–10, 120). Their future reproductive agency can also be determined by the state. In these cases, the state does not notice the strengths of these mothers or how much they might love their children but focuses solely on their weaknesses and their failure to measure up to a middle-class, racial norm of the "good mother." When their children are put into foster care, the children are exposed to the dangers, stigmas, and disruptions of our current foster care system and are at risk of growing up without the love and sense of family that even a troubled mother can provide. An alternative, asset-based approach to these families would respect rather than denigrate the mothers, try to recognize their powerful love and efforts to care for their children under difficult conditions, and help the mothers establish family or community ties to bolster their family (Appell, 1998: 376).

Recently, the U.S. Supreme Court decided a case from South Carolina involving punitive monitoring of pregnant women (*Ferguson, Crystal, v. City of Charleston, et al.*, 2001). This case evolves from a sneaky policy at the Medical University of South Carolina (MUSC) in Charleston of notifying local police when women using the public health clinic tested positive for illegal drugs and were also pregnant. These women were not informed of these possible results of their prenatal care visits and did not give consent to the release of their urine tests to police and prosecutors. Many women were jailed, had their children removed from them, and faced police and state monitoring of their pregnancies.[1] At the time this policy was being implemented, there were not adequate, affordable, or available drug treatment facilities for pregnant women in the area. The MUSC policy was infused with a sense of crisis (the "cocaine baby"), the targeting of a powerless and marginalized population as the problem (poor women, predominately African American, using the health clinic), and an overly narrow definition of the problem (as criminal, not social or medical) (Jos, Marshall, and Perlmutter, 1995: 120; see also Frierson and Binkley, 2001). Socially constructing marginalized and powerless targeted groups as deviant and deserving of punitive social controls is a time-honored device in much public policy-making (A. Schneider and Ingram, 1993). Here, given the adversarial relationship created by authorities between pregnant women and their fetuses, such punitive monitoring of the deviant target population was justified by many state prosecutors. Remarkable also was the mindset of many South Carolina officials who thought that everything had been done to try to help these women; the criminal sanctions were a last resort. Such a consensus was established, Philip Jos, Mary Faith Marshall, and Martin Perlmutter report, "despite the lack of support (such as transportation, child care, and the like) that might have made rehabilitation visits possible, and the lack of adequate long-term residential treatment centers with child care capabilities and women only services. A women-only residential treatment center for substance abusing pregnant women did not exist in Charleston or anywhere else in the State of South Carolina at the time the Interagency Policy was adopted" (1995: 124). Instead, the problem was individualized to the woman herself, and proposals to make social services available to help her were explicitly rejected in South Carolina. Consequently, the health of the addicts was compromised (Jos, Marshall, and Perlmutter, 1995: 126).

Amicus briefs in this case were submitted by dozens of health care groups (the AMA, the American Nurses Association, and the Obstetricians-Gynecologists, to name a few) articulating their dismay at being placed in the role of pregnancy police instead of trusted and confidential health care healers for this vulnerable and powerless population of women. The brief for the National Association of Alcoholism and Drug Abuse Counselors et al. argued that such punitive policies were the opposite of what addicted people need to get well (1998).

When the policy was implemented at MUSC, hospital officials proclaimed it was working very well. Their evidence was that very few women now coming into the clinic tested positive for illegal drugs. What went without saying was that many women had stopped seeking prenatal care altogether.

The U.S. Supreme Court ruled that the use of the urine tests without the women's consent was an unlawful search and seizure. The Court's decision in *Ferguson* was based on search and seizure law but warns jurisdictions not to violate women's rights in collecting evidence from their bodies without their consent. The decision is rather narrow concerning reproductive rights.

Coerced and Punitive Contraception

When pregnant women's drug problems are defined as criminal instead of medical, one response is mandatory birth control. A collection of essays by researchers at the Hastings Center, a research institute that addresses ethical issues in health and medicine, raises many concerns about whether governments can make receipt of government social welfare funds contingent on the applicant's agreement to use long-acting, reversible contraceptives and whether judges can offer convicted female child abusers the choice of jail or a long-acting contraceptive device, such as Norplant (Moskowitz and Jennings, 1996).

Many of the authors in this volume acknowledge the sorry history of government interference in private reproductive decisions and the often racist, class-biased, and sexist results. Some of the authors recognize the suspicion of many groups that might be disproportionately targeted by coerced contraception policies and programs. However, only some of the authors incorporate government authorities' past abuses of long-acting contraceptive devices into their analysis.

The volume does provide an accessible overview of the moral and ethical issues involved in many aspects of reproductive choice. Authors discuss quality of life issues, the ethics of deciding ahead of time (through offering some women the choice of going to jail or consenting to Norplant insertion) that hypothetical future children would be better off not being conceived to begin with, and legitimate governmental incentives, sanctions, and policies for shaping individual's reproductive options. Several scholars in this volume note that coerced contraception does nothing to address the systemic problems of violence, poverty, substance abuse, racism, and sexism, to name a few, which foreground many of the personal histories of the women presented with such "choices."

A couple of authors in this study note the double standard when judicial sentences from child abuse or neglect convictions focus on the *women alone* for possible coercive contraception "choices." The men involved in the abuse or neglect are not considered for similar sanctions, lectures, monitoring, admonitions, or controls over their fertility and possible future parenthood (see also Pollitt, 1995; and Baer, 1999). Given, however, the gender specific nature of these contraceptive policies, a fuller and more thoroughly integrated discussion of gender politics throughout these discussions would be more useful. As Judith Baer observes, men are often not held responsible for the harm they inflict on other people, while women are held responsible disproportionate to their powers and agency:

> When we compare these attitudes toward crimes against women to the increasing use of criminal sanctions on women, the notion of derivative responsibility emerges as the common theme. Because women are responsible, we punish them for drinking while pregnant or for not preventing their children's deaths at the hands of their drunken father. Because women are responsible, we do not hold men accountable for violent sexual acting out or for exposing their children to danger. By selective exculpating and inculpating, society uses criminal law to reinforce women's disproportionate vulnerability and responsibility. (1999: 164–65)

Some scholars do stress societal obligations, duties, and responsibilities, as well as those of individual parents (usually mothers), to nurture, support, and provide for children when assessing punitive and coercive contraceptive orders. Too many, however, ignore societal roles and obligations and frame the discussion around presumedly autonomous individuals who are completely free to make their own choices. Government power invoked to sanction women's wanton behavior, then, seems legitimate. Evidence of this unevenness occurs when scholars mention contraceptives that appear to satisfy many of the problems for a judge wanting to safely limit the reproduction of a convicted female with long-acting, virtually error proof, reversible birth control, such as Norplant, IUDs, or Depo-Provera, but overlook the fact that these contraceptives are not "safe" for many of the women involved because they will not protect the women from sexually transmitted diseases. These devices are analyzed by a few pundits and scholars as if the real public health crisis of sexually transmitted diseases can be assumed away. Denied, also, is the issue of whether women truly control sexual access to their bodies at all times. Policy recommendations such as these do not fully incorporate the context of women's complex lives.

Comparing reproductive laws and practices internationally is very important to this debate. Experiences of abuses of individual rights in other countries, insensitivity to group cultures and religious beliefs, and the disproportionate impact governmental controls, incentives, and surveillance of women's reproduction have on the least powerful ethnic, religious, and economic groups in many countries should inform analysis of U.S. policies as well.

Finally, it is curious that these authors discuss the United States and the ethics of coerced contraceptives as if safe, legal abortions do not currently exist. The true nature of abortion as a choice needs to be woven into any analysis of modern reproductive ethics and politics. If women using illegal drugs are pushed to have abortions because their only alternative is to go to jail, lose custody of existing children, and entangle themselves in the criminal justice system, we need to scrutinize carefully whether they are really freely choosing these abortions.

Coerced contraception is increasingly used or considered by judges and policymakers. Feminist ethics must address the potentials, both positive and negative, that new, long-acting, reliable, and reversible birth control devices present. Central to the debate is whether requiring these devices for some women or letting them "choose" them under difficult and personally painful circumstances allows society to avoid more systemic, costly, but more humane and less ethically troubling policies and programs.

Punitive Monitoring and Control

Why should we care about how pregnant substance-abusing women are treated in the legal system? First of all, we should care about the health of all people, including pregnant women. We also should care about a fetus a woman chooses to bring to term and hope it is healthy at birth. Even after a fetus is born, most people hope that the child has a safe home, plenty to eat, quality and affordable health care, education, public transportation, and a clean and safe environment. Interestingly, although much legislative attention these days is focused on the safety of fetuses, those in power do not pay much attention to them after they are born.

We need to examine the situation of all people (pregnant or not) who engage in self-destructive behavior by looking at their lives. The unique and remarkable study by Sheigla Murphy and Marsha Rosenbaum examines 120 California women who were pregnant and using illegal drugs. "Their stories," they write, "reveal how years of instability, insecurity, and violence conspired to deny them, first, the fundamental right to control their own bodies and, later, the right to mother their own children" (1999: 19). These women "had never felt in control of any part of their lives, including their own bodies" (S. Murphy and Rosenbaum, 1999: 50).

Reforms need to incorporate the multidimensional nature of women, particularly mothers, and their economic marginalization (Slaughter, 1995). Women's substance abuse is often related to their poverty, their experiences of violence, their position in patriarchal and racist institutions, cultural and social norms, and their interpersonal relationships. We should not look away from the inequalities, past abuses, and violence that shape contemporary behavior. To resign ourselves to not investing in the expensive and long-term efforts to help pregnant women out of poverty, violent relationships, and self-destructive behaviors encourages us to, in Marie Ashe's words, "cease our inquiries into their cultural contexts" (1995: 159; see also Rhode, 1993: 324).

Discussions on state policy on substance-abusing pregnant women must also recognize the difficulty these women face in providing safe, affordable child care for their children while they grapple with their substance-abuse problems. Policies must also ensure that pregnant women who seek treatment for substance abuse not risk losing custody of any existing children as a result of their getting help for these problems. Pregnant women under treatment for substance abuse must now also worry about whether their lack of full-time employment while they seek treatment will jeopardize their eligibility for social welfare programs. It is doubtful that the current Republican congressional majority is considering the real needs of these pregnant women as Congress restructures these programs and turns them over to the states.

I wonder about the real purpose of some of the rhetoric to get tough on "bad" mothers, during a period when the very same policymakers have cut funding to help pregnant women, mothers, and children in need. Some of the rhetoric might be soothing, symbolic reassurances to imply that these politicians do care very deeply about children, hence their ferocious demonizing of illegal substance–abusing "bad" mothers. The very same politicians, however, might provide no programs or social supports to actually help pregnant women who use illegal drugs. Hence, they have "words that succeed and policies which fail," as Murray Edelman has shown with many previous social welfare programs (1977).

It is interesting to contrast recommendations for pregnant, illegal substance abusers with the U.S. Supreme Court's majority opinion in *International Union v. Johnson Controls, Inc.* (1991). In *Johnson Controls,* the majority ruled that female workers of child-bearing age may choose for themselves whether to work in occupations in a battery-making factory that might harm future or present fetuses. To do otherwise would constitute sex discrimination. In *Johnson Controls,* then, women's autonomy is recognized. To discuss the "choices" these working women actually have in their lives (the jobs with more health risks also paid more), and whether other options that might have been more expensive and cumbersome for factory owners could have been created is beyond the scope of this work (see Cornell, 1998: 71–81). My point here is that women as potential breeders are treated differently depending on whether the potential fetus-harming activity is legal or illegal. Working at Johnson Controls would not land them in a treatment program, nor would smoking legal cigarettes (although smoking illegal substances would) or drinking wine at a restaurant, at least not yet. Although tobacco use and alcohol consumption are also not recommended prenatal care, the women who use tobacco and alcohol still have the power to be sure that their behavior is not categorized as a public problem (S. Murphy and Rosenbaum, 1999: 141; see also Gusfield, 1981). "There are ideological explanations for why these infants continued to be labeled 'crack babies' rather than, in light of scientific findings, 'poverty babies,'" Murphy and Rosenbaum point out. "In an era of fiscal retrenchment, the notion of poverty babies might engender public sympathy and interfere with the conservative drive to demolish social welfare programs" (1999: 141). If the babies and their mothers were framed as suffering from poverty, possible state responses would be different. For one thing, the pregnant women would not be jailed just for being poor.

Although I am not belittling the harms of illegal substances for all people's health, including pregnant women, fetuses, and future children, the kinds of pregnant women who will be monitored and controlled by these policies is troublesome. In addition, it is not clear what the effects of illegal substance use are on fetuses and children over time (Chavkin, 2001; Frank et al., 2001). What is incontrovertible, though, is all the data that show that poverty, violence (the American Medical Association recently reported that domestic violence is probably one of the largest causes of birth defects), and all the concomitant effects of poverty and violence have a devastating effect on women and their children. Maybe if we start highlighting that poverty and violence also harm fetuses, politicians and prosecutors will do something to prevent them.

Discussions on policies for substance-abusing pregnant women should also acknowledge that "bad" and "unfit" mothers have often been judged based on their social location, which has had dire consequences for disabled, black, Native American, immigrant, lesbian, single, poor, and young women (Ladd-Taylor and Umansky, 1998; Kline, 1995: 120). The state, for instance, has always been very willing to intrude on the autonomy of black mothers (D. Roberts, 1995: 231). Even though behaviors that might harm fetuses cross class and race lines, the vast majority of women tested for substance abuse during pregnancy, reported to government agencies, and charged with such crimes as using illegal drugs during pregnancy are black women (D. Roberts, 1995: 232).

It is important to see that these are not simply the "personal lifestyles" or "personal choices" of pregnant women but are embedded in their social situations and their relationships with other people. For instance, substance-abusing husbands or partners facilitate, encourage, or exacerbate the unhealthy habits of women and pose dangers to fetuses, babies, and children in their households, yet these significant others are not drawn into mandatory treatment programs. Quite often a mother-blaming dynamic is at work, whereby, in Marlee Kline's words, "characterization of battering and alcohol and drug dependency as personal problems reinforces the placing of blame for child neglect on the deficiencies of individual mothers" (Kline, 1995: 126; see also D. Roberts, 1999; and Sanger, 1996). But, as Kline points out, "[t]he individualizing and obfuscating effects of the ideology of motherhood do not always take the form of mother-blaming. They also submerge contradictions between the liberal framework of 'choice' and the coercive and ideological forces in women's lives that make 'options,' such as giving one's child up for adoption, appear viable" (1995: 129–30).

From their interviews with 120 pregnant women using illegal drugs, Murphy and Rosenbaum document how these women have been used and abused since birth, but they also note, "The 1990s brought a different and, in some ways, more virulent kind of abuse. Pregnant drug users were now used as part of a larger ideological offensive to legitimate the wholesale reduction of social welfare services to all poor women and children. We believe that history may prove this last to be the most devastating abuse of all" (1999: 156).

Conclusion: Healthy and Safe Moms and Babies

Societal disapproval and sanction of the nonconforming mother fit into a colonizing pattern (see Fineman and Karpin, 1995; and Fineman, 1995b and 1999). Murphy and Rosenbaum conclude from their examination of the lives and circumstances of 120 pregnant women who used illegal drugs, "Women's drug use during pregnancy cannot be understood apart from the social and economic contexts in which these experiences were embedded. The greatest threat to effective parenting and child survival is a system that perpetuates poverty, violence, hardship, and desperation. Rather than indicting pregnant drug users for their addictions and compulsions, we would do well to look at the impossible conditions in which these women and their children are forced to live their lives" (1999: 157). The punitive monitoring of pregnant women in these and similar cases is based on the state's viewing women's bodies as mere vehicles for the production of children. The welfare of the women, per se, is neglected or erased. Instead, as Wendy Chavkin points out, the trends "in the social perception of women positions a pregnant woman as antagonist to the fetus whenever she asserts her own primacy" (1992: 194).

We need to remember that how we treat pregnant substance abusers affects women's social standing and creates a climate wherein, as Janice Raymond put it, "women are wombs" (1993), who have been "skinned" by new reproductive technologies so that their innards can be examined, monitored, and possibly controlled by medical professionals and the state (C. Daniels, 1993; Duden, 1993; Woliver, 1989a, 1989c, and 1990c). Biomedical discourse, Nathan Stormer asserts, uses "spatial rhetorics whereby women's wombs are coordinated with the general social topography," and the effect is a "shifting topography of public and private worlds" (2000: 111). These merging temporal plates shift the territory of women's reproduction powers from women themselves, creating publicly monitored pregnancies observed by the colonizing biomedical experts.

Primary attention to the foundational aspects of women's well-being is required. "The social construction of adequate mothering must be analyzed in its historical, political, and economic contexts," Murphy and Rosenbaum declare (1999, 136). Chavkin believes that the arguments about fetuses and bad mothers are really in a code; "decoded, the struggle is over our social understanding of women as female roles change in the society. The innocence ascribed to the fetus and the punitive anger expressed toward the pregnant woman considered to be its selfish adversary, express metaphorically the pain and rage of those who no longer find the family to be a 'haven in a heartless world,' and who perceived the loss of the mother as central to family dissolution (rather than structural changes in the economy)" (1992: 200). Hostile focus on errant mothers also serves a diversionary, deflective role, providing a sleight of hand to detract us from social structures, social failures, male violence, and control (Woliver, 1989a and 1989c; Chavkin, 1992: 200). Low birth weight would not be eliminated even if all illegal substance–abusing pregnant women were in treatment (for background, see Merrick and Blank, 1993). As Drucilla Cornell points out, to help babies and children, the "first step is to render justice to women" (1998: 85), not to increase the injustices heaped on them. The strongest single indicator of a baby's health is still the mother's zip code. We must therefore consider the social cost to women's rights of these mandatory treatment policies and the ways they possibly deflect us from more systematic ways to help pregnant women and their children, even if they are more expensive.

Note

An earlier version of this chapter was presented at the Western Political Science Annual Meeting, San Jose, California, March 24–26, 2000. Parts of the discussion in the section "Coerced and Punitive Contraception" draw from Woliver, 1998b. The section "Punitive Monitoring and Control" derives from Woliver, 1996c.

1. Of the approximately thirty women jailed, twenty-nine were African American. The remaining woman was white and in a partnership with an African American man.

CONCLUSION: THE CHANGING
GEOGRAPHIES OF MOTHERHOOD
AND REPRODUCTION

> Male fascination with the reproductive affairs of female group members predates our species.
>
> —Sarah Hrdy, *Maternal Instincts and How They Shape the Human Species*

"We are all cyborgs now," Donna Haraway asserts (1997: 12). The offspring of implosions of subjects and objects, blurred and blended boundaries between the natural and artificial, interwoven machines and organic bodies, economic markets and lives make up enhanced cyborg figures (Haraway, 1997: 14). "Artificial" machines and "natural" human boundaries become blurred in postmodern identities since, as Anne Balsamo points out, "cyborg identity is predicated on transgressed boundaries. They fascinate us because they are not like us and yet are just like us" (1996: 32). The problem is that technologies rapidly gut our ethics, and new procedures become rights (Elshtain, 1998: 185). A market-driven biotechnocracy emerges before ethical reflection (Tracy, 1998: 192). "Whatever happened to accepting embodied limits with better grace?" Jean Elshtain wonders (1998: 187). Instead, what occurs is that life is "enterprised up" wherein, in Haraway's words, "in the dyspeptic version of the technoscientific soap opera, the species becomes the brand name and the figure becomes the price. Ironically, the millenarian fulfillment of development is the excessive condensation of implosion" (1997: 12).

There are many ways manifest even in our popular culture where the natural body has been dramatically dismembered, enterprised up, and re-fashioned through the application of new technologies of corporeality. These new "[t]echno-bodies are healthy, enhanced, and fully functional— more real than real" Balsamo asserts. Yet "[o]ten obscured are the disciplining and surveillant consequences of these technologies—in short, the bio-politics of technological formations" (Balsamo, 1996: 5). New visualization technologies, new tests, new devices, "anonymous 'health' guardians (often appointed by the state) monitor intrauterine fetal blood composition to determine the possibility of cocaine-addicted infants. Fractured body parts are taken up as elements in the construction of cultural identities— agent of infection, cocaine mother, drug uses—or that, as unknowing subjects of a disembodied technological gaze, our bodies betray us. Nowhere to hide from our bodies ourselves, we have no other choice but to comply and live cleanly; docile creatures practice safe sex or self-destruct" (Balsamo, 1996: 6).

Viewing the social impact of new reproductive science through the situated knowledge used by Haraway for "[c]hallenging the material-semiotic practices of technoscience is in the interests of a deeper, broader, and more open scientific literacy" (1997: 11). The situated knowledge recognized by the modest witness to these scientific and patentable developments illuminates, in Haraway's words, that the "chip, seed, or gene is simultaneously literal and figurative. We inhabit and are inhabited by such figures that map universes of knowledge, practice and power" (1997: 11). What Haraway's modest witness (not an authoritative expert but someone who is aware of the context, cultural differences, and situated knowledge of both subjects and objects) seeks is to question "the elaborately constructed and defended confidence of this civic man of reason in order to enable a more corporeal, inflected, and optically dense, if less elegant, kind of modest witness to matters of fact to emerge in the worlds of technoscience" (1997: 24). Modern biological thinking and teaching could diminish the importance of social and political structures and choices that also shape the human condition. Haraway writes about one university biology course with which she was involved: it "aimed to persuade students that natural science alone, not politics or religion, offered hope for secular progress not infected by ideology" (1997: 104). She argues that "we need a critical hermeneutics of genetics *as a constitutive part of scientific practice* more urgently than we need better map resolution for genetic markers in yeast, human, or canine genomes" (1997: 160). Genetics, technoscience, and patents on life forms and mapped genes ratchet up the economic and political stakes in human reproduction, making women's bodies more publicly visible and publicly held assets.

Feminist Praxis: Political Challenge

Rejecting untenable choices (for example, aborting female fetuses or bringing them into a world where they are unwanted) and instead addressing the underlying injustices are necessary to delineate guidelines for the shifting terrain of reproductive decision making. Rosalind Petchesky, in her study of abortion, for instance, concludes, "In short, making authentic moral judgments about abortion and having choices that are real involve changing the world" (1984: 360).

The women's health movement of the 1970s and 1980s mobilized in response to some of the alienating practices of modern medicine. The best-selling successive editions of the feminist self-help health manual *Our Bodies, Ourselves* is one indicator of the widespread interest women have in empowering themselves through learning about their bodies. Particularly with pregnancy and childbirth, many scholars note, women are monitored and controlled in a manner that doubts their birth powers, pathologizes all their pregnancies, and seeks to control, manage, and profit from what could be a woman-centered and affirming experience.[1] Robbie Pfeufer Kahn articulates this alternative vision of birth: "The language of birth should be a language of touch, of the relational self grounded in the body. Yet, nothing in this text [*Williams Obstetrics*, a widely used textbook] acknowledges touch as a language. Touching becomes a way of looking with the hand in order to make a clinical judgment: to grasp, to take apart" (1995: 209). *Williams Obstetrics* deeply affects our birth experiences because it is now the standard of care, the template for obstetric protocols, and the text of authoritative knowledge that doctors defend themselves with or against in malpractice lawsuits. These protocols construct a reality that the doctors must adhere to or face professional discipline (Kahn, 1995: 215).

In response to these issues, in 1984 feminists from all over the world organized the Feminist International Network on the New Reproductive Technologies (FINNRET). A journal published from 1988 to 1992, *Reproductive and Genetic Engineering: Journal of International Feminist Analysis*, sought to "make a feminist analysis of the technologies more consistently central in the educational, public policy, and informational realms, as well as to address the everchanging and rapid developments in this area" ("Editorial," 1988: 1) and thus expose and counter the impact these technologies have on women.

Feminist Praxis: Imperfect Individuals and Connected Communities

From conversations with abortion workers and fieldwork observations of them, Wendy Simonds concludes that we should take a holistic approach to reproductive issues and understand the depth and complexity of such reproductive decisions as abortion (1996: 1). "Center women found abortion to be more complicated than pro-choice rhetoric allows, but the pro-choice moral framework remained unchanged except for their belief that thinking through the complexity gave their position increased strength," Simonds writes (1996: 102). The abortion workers, Simonds reports, also learned that "choice" was a weak expression of what aborting women exercised; many clients were painfully trapped in situations in which their own agency seemed impossible. Abortion could be seen as an act of protest against an unhappy biological consequence of sexual expression (though for many women, sexual expression might have had little to do with the act that led to unwanted pregnancy). Abortion could be seen as an "only choice" some women made in order to gain a modicum of control in circumstances that allowed for little freedom in the first place. (1996: 228)

The workers Simonds studied "depicted abortion as a potentially profound organizing force, a representative symbol in the struggle to advance women's agency to protect sexual and procreative freedom and to ensure women's very survival" (1996: 231). As one worker put it to Simonds, "'Part of what abortion is about is a woman's *wholeness*. . . . It's whether the world has enough room for you'" (1996: 231).

Listening to the ongoing interpretations of the relationships mothers have with "defective" children at birth and as they are raised reveals the impact new medical technologies are having on motherhood, the complex ways that women mother, and the prejudices against people who are less than "perfect." However, people do not often listen to mothers, especially health care professionals.

The anthropologist Gail H. Landsman, herself the mother of three children, one with disabilities, thoughtfully and empathetically listened to mothers of disabled babies and children. Her interviews uncover the complexities of these relationships, the sorrows, joys, and pressures these women feel, given our shifting geographies of pregnancy, childbirth, and what are considered "productive" and "worthwhile" outcomes. Parents of children with disabilities, Landsman found, often feel miscast, partly because medical technologies, selective abortions, and authoritative knowledge by medical authorities "produce an illusion of control and of the potential for 'perfect' babies for mothers of all socioeconomic classes who have access to and utilize the medical system; and because discrimination against persons with disabilities extends broadly across class lines in U.S. culture" (2000: 185).

As Landsman points out, "Examining how mothers of infants with disabilities define and redefine their identities in the course of mothering contributes to the knowledge of how motherhood is constituted in various contexts, in this case, a context of 'difference' and societal devaluation, as well as one of extensive maternal interaction with medical experts, new technologies, and government bureaucracies" (1998: 79).

Medical technologies are now constantly embedded in these families' lives. When presenting the need to make decisions for a baby's treatment, medical personnel describe it as a "choice." Landsman helps us see what these so-called choices feel like for the parents. "These parental obligations are often first experienced in the context of having to make decisions in the neonatal intensive care unit (NICU) of a hospital. Such decisions are presented to parents under the guise of choice and informed consent," Landsman writes (1998: 72–71). The narratives of mothers with sick, premature, or disabled babies, however, "are full of the agonies of decision making in the NICU and demonstrates the cruel irrelevance of a rhetoric of choice in such a situation" (Landsman, 1998: 72). "Connecting the stories is a discourse of love for a child whom they once might have imagined to be unlovable. The rhetoric of choice is inadequate for dealing with the inherent ambiguities of bringing into the world, making decisions about, and caring for infants with disabilities. In an age of 'perfect' babies, these mothers must break new ground and struggle with developing a vocabulary to explain the meaning of their children and of their own motherhood" (Landsman, 1998: 92).

Mothers' experiences of raising and loving children with disabilities make them grapple with societal norms of "lives worth living," "defections," "choice," and "personhood," to name a few. "For the woman whose infant is born 'damaged,' however, the 'other' is no longer a hypothetical possibility but a member of the family," Landsman observes (1998: 73). What occurs is a transformational "move from one's prior identity to one's newly emerging identity as a mother of a disabled child" (Landsman, 1998: 76). Sensitive scholars like Landsman admonish us to study the agency of mothers of children with disabilities "to examine how they may accept, reject, or reconstruct cultural representations of reproduction, medical science, and technology through their own experiences of mothering a child with disabilities" (Landsman, 1998: 82). The disabled "child's ability to give and receive love . . . appears most often in narratives as a defining feature of his or her humanity," Landsman reports (1998: 93). Once again, a nurturance ethic is evident in these mother-child narratives. While every mother's story is different and some reject their children with disabilities, many mothers construct a narrative of hope, "attributing to their infants culturally valued qualities that may not be readily apparent to outside observers or medical staff" (Landsman, 1998: 78). These include pointing out the child's strength in overcoming obstacles, their grit for surviving, their happiness as babies and children, and the love they have brought to their families.

Many mothers also attempt to fit their disabled child into a narrative of progress. The culturally available discourse of progress, Landsman notes, "enables U.S. mothers simultaneously to hold negative attitudes about people with disabilities *and* to attribute personhood passionately to their own children" (1998: 78). Landsman found, "The stories told by most mothers in the study suggest that what the literature refers to as a process of parental adjustment may be a matter not of becoming resigned to the tragedy of not having a normal child but rather of being challenged by, and redefining through experience, existing cultural understandings of what constitutes normality and perfection" (1998: 93). Such a standpoint, based on lived experience, illuminates the diverse responses of caregivers as they build and sustain their families.

Prenatal screening is profoundly changing the ethos of pregnancy and the culture of motherhood. Underlying its availability and widespread use is an implicit assumption, according to Nancy Press and her colleagues: "The prenatal detection of conditions that cannot be cured logically entails the belief that these conditions are so devastating that pregnant women should be given the opportunity to avoid the birth of babies so affected" (N. Press et al., 1998: 50).

The political and cultural shifting in the geography of pregnancy filters new layers of guilt onto mothers. The availability of prenatal screening, a study of three European countries shows, factors into blaming mothers of children with Down's syndrome (Marteau and Drake, 1995). As Landsman highlights about the European study, it "not only demonstrates that mothers' access to an informed choice allows blame to be placed on them but also contains an implicit assumption that the birth of a child with a disability requires assignment of blame" (1998: 94–95). Landsman's analysis of the narratives of mothers of children with disabilities reveals that the "fundamental unfairness of bearing infants with disabilities despite the promises of genetic screening, prenatal testing, and high-tech nurseries and despite the mother's compliance with the best scientific prescriptions for producing positive pregnancy outcomes is in many mothers' stories tied to an affirmation of the role of mother. However, the role focuses on commitment to nurturance of and advocacy for the child, rather than on the maternal responsibility for biological 'quality control' that pregnancy in the age of new reproductive technologies seems to imply" (1998: 83). She adds, "'Real" motherhood exists as an issue for mothers of disabled infants in part because they hold themselves accountable, or feel they are held accountable by others, for the failure to produce a perfect child despite their access to expert medical knowledge" (1998: 85). Mothers of children with disabilities do not romanticize their situations. "Well aware of the 'downside' to disability and the financial and emotional costs, many mothers have nevertheless normalized both their children and their own experiences; whether already knowing or coming to learn through nurturing that their disabled children are as fully human and valuable as any other children, they have also come to define their own motherhood, while counter to expectations, as nevertheless normal in its own terms," Landsman reports (1998: 93). The mothers of children with disabilities, through their day-to-day labors and work with these children, come to see the child as gift giver, bestowing the experience of unconditional love (Landsman, 1999).

Careful research also reveals that some mothers do not bond with their children; the "maternal instinct" ideal sometimes blinds us to the reality that some mothers and other caretakers of disabled, highly dependent, or different children harm, neglect, or kill these children (Hrdy, 1999; Bourgois, 1998; Goldstein, 1998; M. Weiss, 1998; Korbin, 1998). The nurturing that primate mothers (including us human moms) give our babies depends on the context of our lives (Hrdy, 1999). Mothers who kill, whether the child is disabled or not, are depicted as monsters. Fathers who kill children are not as fascinating or inexplicable in many cultures. The well-being and survival of children, disabled or not, are linked to the well-being of their mothers or other caretakers.

Faye Ginsburg's (1989) insights into how nurturance has been transformed from an ascribed to an achieved feature in modern U.S. gender identity "becomes all the more critical for mothers who have given birth to 'less-than-perfect' babies" (Landsman, 1998: 86; see also Kittay, 1999a: 176, and 1999b).

Landsman sums up many of these dilemmas: "The eugenic implications of prenatal screening technologies and of selective abortion of defective fetuses have led to conflicts within feminism, with many arguing the need to reflect on whether genetic research and reproductive technologies truly provide more data for women's informed choices or instead support existing socially constructed attitudes toward disabled children" (1998: 80).

The label "disabled" might in the future expand to include many attributes deemed undesirable in a particular culture or society. "Disabled," Landsman maintains, should also be interpreted "to include those who have traits that, given the availability of prenatal screening and the widespread belief in the genetic basis of behavior, may be so labeled (and hence 'chosen against') in the future: homosexuals, people with obesity or short stature, and those determined to have a genetic predisposition for a chronic illness or lower-than-average IQ score, among others" (1998: 95).

Unfortunately, as Barbara Rothman points out, "[t]he keening of mothers has never made much difference in our world" (1994: 261). The

gendered polarities of dependence/independence also mean that efforts
to nurture or help the nurturers of the world is seen as weak. Jessica
Benjamin explains:

> Internalization of authority proceeds by turning the frustrated wish for
> power inward: we may not be able to affect the world, but we can at least
> control ourselves; we may not be able to truly achieve independence from
> all other creatures, but we can distance ourselves from them so that we
> *appear* completely autonomous. That this acceptance of powerlessness
> in the guise of autonomy may deny our responsibility to care for others
> is rationalized by the notion that we can, after all, do nothing to help
> them. (1988: 179–80)

A comparative study of women in seven countries paints a picture of how
women often see themselves as individuals with rights yet embedded in
an interconnected and interdependent nexus of community. Western
rights discourses based on "privacy" and "individualism" do not capture
the complex standpoints of women comparatively. One team of comparative scholars therefore adopted a research approach that invokes "a subversive tradition of autonomy and self-ownership that exists in popular
European, African American and many non-Western cultures, one that
postulates the self as *both* individual *and* constructed through ongoing
interaction and interdependency with others" (Petchesky, 1998b: 15). The
comparative study revealed that "women in their everyday deliberations
over matters of fertility, sexuality, work, and child care do not necessarily experience their own entitlement and that of their families, especially their children, as operating on different or conflicting levels of decision making. Rather, they interweave the self-other relationship in their
moral calculations all the time, rooting their individual identity in family and community" (Petchesky, 1998b: 15). Here is the nurturance ethic displayed cross-culturally.

What society could move toward is a "caring jurisprudence" that does
not frame issues as zero-sum struggles in which one side wins all and the
other loses everything. This caring jurisprudence would draw from the
ethic of justice and the ethic of care, which incorporates nurturance into
the human condition. Including patients' stories in policy-making would
add to decision makers' information in two ways: one, the particularized
knowledge of the patient might challenge more generalized knowledge;
two, personal accounts, especially when collectively accumulated, might
place an issue within a large social context for decision makers (Behuniak, 1999: 23). Currently, however, physicians' interests are protected
at the expense of patients, such as women who seek abortions (Behuniak,
1999: 29).

Mothers of children with disabilities are especially good reminders of the links between experience and theory. Their lived daily reality of dependency, nurturance, and relationship to sustain human life pertains to all of us at some time in our existence. Feminist praxis centers the ongoing dialectic between experience and theory, as Eloise Buker explains:

> Turning away from early Enlightenment emphases on neutrality brings citizens closer to classic Greek notions that emphasize the connection between social theory and action. Praxis explains this connection as a dialectic in which theory is shaped out of social experiences and social experiences are viewed through the lens of theory. Good social analysis means continually being open to the dialectical changes that this tension produces. However, openness does not mean beginning an analysis with a blank slate (that is, no prejudice) because some pre-judgment position makes analysis possible. Reflection emerges by critically examining the pre-judgments that frame the inquiry and the new insights produced by inquiry. (1999: 66)

Theories are not isolated from politics, Buker goes on to explain: "This understanding of theory is often called praxis because its holders argue that practices shape the formulation of theories, and theories shape the sort of actions that believers select. Thus, theories are more accurately the result of political experiences than the wild imaginations of either good or bad visionaries" (1999: 6). Often, then, theories of the natural world have been constructed to mirror (and justify) the social world, even in cell research. "Feminist scientific questions," Buker relates, "illuminated unspoken assumptions and gave support to the hypothesis that scientists had projected their own social images onto their research observations" (1999: 88). Situated modest witnesses, such as Donna Haraway, advocate that scientists turn their mirrors around and be more philosophically reflective of their own work. As Buker comments regarding Haraway's line of analysis, "Put more crudely, scientists expected the male primates that they observed to be aggressive and to dominate females, and then those scientists used these observations as data to support claims that male primates, including male humans, are naturally dominant. The political implication of their research was that human females should be satisfied with secondary citizenship status; men should run things as nature dictates" (1999: 88). Mother nature, however, did not construct this binary vision. Mothers of children with disabilities and nurturers of all sorts experience the interconnectedness of all human lives. As Joan Tronto points out, an ethic of care and a more caring jurisprudence would recognize that "[t]hroughout our lives, all of us go through varying degrees of dependence and independence, of autonomy and vulnerability. A political order that presumes only independence and autonomy as the nature of human life thereby misses a great deal of human experience, and must somehow hide this point elsewhere. For example, such an order must rigidly separate public and private life" (1993: 135). The acknowledgment of our interconnectedness and mutual dependencies through the social experiences nurturers have dialectically speaks to feminist theory and praxis. The interconnectedness manifest in ecofeminism echoes these ethics of care, acknowledgement of human dependency, and validation of nurturing work (McLeod, 1999). Ecofeminism does not use hierarchical or anthropocentric worldviews. Ecofeminism blends community and human nurturance with ecological thinking that centers on the interconnectedness of all life. Instead of perpetuating the idea of isolated individuals making rational economic choices and producing perfect babies and enhanced, enterprised-up human products, feminist praxis (1) critiques the idea of objective science; (2) asks what the view of gender, race, class, and sexuality is in any science; (3) based on experiences of dependency and nurturing, questions the premises of rational, autonomous individualism; and (4) advocates a more humble science.

The more humble, reflective science can no longer deny the connections between politics, science, and truth (Buker, 1999: 117). Scientists try to discern order out of chaos. Nevertheless, scientists are often bedeviled by contradictory concepts, trivia, errors, and puzzling exceptions to rules. Often their scientific findings draw them into passionate political controversies. The static and feuds are ever-present background elements in science, and, as Bruno Latour and Steve Woolgar point out, "it is only rarely that a pocket of stability emerges from it. The revelation of the diversity of accounts and inconsistency of scientific arguments should therefore come as no surprise: on the contrary, the emergenc[e] of an accepted fact is the rare event which should surprise us" (1979: 252).

Especially important for my topic—the new and shifting terrains of reproductive politics—a more reflective science must explore how gender is characterized, assumed, stereotyped, controlled, and shaped in the process. As Buker writes, "A key step in reflective scientific discourse is an explicit examination of how scientific projects articulate the relationship between men and women. This means that scientists and citizens need to review how projects characterize females" (1999: 129).

Feminist Justice: Ethics of Care, Human Dependency, and Nurturing

The feminist psychoanalyst Jessica Benjamin notes, "While the values of competition, success, and hard work seem to thrive as ever, the values of collective nurturance and responsibility for others have suffered. Of course, these are not intrinsically female values, but in our society they are almost exclusively familial and private, and thus associated with women" (1988: 203). Yet, she adds, "[t]he inner core of need (still seen as infantile since the autonomous adult should not need anyone) can never be revealed 'outside,' in public, except as weakness" (1988: 205).

Part of our reflections must include attentive listening to what women experience while they try to negotiate their reproductive lives, how mothers see nurturing, and what the context is for the pleasures and worries of mothering/nurturing a child with a disability. We must incorporate into our social theories the fact that we are all interdependent and that every one of us has the chance to be disabled and dependent once again (as we were when we were infants and children and will be again when we are dying).[2] This form of listening is not advanced by defensiveness or combativeness on the part of any party. Feminist praxis helps here, too, according to Buker: "the mechanism of so-called objective descriptions and skeptical approaches often endangers critiques because combative questions silence intellectual exchanges. Neither academic feminists nor feminists in other settings will stay in a conversation for long if its form or telos is verbal combat. Feminists alert to the problems of the permanent other are often intolerant of playing subordinate roles" (1999: 221). Human dependency, interdependency, and interconnectedness are experiences that nurturers (often, but not always women) bring to feminist praxis and theory. The dependency work of nurturers and caregivers is part of the human condition of constant interdependency that, in Eva Kittay's words, "begins with the dependency of an infant, and often ends with the dependency of a very ill or frail person close to dying" (Kittay, 1999a: xii). Kittay, the mother of a severely disabled daughter, lives and breaths what I and others mean by feminist praxis. Kittay writes about what it means to mother a child with severe disabilities, "all the while continuing to use my own experiences with my daughter as a source of reflection and as a tether that prevents me from wandering away from the lived reality" (1999a: 162). Mothering a child with a disability helped Kittay learn "that the differences we encounter redefine sameness. Raising a child with a severe disability is not just like parenting a normal child—but more so. It is often very different. Yet in that difference, we come to see features of raising any child that otherwise escape attention or that assume a new valence. One notices aspects of maternal practice that are not highlighted when we begin our theorizing from the perspective of the mother of the normal child" (Kittay, 1999a: 163). Her experience has taught her much more: "More than any abstract theorizing could, it has made me see that we cannot understand the demands of social organization if we cannot take the fact of dependency as one of the circumstances of justice" (1999a: 165).

Recognition of the ubiquity of dependency and the importance of nurturing, Kittay argues, is mandatory: "To function free of vulnerability to exploitation due to paid or familial dependency work, and free to engage with the full resonance of their voices, women must have access to a universal provision that recognizes the indispensable role of dependency workers and the importance of their participation as full citizens" (1999a: 146). Acknowledgment of our inability to escape dependency in our lifetime would "cut through the fiction of our independence," where dependency is wrongly considered abnormal (Kittay, 1999a: xiii). Dependency, from infancy, disability, sickness, and dying, is unavoidable, and caring for dependents is a mark of our humanity (Kittay, 1999a: 29). Dependency when an infant, disabled, sick, and dying is a part of the human condition. Moral and political theories need to incorporate this fact of dependency and nurturance rather than the myths of independence, equality of circumstances, and autonomous individualism as universal human constants. Perhaps the human genome maps will convince us of this instead of dividing us into more hierarchical categories. As Buker writes, "Citizens, like family members, live connected lives" (1999: 41). However, in our current "dialectic of dependency," women, who mainly perform the dependency work in the world, often suffer poverty, abuse, and secondary citizenship status because of this work. Kittay illustrates how liberal theory, wherein public space is the terrain of free, equal, rationally self-interested autonomous economic beings, does not include the lived experience (feminist praxis) of dependency workers. She elaborates: "The exercise of an unfettered, rational self-interest presumed possible for the putatively nondependent and independent worker is not possible for the dependency worker whose responsibilities to her charge remain primary" (1999a: 41).

The feminist ethic of care, embedded in feminist praxis, goes against the grain of dominant liberalism with its frame of autonomous individuals (in denial that they once were all helpless, dependent infants) engaging in market exchanges. Virginia Held argues that "care is a value of no less importance than justice, and that it is highly relevant to 'public' as well as 'private' contexts" (1999: 288). She explains the ethic of care requires another viewpoint:

> When, for instance, I suggest that in trying to understand social relations between persons we should think about how they would look if we used as a model the relation between a mothering-person and child instead of the more usual model of contracts between self-interested strangers, my point is to suggest the alternative model as an exercise of the imagination. . . . I wish to claim not that there is no room for standard liberal individual autonomy but that liberal ideology increasingly leaves no room for anything else. There must be room for much more than liberal individualism for either individuals or societies to flourish. (1999: 289)

Theories that do not incorporate the cornerstones of dependency work that sustain societies result in not seeing the dependency needs of people (infants, the infirm, the elderly, the sick, and the dying) and enable the strong and privileged to "imagine that dependencies do not exist" (Held, 1999: 298; see also Kittay, 1999a).

"On the horizon are critical issues for feminist cultural studies of science and technology," Anne Balsamo foresees, "the politics of information, the global division of technological labor, and the reproductive exploitation of women. These issues are not, in a simple determinist sense, brought into being solely through the development of new technologies; rather they emerge through the articulation between technologies, cultural narratives, social, economic, and institutional forces" (1996: 162). Balsamo asks, "When the human body is fractured into organs, fluids, and genetic codes, what happens to gender identity?" (1996: 6). She continues:

> The widespread technological refashioning of the 'natural' human body suggests that gender too would be ripe for reconstruction. Advances in reproductive technology already decouple the act of procreation from the act of sexual intercourse. Laparoscopy has played a critical role in the assessment of fetal development, with the attendant consequence that the "fetal body" has been metaphorically (and sometimes literally) severed from its natural association with the female body and is now proclaimed to be the new and primary obstetric patient. (1996: 9)

Adele Clarke argues, based on her examination of the "illegitimate science" of reproduction, "that what is in decline is science as an *autonomous* force, and that it is science's autonomy and its lack of social accountability that are being and will continue to be challenged by different

168   *Conclusion*

constituencies to allow broader democratic participation" (1998: 236). Haraway contends that biotechnology serves corporations instead of people:

> Biotechnology in the service of corporate profit is a revolutionary force for remaking the inhabitants of planet Earth, from viruses and bacteria right up to the now repudiated chain of being to *Homo sapiens* and beyond. Biological research globally is progressively practiced under the direct auspices of corporations, from the multinational pharmaceutical and agribusiness giants to venture-capital companies that fascinate the writers for the business sections of daily newspapers. Molecular biology and molecular genetics have become nearly synonymous with biotechnology as engineering and redesign disciplines. (1997: 245)

Life becomes, as Haraway argues, enterprised up, copyrighted, patented, "registered for commerce; and, above all, highly flexible. In a world where the artifactual and the natural have imploded, nature itself, both ideologically and materially, has been patently reconstructed. Structural adjustment demands no less of bacteria and trees as well as of people, businesses, and nations" (1997: 245).

Analysis, policies, laws, and practices that incorporate the real lives of girls and women are needed to work toward possibly just uses of new reproductive arrangements and possibilities. There will most likely be no *one* rule to apply to all these scenarios and disputes over human reproduction. The goal is not a clear endpoint, a template of justice where everyone's lives must fit into the decision rules. The process, however, should include the voices and lives of girls and women of all social classes and circumstances. Acknowledging that study after study confirm that money spent on legal abortions and family planning produces direct and significant public health benefits (McFarlane and Meier, 2001: 153) is also required.

Ethical challenges from these reproductive arrangements are ineluctable and ongoing. Many of these choices set up by new technologies have, in Dena Davis's words, "the alchemy to turn a hope into a virtual entitlement" (2001: 33). Hoping that a child will grow up to be a certain way and deliberately paying for the cloning, genetic therapy, or surrogate to ensure a certain result are different pathways. "Deliberately creating a child who will be forced irreversibly into the parents' notion of the good life," Davis charges, "violates the Kantian principle of treating each person as an end in herself and never as a means only" (2001: 34).

Policies and laws should incorporate the fact of the interdependency of humans and the enormous dependency work that unsung people (mostly women) continuously do. As with abortion politics, the new reproductive arrangements must imagine women's bodily integrity as essential to an integrated, coherent, individuated whole. Writing on abortion law, ethics, and practices, Drucilla Cornell declares, "My emphasis is on empowering women to do just that—give their own meaning to their abortion, to imagine their own bodies, and to represent their 'sex' with joy within sexual difference" (1995: 91). "My argument that women be recognized in their feminine sexual difference as equal," she writes, "leads to this insistence that it must be *the imaginary domain of women themselves* that is allowed to determine the meaning of abortion for *themselves* at any particular time" (1995: 86). The meaning of abortion, she asserts (and I would stretch this to encompass all reproductive acts), "including the value that a woman gives to the act, must be left to her imaginary domain" (1995: 82).

Conclusion: Empowering Women, Remapping Reproduction

My children may become parents in a world that has already incorporated many of the reproductive technologies; genetic maps and patents; adoption, surrogacy, and abortion laws; and punitive surveillance policies I have discussed. My students foresee already that they will have many heart-wrenching choices to make as they form and nurture their families. I hope that they will all have true choices, not "Sophie's Choices," that enable them and their loved ones to flourish. I hope their childbirths are also one of "the best things" they ever did.

Notes

1. A clear example of patriarchal medicine intersecting with capitalism and profits is the expanded use of fetal heart monitors so that they are now a standard of care protocol (Kahn, 1995: 220).

2. A recent study found that women do most of the care when people are dying. Women do even complex nursing tasks day and night. The study mentions the stress caregivers themselves experience and advises all of us to pay attention to the health of these caregivers ("Women Give Most Care to Dying, Study Finds," 1999).

BIBLIOGRAPHY

Abate, Tom. 2001. "Embryonic Stem Cell Debate Is More Than Science vs. Religion." *San Francisco Chronicle*, May 28.

"Abortion Protest Expected." 1992. *Greenville News*, March 21.

Abzug, Bella, and others. 1996. Letter from the International Coalition to Protect the Human Genome, March 21. In possession of author.

"Active Activism and Updates." 1999. *South Carolina Advocates for Pregnant Women* 1, no. 2 (June): 1.

Adams, Greg D. 1997. "Abortion: Evidence of an Issue Evolution." *American Journal of Political Science* 41, no. 3 (July): 718–37.

Adams, Susan L. et al. 2000. "Don't Turn Doctors into Cops: An Open Letter to United States Surgeon General David Satcher, M.D." *The Hill* (Washington, D.C.), October 4.

Aho, James. 1996. "Popular Christianity and Political Extremism." In *Disruptive Religion: The Force of Faith in Social Movement Activism*, edited by Christian Smith, 189–204. New York: Routledge.

Akhtar, Farida. 1987. "Wheat for Statistics: A Case Study of Relief Wheat for Attaining Sterilization Target in Bangladesh." In *Made to Order: The Myth of Reproductive and Genetic Progress*, edited by Patricia Spallone and Deborah Lynn Steinberg, 154–60. New York: Pergamon.

Akron v. Akron Center for Reproductive Health, 462 U.S. 446 (1983).

Alinsky, Sol D. 1946. *Reveille for Radicals*. Chicago: University of Chicago Press.

———. 1971. *Rules for Radicals: A Pragmatic Primer for Realistic Radicals*. New York: Vintage Books.

American Medical Association. 1990. "Legal Interventions during Pregnancy: Court-Ordered Medical Treatments and Legal Penalties for Potentially Harmful Behavior by Pregnant Women." *JAMA: The Journal of the American Medical Association* 264, no. 20 (November 28): 2663.

American Public Health Association et al. 2001. "Amicus Brief in Support of Appellant, Brenda Peppers." In *State of South Carolina v. Brenda Kay Peppers*, Supreme Court of the State of South Carolina, May 20, 2001.

American Society of Human Genetics. 1994. "Statement of the American Society of Human Genetics on Genetic Testing for Breast and Ovarian Cancer Predisposition." *American Journal of Human Genetics* 55: i–iv.

"Amicus Brief of Feminist for Life in *Bray v. Alexandria Women's Health Clinic*." 1994. In *Feminist Jurisprudence: Taking Women Seriously, Cases and Materials,* edited by Mary Becker, Cynthia Grant Bowman, and Morrison Torrey, 409–10. St. Paul, Minn.: West Publishing.

"Amicus Brief of 274 Organizations in Support of *Roe v. Wade* in *Turnock v. Ragsdale* (1994)." In *Feminist Jurisprudence: Taking Women Seriously, Cases and Materials,* 2d ed., edited by Mary Becker, Cynthia Grant Bowman, and Morrison Torrey, 559–62. St. Paul, Minn.: West Publishing.

Anagnost, Ann. 1995. "A Surfeit of Bodies: Population and the Rationality of the State in Post-Mao China." In *Conceiving the New World Order: The Global Politics of Reproduction,* edited by Faye D. Ginsburg and Rayna Rapp, 22–41. Berkeley: University of California Press.

Andrews, Lori B. 1988. "Surrogate Motherhood: The Challenge for Feminists." *Law, Medicine and Health Care* 16, no. 1–2: 72–80.

———. 1989a. "Alternative Modes of Reproduction." In *Reproductive Laws for the 1990s,* edited by Sherrill Cohen and Nadine Taub, 361–403. Clifton, N.J.: Humana.

———. 1989b. *Between Strangers: Surrogate Mothers, Expectant Fathers, and Brave New Babies.* New York: Harper and Row.

Andrews, Lori B., Jane E. Fullarton, Neil A. Holtzman, and Arno G. Motulsky, eds. 1994. *Assessing Genetic Risks: Implications for Health and Social Policy.* Committee on Assessing Genetic Risks, Division of Health Sciences Policy, Institute of Medicine. Washington, D.C.: National Academy Press.

Angier, Natalie. 1993a. "Heredity's More Than Genes, New Theory Proposes." *New York Times,* January 3.

———. 1993b. "Scientists Isolate Gene That Causes Cancer of Colon." *New York Times,* December 3.

———. 1994a. "Gene Experiment to Reverse Inherited Disease Is Working." *New York Times,* April 1.

———. 1994b. "Genetic Mutations Tied to Father in Most Cases." *New York Times,* May 17.

———. 1995. "Disputed Meeting to Ask if Crime Has Genetic Roots." *New York Times,* September 19.

———. 1999. *Woman: An Intimate Geography.* Boston: Houghton Mifflin.

Annas, George J. 1988. "Fairy Tales Surrogate Mothers Tell." In *Surrogate Motherhood: Politics and Privacy,* edited by Larry Gostin, 43–55. Bloomington: Indiana University Press.

———. 1995. "Editorial: Genetic Prophecy and Genetic Privacy—Can We Prevent the Dream from Becoming a Nightmare?" *American Journal of Public Health* 85, no. 9 (September): 1196–97.

Appell, Annette R. 1998. "On Fixing 'Bad' Mothers and Saving Their Children." In *"Bad" Mothers: The Politics of Blame in Twentieth-Century America,* edited by Molly Ladd-Taylor and Lauri Umansky, 356–80. New York: New York University Press.

Arnold, Erik, and Wendy Faulkner. 1985. "Smothered by Invention: The Masculinity of Technology." In *Smothered by Invention: Technology in Women's Lives,* edited by Wendy Faulkner and Erik Arnold, 18–50. London: Pluto.

Asch, Adrienne. 1989. "Reproductive Technology and Disabilities." In *Reproductive Laws for the 1990s*, edited by Sherrill Cohen and Nadine Taub, 69–124. Clifton, N.J.: Humana.

Asch, Adrienne, and Gail Geller. 1996. "Feminism, Bioethics, and Genetics." In *Feminism and Bioethics: Beyond Reproduction*, edited by Susan M. Wolf, 318–50. New York: Oxford University Press.

Ashe, Marie. 1995. "Postmodernism, Legal Ethics, and Representation of 'Bad Mothers.'" In *Mothers in Law: Feminist Theory and the Legal Regulation of Motherhood*, edited by Martha Albertson Fineman and Isabel Karpin, 142–66. New York: Cambridge University Press.

Austin, Katherine Duffin, and Judith G. Hall. 1992. "Nontraditional Inheritance." *Pediatric Clinics of North America* 39, no. 2 (April): 337–48.

Babb, L. Anne. 1999. *Ethics in American Adoption*. Westport, Conn.: Bergin and Garvey.

Baer, Judith A. 1999. *Our Lives before the Law: Constructing a Feminist Jurisprudence*. Princeton, N.J.: Princeton University Press.

Baker, Brenda M. 1996. "A Case for Permitting Altruistic Surrogacy." *Hypatia* 11, no. 2 (Spring): 34–48.

Balsamo, Anne. 1996. *Technologies of the Gendered Body: Reading Cyborg Women*. Durham, N.C.: Duke University Press.

Barone, Michael, and Grant Ujifusa. 1998. *The Almanac of American Politics*. Washington, D.C.: National Journal.

Barroso, Carmen, and Sonia Correa. 1995. "Public Servants, Professionals, and Feminists: The Politics of Contraceptive Research in Brazil." In *Conceiving the New World Order: The Global Politics of Reproduction*, edited by Faye D. Ginsburg and Rayna Rapp, 292–306. Berkeley: University of California Press.

Bartholet, Elizabeth. 1992. "In Vitro Fertilization: The Construction of Infertility and of Parenting." In *Issues in Reproductive Technology*, edited by Helen Bequaert Holmes, 253–60. New York: Garland.

———. 1993. *Family Bonds: Adoption and the Politics of Parenting*. Boston: Houghton Mifflin.

———. 1999. "Reporting on Child Welfare and Adoption Policies." *Nieman Reports* 53, no. 3 (Fall): 74.

Bashevkin, Sylvia. 1998. *Women on the Defensive: Living through Conservative Times*. Chicago: University of Chicago Press.

Baslington, Hazel. 1996. "Anxiety Overflow: Implications of the IVF Surrogacy Case and the Ethical and Moral Limits of Reproductive Technologies in Britain." *Women's Studies International Forum* 19, no. 6 (November/December): 675–84.

Bass, Marie. 1998. "Toward Coalition: The Reproductive Health Technologies Project." In *Abortion Wars: A Half Century of Struggle, 1950–2000*, edited by Rickie Solinger, 251–68. Berkeley: University of California Press.

Bassin, Donna, Margaret Honey, and Meryle Mahrer Kaplan. 1994. Introduction to *Representations of Motherhood*, edited by Donna Bassin, Margaret Honey, and Meryle Mahrer Kaplan, 1–15. New Haven, Conn.: Yale University Press.

Basu, Amrita, ed. 1995. *The Challenge of Local Feminisms: Women's Movements in Global Perspective.* Boulder, Colo.: Westview.

Beardsley, Tim. 1996. "Vital Data." *Scientific American* 274, no. 3 (March): 100–105.

Beaulieu, Anne, and Abby Lippman. 1995. "'Everything You Need to Know': How Women's Magazines Structure Prenatal Diagnosis for Women over Thirty-Five." *Women and Health* 23, no. 3: 59–74.

Becker, Gay. 2000. *The Elusive Embryo: How Women and Men Approach New Reproductive Technologies.* Berkeley: University of California Press.

Becker, Mary, Cynthia Grant Bowman, and Morrison Torrey. 1994. *Feminist Jurisprudence: Taking Women Seriously.* American Casebook Series. St. Paul, Minn.: West Publishing.

Begley, Sharon. 2000. "Cloning the Endangered." *Newsweek* 136, no. 16 (October 16): 56–57.

Behuniak, Susan M. 1999. *A Caring Jurisprudence: Listening to Patients at the Supreme Court.* Lanham, Md.: Rowman and Littlefield.

Belenky, Mary Field, Blythe McVicker Clinchy, Nancy Rule Goldberger, and Jill Mattuck Tarule. 1986. *Women's Ways of Knowing: The Development of Self, Voice, and Mind.* New York: Basic Books.

Benjamin, Jessica. 1988. *The Bonds of Love: Psychoanalysis, Feminism, and the Problem of Domination.* New York: Pantheon Books.

Berenson, Alex, and Nicholas Wade. 2000. "A Call for Sharing of Research Causes Gene Stocks to Plunge." *New York Times,* March 15.

Bernard, Jessie. 1974. *The Future of Motherhood.* New York: Dial.

Biesele, Megan. 1997. "An Ideal of Unassisted Birth: Hunting, Healing, and Transformation among the Kalahari Ju/'hoansi." In *Childbirth and Authoritative Knowledge: Cross-Cultural Perspectives,* edited by Robbie E. Davis-Floyd and Carolyn F. Sargent, 474–92. Berkeley: University of California Press.

Binion, Gayle. 1991. "Towards a Feminist Regrounding of Constitutional Law." *Social Science Quarterly* 72, no. 2 (June): 207–20.

Birenbaum-Carmeli, Daphna. 1998. "Reproductive Partners: Doctor-Woman Relations in Israeli and Canadian IVF Contexts." In *Small Wars: The Cultural Politics of Childhood,* edited by Nancy Scheper-Hughes and Carolyn Sargent, 75–92. Berkeley: University of California Press.

Black, Rita Beck. 1994. "Reproductive Genetic Testing and Pregnancy Loss: The Experience of Women." In *Women and Prenatal Testing: Facing the Challenges of Genetic Technology,* edited by Karen H. Rothenberg and Elizabeth J. Thomson, 271–94. Columbus: Ohio State University Press.

Blanchard, Dallas A. 1994. *The Anti-Abortion Movement and the Rise of the Religious Right: From Polite to Fiery Protest.* New York: Twayne.

Blank, Robert H. 1981. *The Political Implications of Human Genetic Technology.* Boulder, Colo.: Westview.

———. 1984a. "Judicial Decision Making and Biological Fact: Roe v. Wade and the Unresolved Question of Fetal Viability." *Western Political Quarterly* 37 (December): 584–602.

———. 1984b. *Redefining Human Life: Reproductive Technologies and Social Policy.* Boulder, Colo.: Westview.

———. 1988. *Rationing Medicine.* New York: Columbia University Press.

Bleier, Ruth. 1984. *Science and Gender: A Critique of Biology and Its Theories on Women.* New York: Pergamon.

———. 1988. *Feminist Approaches to Science.* Elmsford, N.Y.: Pergamon.

Blum, Virgil C. 1975. "Abortion: A New Kind of Exorcism in America." *Denver Post*, March 23.

Blumberg, Lisa. 1994a. "Eugenics vs. Reproductive Choice." *Disability Rag and Resource*, January/February, 3–11.

———. 1994b. "Proposals for Positions to Be Taken by Disability Rights Groups." *Disability Rag and Resource*, January/February, 10.

Bonavoglia, Angela. 1997. "Late Term Abortion: Separating Fact from Fiction." *Ms.* 7, no. 6 (May/June): 54–63.

Boston Women's Health Book Collective. 1971. *Our Bodies, Ourselves.* Boston: New England Free Press.

———. 1984. *The New Our Bodies, Ourselves.* New York: Simon and Schuster.

Botsch, Robert E. 1992. "South Carolina: The Rise of the New South." In *Interest Group Politics in the Southern States*, edited by Ronald J. Hrebenar and Clive S. Thomas, 209–30. Tuscaloosa: University of Alabama Press.

Boukhari, Sophie, and Amy Otchet. 1999. "Uncharted Terrain on Tomorrow's Genetic Map." *UNESCO Courier* 52, no. 9 (September): 18–19.

Bourgois, Philippe. 1998. "Families and Children in Pain in the U.S. Inner City." In *Small Wars: The Cultural Politics of Childhood*, edited by Nancy Scheper-Hughes and Carolyn Sargent, 331–51. Berkeley: University of California Press.

Bowers, James R. 1994. *Pro-Choice and Anti-Abortion: Constitutional Theory and Public Policy.* Westport, Conn.: Praeger.

Bowman, James E. 1994. "Genetic Screening: Toward a New Eugenics?" In *"It Just Ain't Fair": The Ethics of Health Care for African Americans*, edited by Annette Dula and Sara Goering, 165–81. Westport, Conn.: Praeger.

Boyd, Robert S. 1996. "Discarding the Biological Race Card: Among Scientists, Genetic Differences Now a Moot Concept." *The State* (Columbia, S.C.), October 13.

Bray v. Alexandria Women's Health Clinic, 506 U.S. 263 (1993).

Browner, Carole H., and Nancy Ann Press. 1995. "The Normalization of Prenatal Diagnostic Screening." In *Conceiving the New World Order: The Global Politics of Reproduction*, edited by Faye D. Ginsburg and Rayna Rapp, 307–22. Berkeley: University of California Press.

———. 1997. "The Production of Authoritative Knowledge in American Prenatal Care." In *Childbirth and Authoritative Knowledge: Cross-Cultural Perspectives*, edited by Robbie E. Davis-Floyd and Carolyn F. Sargent, 113–31. Berkeley: University of California Press.

Brunger, Fern, and Abby Lippman. 1995. "Resistance and Adherence to the Norms of Genetic Counseling." *Journal of Genetic Counseling* 4, no. 3 (June): 151–67.

Bryant, Kathryn. 1996. "The Politics of Adoption: A Question of Standards." Master's thesis, Department of Political Science, University of South Carolina at Columbia.

———. Forthcoming. "The Social Construction of Single Motherhood and Adoption Policy: Diverging Experiences—Fragmented Realities." *Policy Studies Journal.*

Buker, Eloise A. 1999. *Talking Feminist Politics: Conversations on Law, Science, and the Postmodern.* Lanham, Md.: Rowman and Littlefield.

Bumiller, Kristen. 1988. *The Civil Rights Society: The Social Construction of Victims.* Baltimore: Johns Hopkins University Press.

Bunkle, Phillida. 1984. "Calling the Shots? The International Politics of Depo-Provera." In *Test-Tube Women: What Future for Motherhood?* edited by Rita Arditti, Renate Duelli Klein, and Shelley Minden, 165–87. London: Pandora.

Burfoot, A. 1988. "A Review of the Third Annual Meeting of the European Society of Human Reproduction and Embryology." *Reproductive and Genetic Engineering: Journal of International Feminist Analysis* 1, no. 1: 107–11.

Bush, Corlann Gee. 1983. "Women and the Assessment of Technology: To Think, to Be; To Unthink, to Free." In *Machina Ex Dea: Feminist Perspective on Technology,* edited by Joan Rothschild, 151–68. New York: Pergamon.

Butler, Judith. 1990. *Gender Trouble.* New York: Routledge.

Buzzanca v. Buzzanca, 72 Cal. Rptr. 2d 280 (Cal. App. 4th Dist. 1998).

Byrnes, Timothy A. 1995. "Conclusion: The Future of Abortion Politics in American States." In *Abortion Politics in American States,* edited by Mary C. Segers and Timothy A. Byrnes, 246–64. Armonk, N.Y.: M. E. Sharpe.

Callahan, Joan C., and James W. Knight. 1992. "Prenatal Harm as Child Abuse?" In *The Criminalization of a Woman's Body,* edited by Clarice Feinman, 127–55. New York: Haworth.

Campion, Frank D. 1984. *The AMA and U.S. Health Policy since 1940.* Chicago: Chicago Review.

Cannold, Leslie. 2000. *The Abortion Myth: Feminism, Morality, and the Hard Choices Women Make.* Hanover, N.H.: Wesleyan University Press.

Cantor, Charles. 1992. "The Challenges to Technology and Informatics." In *The Code of Codes: Scientific and Social Issues in the Human Genome Project,* edited by Daniel J. Kevles and Leroy Hood, 98–111. Cambridge, Mass.: Harvard University Press.

Caplan, Arthur L. 1993. "The Neutrality Is Not Morality: The Ethics of Genetic Counseling." In *Prescribing Our Future: Ethical Challenges in Genetic Counseling,* edited by Dianne M. Bartels, Bonnie S. LeRoy, and Arthur L. Caplan, 127–44. New York: Aldine de Gruyter.

Capron, Alexander M., and Margaret J. Radin. 1988. "Choosing Family Law over Contract Law as a Paradigm for Surrogate Motherhood." In *Surrogate Motherhood: Politics and Privacy,* edited by Larry Gostin, 59–76. Bloomington: Indiana University Press.

Carp, E. Wayne. 1998. *Family Matters: Secrecy and Disclosure in the History of Adoption.* Cambridge, Mass.: Harvard University Press.

Caskey, C. Thomas. 1992. "DNA-Based Medicine: Prevention and Therapy." In *The Code of Codes: Scientific and Social Issues in the Human Genome Project,* edited by Daniel J. Kevles and Leroy Hood, 112–35. Cambridge, Mass.: Harvard University Press.

Chacko, Arun. 1982. "Too Many Daughters? India's Drastic Cure." *World Paper* (November): 8–9.

Chalmers, Beverley. 1997. "Changing Childbirth in Eastern Europe: Which Systems of Authoritative Knowledge Should Prevail?" In *Childbirth and Authoritative Knowledge: Cross-Cultural Perspectives,* edited by Robbie E. Davis-Floyd and Carolyn F. Sargent, 263–83. Berkeley: University of California Press.

Charo, R. Alta, and Karen H. Rothenberg. 1994. "'The Good Mother': The Limits of Reproductive Accountability and Genetic Choice." In *Women and Prenatal Testing: Facing the Challenges of Genetic Technology,* edited by Karen H. Rothenberg and Elizabeth J. Thomson, 105–30. Columbus: Ohio State University Press.

Chavkin, Wendy. 1992. "Women and Fetus: The Social Construction of Conflict." In *The Criminalization of a Woman's Body,* edited by Clarice Feinman, 193–202. New York: Haworth.

———. 2001. "Cocaine and Pregnancy—Time to Look at the Evidence." *JAMA: The Journal of the American Medical Association* 285, no. 12 (March 28): 1626–28.

Chesler, Phyllis. 1987. *Mothers on Trial: The Battle for Children and Custody.* New York: McGraw-Hill.

Chodorow, Nancy. 1978. *The Reproduction of Mothering: Psychoanalysis and the Sociology of Gender.* Berkeley: University of California Press.

Chong, D. 1991. *Collective Action and the Civil Rights Movement.* Chicago: University of Chicago Press.

Clark, Janet. 1991. "Getting There: Women in Political Office." *Annals of the American Academy of Political and Social Science* 515 (May): 63–76.

Clarke, Adele E. 1984. "Subtle Forms of Sterilization Abuse: A Reproductive Rights Analysis." In *Test-Tube Women: What Future for Motherhood?* edited by Rita Arditti, Renate Duelli Klein, and Shelley Minden, 188–212. London: Pandora.

———. 1998. *Disciplining Reproduction: Modernity, American Life Sciences, and "the Problems of Sex."* Berkeley: University of California Press.

Clayton, Ellen Wright. 1994. "What the Law Says about Reproductive Genetic Testing and What It Doesn't." In *Women and Prenatal Testing: Facing the Challenges of Genetic Technology,* edited by Karen H. Rothenberg and Elizabeth J. Thomson, 131–78. Columbus: Ohio State University Press.

"Cocaine and Pregnancy. . . What Do We Know?" 1999. *South Carolina Advocates for Pregnant Women* 1, no. 2 (June): 1.

Cock, Jacklyn. 1997. "Women in South Africa's Transition to Democracy." In *Transitions, Environments, Translations: Feminisms in International Politics*, edited by Joan W. Scott, Cora Kaplan, and Debra Keates, 310–33. New York: Routledge.

Cogbian, Andy. 1994. "Hidden Costs of a Clean Inheritance." *New Scientist* 29 (May 14): 14–15.

Cohan, Alvin. 1986. "Abortion as a Marginal Issue: The Use of Peripheral Mechanisms in Britain and the United States." In *The New Politics of Abortion*, edited by Joni Lovenduski and Joyce Outshoorn, 27–48. Newbury Park, Calif.: Sage Publications.

Cohen, Joel E. 1995. *How Many People Can the Earth Support?* New York: W. W. Norton.

Cohen, Sherrill, and Nadine Taub, eds. 1989. *Reproductive Laws for the 1990s*. Clifton, N.J.: Humana.

Colen, Shellee. 1995. "'Like a Mother to Them': Stratified Reproduction and West Indian Childcare Workers and Employers in New York." In *Conceiving the New World Order: The Global Politics of Reproduction*, edited by Faye D. Ginsburg and Rayna Rapp, 78–102. Berkeley: University of California Press.

Coles, Robert. 1988. "'So, You Fell in Love with Your Baby.'" *New York Times Book Review* 93 (June 26): 1, 34–35.

Colker, Ruth. 1990. "Feminist Litigation: An Oxymoron?—A Study of the Briefs Filed in *William L. Webster v. Reproductive Health Services.*" *Harvard Women's Law Journal* 13 (Spring): 137–88.

———. 1992. *Abortion and Dialogue: Pro-Choice, Pro-Life, and American Law*. Bloomington: Indiana University Press.

Collins, Jeffrey. 2001. "Mom Gets Twelve Years in Drug Death of Fetus." *The State* (Columbia, S.C.), May 17.

Collins, Patricia Hill. 1991. *Black Feminist Thought: Knowledge, Consciousness, and the Politics of Empowerment*. New York: Routledge.

———. 1994. "Shifting the Center: Race, Class, and Feminist Theorizing about Motherhood." In *Representations of Motherhood*, edited by Donna Bassin, Margaret Honey, and Meryle Mahrer Kaplan, 56–74. New Haven, Conn.: Yale University Press.

Condit, Celeste Michelle. 1990. *Decoding Abortion Rhetoric: Communicating Social Change*. Urbana: University of Illinois Press.

Connolly, Deborah. 2000. "Mythical Mothers and Dichotomies of Good and Evil: Homeless Mothers in the United States." In *Ideologies and Technologies of Motherhood: Race, Class, Sexuality, Nationalism*, edited by Heléna Ragoné and France Winddance Twine, 263–94. New York: Routledge.

Conway, M. Margaret, Gertrude A. Steuernagel, and David W. Ahern. 1997. *Women and Political Participation: Cultural Change in the Political Arena*. Washington, D.C.: Congressional Quarterly.

Cooey, Paula M. 1999. "'Ordinary Mother' as Oxymoron: The Collusion of Theology, Theory, and Politics in the Undermining of Mothers." In *Mother Troubles: Rethinking Contemporary Maternal Dilemmas*, edited by Julia E. Haningberg and Sara Ruddick, 229–49. Boston: Beacon.

Cook, Elizabeth Adell, Ted G. Jelen, and Clyde Wilcox. 1994. "Issue Voting in Gubernatorial Elections: Abortion and Post-*Webster* Politics." *Journal of Politics* 56, no. 1 (February): 187–99.

Cook-Deegan, Robert. 1994. *The Gene Wars: Science, Politics, and the Human Genome*. New York: W. W. Norton.

Cool, Lisa Collier. 1999. "Forgotten Women: How Minorities Are Underserved by Our Health Care System." *American Health for Women*, May 1997, reprinted in *Annual Editions: Women's Health 99/00*, edited by Maureen Edwards and Nora L. Howley, 12–14. Boston: McGraw-Hill/ Dushkin.

Corea, Gena. 1985a. *The Hidden Malpractice: How American Medicine Mistreats Women*. Updated ed. New York: Harper Colophon Books.

———. 1985b. *The Mother Machine: Reproductive Technologies from Artificial Insemination to Artificial Wombs*. New York: Harper and Row.

Corea, Gena, Jalna Hanmer, Renate D. Klein, Janice Raymond, and Robyn Rowland. 1987. Prologue to *Made to Order: The Myth of Reproductive and Genetic Progress*, edited by Patricia Spallone and Deborah Lynn Steinberg, 1–12. New York: Pergamon.

Corea, Gena, and Susan Ince. 1987. "Report of a Survey of IVF Clinics in the USA." In *Made to Order: The Myth of Reproductive and Genetic Progress*, edited by Patricia Spallone and Deborah Lynn Steinberg, 133–45. New York: Pergamon.

Cornell, Drucilla. 1995. *The Imaginary Domain: Abortion, Pornography, and Sexual Harassment*. New York: Routledge.

———. 1998. *At the Heart of Freedom: Feminism, Sex, and Equality*. Princeton, N.J.: Princeton University Press.

———. 1999a. *Beyond Accommodation: Ethical Feminism, Deconstruction, and the Law*. New ed. Lanham, Md.: Rowman and Littlefield.

———. 1999b. "Reimagining Adoption and Family Law." In *Mother Troubles: Rethinking Contemporary Maternal Dilemmas*, edited by Julia E. Haningberg and Sara Ruddick, 208–28. Boston: Beacon.

Costain, Anne N. 1992. *Inviting Women's Rebellion: A Political Process Interpretation of the Women's Movement*. Baltimore: Johns Hopkins University Press.

Costa-Lascoux, Jacqueline. 1994. "Reproduction and Bioethics." In *A History of Women in the West*, vol. 5, *Toward a Cultural Identity in the Twentieth Century*, edited by Francoise Thébaud, 567–86. Cambridge, Mass.: Belknap Press of Harvard University Press.

Cowan, Ruth Schwartz. 1992. "Genetic Technology and Reproductive Choice: An Ethics for Autonomy." In *The Code of Codes: Scientific and Social Issues in the Human Genome Project*, edited by Daniel J. Kevles and Leroy Hood, 244–63. Cambridge, Mass.: Harvard University Press.

————. 1994. "Women's Roles in the History of Amniocentesis and Chorionic Villi Sampling." In *Women and Prenatal Testing: Facing the Challenges of Genetic Technology*, edited by Karen H. Rothenberg and Elizabeth J. Thomson, 35–48. Columbus: Ohio State University Press.

Crary, David. 2000. "Adoptees Battle Secrecy Records." Associate Press (Internet article), November 11.

Critchlow, Donald T. 1999. *Intended Consequences: Birth Control, Abortion, and the Federal Government in Modern America*. New York: Oxford University Press.

Cussins, Charis. 1998. "Producing Reproduction: Techniques of Normalization and Naturalization in Infertility Clinics." In *Reproducing Reproduction: Kinship, Power, and Technological Innovations*, edited by Sarah Franklin and Heléna Ragoné, 66–101. Philadelphia: University of Pennsylvania Press.

Dalton, Susan. 2000. "Nonbiological Mothers and the Legal Boundaries of Motherhood: An Analysis of California Law." In *Ideologies and Technologies of Motherhood: Race, Class, Sexuality, Nationalism*, edited by Heléna Ragoné and France Winddance Twine, 191–232. New York: Routledge.

Daly, Herman E. 1998. "The Perils of Free Trade." In *Green Planet Blues: Environmental Politics from Stockholm to Kyoto*, 2d ed., edited by Ken Conca and Geoffrey D. Dabelko, 187–94. Boulder, Colo.: Westview.

Daly, Mary. 1978. *Gyn/Ecology: The Metaethics of Radical Feminism*. Boston: Beacon.

D'Amato, Anthony. 1999. "Globalizing Adoption." *Christian Century* 116, no. 19 (June 30): 668.

Daniels, Cynthia R. 1993. *At Women's Expense: State Power and the Politics of Fetal Rights*. Cambridge, Mass.: Harvard University Press.

————. 1997. "Between Fathers and Fetuses: The Social Construction of Male Reproduction and the Politics of Fetal Harm." *Signs: Journal of Women in Culture and Society* 22, no. 3 (Spring): 579–616.

Daniels, Ken, and Erica Haimes, eds. 1998. *Donor Insemination: International Social Science Perspectives*. Cambridge: Cambridge University Press.

Darcy, R., Susan Welch, and Janet Clark. 1987. *Women, Elections, and Representation*. Lincoln: University of Nebraska Press.

Darnovsky, Marcy, Barbara Epstein, and Richard Flacks, eds. 1995. *Cultural Politics and Social Movements*. Philadelphia: Temple University Press.

Das, Veena. 1995. "National Honor and Practical Kinship: Unwanted Women and Children." In *Conceiving the New World Order: The Global Politics of Reproduction*, edited by Faye D. Ginsburg and Rayna Rapp, 212–33. Berkeley: University of California Press.

Davis, Angela Y. 1990. *Women, Culture, and Politics*. New York: Vintage Books.

Davis, Dena S. 2001. *Genetic Dilemmas: Reproductive Technology, Parental Choices, and Children's Futures*. New York: Routledge.

Davis, Peggy Cooper. 1999. "A Reflection on Three Verbs: To Father, to

Mother, to Parent." In *Mother Troubles: Rethinking Contemporary Maternal Dilemmas*, edited by Julia E. Haningberg and Sara Ruddick, 250–78. Boston: Beacon.

Davis-Floyd, Robbie, and Elizabeth Davis. 1997. "Intuition as Authoritative Knowledge in Midwifery and Home Birth." In *Childbirth and Authoritative Knowledge: Cross-Cultural Perspectives*, edited by Robbie E. Davis-Floyd and Carolyn F. Sargent, 315–49. Berkeley: University of California Press.

Davis-Floyd, Robbie, and Carolyn F. Sargent. 1997. "Introduction: The Anthropology of Birth." In *Childbirth and Authoritative Knowledge: Cross-Cultural Perspectives*, edited by Robbie E. Davis-Floyd and Carolyn F. Sargent, 1–51. Berkeley: University of California Press.

Daviss, Betty-Anne. 1997. "Heeding Warnings from the Canary, the Whale, and the Inuit: A Framework for Analyzing Competing Types of Knowledge about Childbirth." In *Childbirth and Authoritative Knowledge: Cross-Cultural Perspectives*, edited by Robbie E. Davis-Floyd and Carolyn F. Sargent, 441–73. Berkeley: University of California Press.

Davis v. Davis, 842 S.W.2d 588 (Tenn. 1992).

Dawla, Aida Seif El, Amal Abdel Hadi, and Nadia Abdel Wahab. 1998. "Women's Wit over Men's: Trade-Offs and Strategic Accommodations in Egyptian Women's Reproductive Lives." In *Negotiating Reproductive Rights: Women's Perspectives across Countries and Cultures*, edited by Rosalind P. Petchesky and Karen Judd, 69–107. London: Zed Books.

Day, Christine L., and Charles D. Hadley. 1997. "The Importance of Attitudes toward Women's Equality: Policy Preferences among Southern Party Elites." *Social Science Quarterly* 78, no. 3 (September): 672–87.

DeBettencourt, Kathleen B. 1990. "The Wisdom of Solomon: Cutting the Cord That Harms." *Children Today* 19, no. 4 (July–August): 17.

De Koninck, Maria. 1998. "Reflections on the Transfer of 'Progress': The Case of Reproduction." In *The Politics of Women's Health: Exploring Agency and Autonomy*, edited by Susan Sherwin, 150–77. Philadelphia: Temple University Press.

de Lesseps, Emmanuele. 1981. "Female Reality: Biology or Society?" *Feminist Issues* 1 (Winter): 77–102.

de Man, Paul. 1978. "The Epistemology of Metaphor." In *On Metaphor*, edited by Sheldon Sacks, 11–28. Chicago: University of Chicago Press.

DeShaney v. Winnebago County Department of Social Services, 489 U.S. 189, 109 S. Ct. 998, 103 L.Ed. 2d 249 (1989).

"Detailed Human Physical Map Published by Whitehead-MIT." 1996. *Human Genome News*, January–March, 5.

DeVault, Marjorie L. 1999. *Liberating Method: Feminism and Social Research*. Philadelphia: Temple University Press.

De Ville, Kenneth A., and Loretta M. Kopelman. 1999. "Fetal Protection in Wisconsin's Revised Child Abuse Law: Right Goal, Wrong Remedy." *Journal of Law, Medicine and Ethics* 27, no. 4 (Winter): 332.

Diamond, Irene. 1988. "Medical Science and the Transformation of Motherhood: The Promise of Reproductive Technologies." In *Women, Power and Policy: Toward the Year 2000*, edited by Ellen Boneparth and Emily Stoper, 155–67. New York: Pergamon.

————. 1990. "Babies, Heroic Experts, and a Poisoned Earth." In *Reweaving the World: The Emergence of Ecofeminism*, edited by Irene Diamond and Gloria Feman Orenstein, 201–10. San Francisco: Sierra Club Books, 1990.

Digeser, Peter. 1994. "Performativity Trouble: Postmodern Feminism and Essential Subjects." *Political Research Quarterly* 47, no. 3 (September): 655–73.

Diniz, Simone Grilo, Cecilia De Mello E Souza, and Ana Paula Portella. 1998. "Not Like Our Mothers: Reproductive Choice and the Emergence of Citizenship among Brazilian Rural Workers, Domestic Workers and Housewives." In *Negotiating Reproductive Rights: Women's Perspectives across Countries and Cultures*, edited by Rosalind P. Petchesky and Karen Judd, 31–68. London: Zed Books.

Dombrowski, Daniel A., and Robert Deltete. 2000. *A Brief, Liberal, Catholic Defense of Abortion*. Urbana: University of Illinois Press.

Dubler, Ariela R. 1996. "Monitoring Motherhood." *Yale Law Journal* 106, no. 3 (December): 935–40.

Duden, B. 1993. *Disembodying Women: Perspectives on Pregnancy and the Unborn*. Cambridge, Mass.: Harvard University Press.

Duerst-Lahti, Georgia, and Rita Mae Kelly, eds. 1995. *Gender Power, Leadership, and Governance*. Ann Arbor: University of Michigan Press.

Dugger, Celia W. 2001. "As India and China Modernize, Ultrasound Means Unborn Girls." *New York Times*, May 7.

Dugger, Karen. 1991. "Race Differences in the Determinants of Support for Legalized Abortion." *Social Science Quarterly* 72, no. 3 (September): 570–87.

Duke, Lois Lovelace, ed. 1996. *Women in Politics: Outsiders or Insiders?* New York: Prentice Hall.

Dula, Annette. 1994. "African American Suspicion of the Healthcare System Is Justified: What Do We Do about It?" *Cambridge Quarterly of Healthcare Ethics* 3: 347–57.

DuPlessis, Rachel Blau, and Ann Snitow. 1998. "Introduction: A Feminist Memoir Project." In *The Feminist Memoir Project: Voices from Women's Liberation*, edited by Rachel Blau DuPlessis and Ann Snitow, 3–24. New York: Three Rivers.

Durfy, Sharon J. 1993. "Case Study, for the Benefit of All, and Commentary." *Hastings Center Report*, September–October, 28–29.

Duryea, Bill. 1996. "'Gray Market' for Adoptions Emerges." *St. Petersburg Times*, May 27.

Dutton, Diana B., Thomas A. Preston, and Nancy E. Pfund. 1988. *Worse Than the Disease: Pitfalls of Medical Progress*. New York: Cambridge University Press.

Dworkin, Andrea. 1983. *Right-Wing Women*. New York: Perigee Books.

Easterwood, Michael. 1984. "The Municipality and South Carolina Government." In *Local Government in South Carolina*, edited by Charlie B. Tyer and Cole Blease Graham Jr., 9–49. Columbia: Bureau of Governmental Research and Service, University of South Carolina.

Edelman, Murray. 1964. *The Symbolic Uses of Politics.* Urbana: University of Illinois Press.

———. 1977. *Political Language: Words That Succeed and Policies That Fail.* New York: Academic.

———. 1989. *Constructing The Political Spectacle.* Chicago: University of Chicago Press.

Edwards, Jeanette, Sarah Franklin, Eric Hirsch, Frances Price, and Marilyn Strathern. 1993. *Technologies of Procreation: Kinship in the Age of Assisted Conception.* Manchester, England: Manchester University Press.

Edwards, Margot, and Mary Waldorf. 1984. *Reclaiming Birth: History and Heroines of American Childbirth Reform.* Trumansburg, N.Y.: Crossing.

Ehrenreich, Barbara, and Deirdre English. 1973. *Complaints and Disorders: The Sexual Politics of Sickness.* New York: Feminist Press.

———. 1978. *For Her Own Good: 150 Years of the Expert's Advice to Women.* New York: Anchor Books.

Eisenstein, Zillah R. 1988. *The Female Body and the Law.* Berkeley: University of California Press.

———. 2001. *Manmade Breast Cancers.* Ithaca, N.Y.: Cornell University Press.

Elder, Charles D., and Roger W. Cobb. 1983. *The Political Uses of Symbols.* New York: Longman.

Elkington, John. 1985. *The Poisoned Womb: Human Reproduction in a Polluted World.* New York: Penguin Books.

Elshtain, Jean B. 1989. "Technology as Destiny: The New Eugenics Challenges Feminism." *Progressive* 53, no. 6 (June): 19–23.

———. 1998. "To Clone or Not to Clone." In *Clones and Clones: Facts and Fantasies about Human Cloning,* edited by Martha C. Nussbaum and Cass R. Sunstein, 181–89. New York: W. W. Norton.

Epstein, Cynthia Fuchs. 1988. *Deceptive Distinctions: Sex, Gender, and the Social Order.* New Haven, Conn.: Yale University Press.

Estrich, Susan. 1987. *Real Rape.* Cambridge, Mass.: Harvard University Press.

Ezzell, Carol. May 1996a. "Gene-Therapy Trial Using BRCA1 to Begin with Ovarian Cancer." *Journal of NIH Research* 8, no. 5 (May): 24–25.

———. May 1996b. "New Genetic Linkages for Manic Depression." *Journal of NIH Research* 8, no. 5 (May): 41–42.

Fabros, Mercedes Lactao, Aileen May C. Paguntalan, Lourdes l. Arches, and Maria Teresa Guia-Padilla. 1998. "From *Sanas* to *Dapat:* Negotiating Entitlement in Reproductive Decision-Making in the Philippines." In *Negotiating Reproductive Rights: Women's Perspectives across Countries and Cultures,* edited by Rosalind P. Petchesky and Karen Judd, 217–55. London: Zed Books.

"Facts You May Not Have Known." 1999. *South Carolina Advocates for Pregnant Women* 1, no. 2 (June): n.p.

Faden, Ruth. 1994. "Reproductive Genetic Testing, Prevention, and the Ethics of Mothering." In *Women and Prenatal Testing: Facing the Challenges of Genetic Technology,* edited by Karen H. Rothenberg and Elizabeth J. Thomson, 88–97. Columbus: Ohio State University Press.

Farrant, Wendy. 1985. "Who's for Amniocentesis? The Politics of Prenatal Screening." In *The Sexual Politics of Reproduction,* edited by Hilary Homans, 96–122. Brookfield, Vt.: Gower.

Fausto-Sterling, Anne. 1992. "Building Two-Way Streets: The Case of Feminism and Science." *NWSA Journal* 4, no. 3 (Fall): 336–49.

Ferguson, Crystal, v. City of Charleston, et al., 186 F.3d 469 U.S. (2001).

Ferree, Myra Marx. 1997. "German Unification and Feminist Identity." In *Transitions, Environments, Translations: Feminism in International Politics,* edited by Joan W. Scott, Cora Kaplan, and Debra Keates, 46–55. New York: Routledge.

Ferree, Myra Marx, and Patricia Yancey Martin, eds. 1995. *Feminist Organizations: Harvest of the New Women's Movement.* Philadelphia: Temple University Press.

Fiedler, Deborah Cordero. 1997. "Authoritative Knowledge and Birth Territories in Contemporary Japan." In *Childbirth and Authoritative Knowledge: Cross-Cultural Perspectives,* edited by Robbie E. Davis-Floyd and Carolyn F. Sargent, 159–79. Berkeley: University of California Press.

Field, Martha A. 1988. *Surrogate Motherhood.* Cambridge, Mass.: Harvard University Press.

———. 1991. "Surrogacy Contracts: Gestational and Traditional: The Argument for Nonenforcement." *Washburn Law Journal* 31, no. 1 (Fall): 1–17.

Fine, Beth. 1993. "The Evolution of Nondirectiveness in Genetic Counseling and Implications of the Human Genome Project." In *Prescribing Our Future: Ethical Challenges in Genetic Counseling,* edited by Dianne M. Bartels, Bonnie S. LeRoy, and Arthur L. Caplan, 101–17. New York: Aldine de Gruyter.

Fineman, Martha A. 1983. "Implementing Equality: Ideology, Contradiction, and Social Change; A Study of Rhetoric and Results in the Regulation of the Consequences of Divorce." *Wisconsin Law Review* 1983, no. 4 (November): 789–886.

———. 1988. "Dominant Discourse, Professional Language, and Legal Change in Child Custody Decisionmaking." *Harvard Law Review* 101, no. 4 (February): 727–74.

———. 1995a. "Images of Mothers in Poverty Discourse." In *Mothers in Law: Feminist Theory and the Legal Regulation of Motherhood,* edited by Martha Albertson Fineman and Isabel Karpin, 205–23. New York: Columbia University Press.

———. 1995b. *The Neutered Mother, the Sexual Family, and Other Twentieth-Century Tragedies.* New York: Routledge.

———. 1999. "Law of the Father." In *Mother Troubles: Rethinking Contemporary Maternal Dilemmas,* edited by Julia E. Haningberg and Sara Ruddick, 139–56. Boston: Beacon.

Fineman, Martha Albertson, and Isabel Karpin, eds. 1995. *Mothers in Law: Feminist Theory and the Legal Regulation of Motherhood.* New York: Columbia University Press.

Finger, Anne. 1984. "Claiming All of Our Bodies: Reproductive Rights and Disability." In *Test-Tube Women: What Future for Motherhood?* edited by Rita Arditti, Renate Duelli Klein, and Shelley Minden, 281–97. London: Pandora.

Finley, Lucinda M. 1986. "Transcending Equality Theory: A Way out of the Maternity and the Workplace Debate." *Columbia Law Review* 86, no. 6 (October): 1118–82.

Firestone, David. 2001. "Woman Is Convicted of Killing Her Fetus by Smoking Cocaine." *New York Times*, May 18.

Firestone, Shulamith. 1970. *The Dialectic of Sex: The Case for Feminist Revolution.* New York: William Morrow.

Fisher, Susan. 1986. *In the Patient's Best Interest: Women and the Politics of Medical Decisions.* New Brunswick, N.J.: Rutgers University Press.

Fitzgerald, Jennifer. 1998. "Geneticizing Disability: The Human Genome Project and the Commodifiction of Self." *Issues in Law and Medicine* 14, no. 2 (Fall): 147–63.

Flammang, Janet A. 1997. *Women's Political Voice: How Women Are Transforming the Practice and Study of Politics.* Philadelphia: Temple University Press.

Flax, Jane. 1990. *Thinking Fragments: Psychoanalysis, Feminism, and Postmodernism in the Contemporary West.* Berkeley: University of California Press.

"Folic Acid Gives Hope in the Fight against Neural Tube Defects." 1994. *New York Times Magazine*, April 3, A6.

Forte, Dianne Jntl, and Karen Judd. 1998. "The South within the North: Reproductive Choice in Three U.S. Communities." In *Negotiating Reproductive Rights: Women's Perspectives across Countries and Cultures,* edited by Rosalind P. Petchesky and Karen Judd, 256–94. London: Zed Books.

Fox-Genovese, Elizabeth. 1990. *Feminism without Illusions: A Critique of Individualism.* Chapel Hill: University of North Carolina Press.

Frank, Deborah A., Marilyn Augustyn, Wanda Grant Knight, Tripler Pell, and Barry Zuckerman. 2001. "Growth, Development, and Behavior in Early Childhood following Prenatal Cocaine Exposure: A Systematic Review." *JAMA: The Journal of the American Medical Association* 285, no. 12 (March 28): 1613–25.

Franklin, Sarah. 1993. "Making Representations: The Parliamentary Debate on the Human Fertilisation and Embryology Act." In *Technologies of Procreation: Kinship in the Age of Assisted Conception,* edited by Jeanette Edwards, Sarah Franklin, Eric Hirsch, Frances Price, and Marilyn Strathern, 96–131. Manchester, England: Manchester University Press.

———. 1995. "Postmodern Procreation: A Cultural Account of Assisted Reproduction." In *Conceiving the New World Order: The Global Politics of Reproduction,* edited by Faye D. Ginsburg and Rayna Rapp, 323–45. Berkeley: University of California Press.

———. 1998. "Making Miracles: Scientific Progress and the Facts of Life." In *Reproducing Reproduction: Kinship, Power, and Technological Inno-*

vations, edited by Sarah Franklin and Heléna Ragoné, 102–17. Philadelphia: University of Pennsylvania Press.

Franklin, Sarah, and Heléna Ragoné, eds. 1998. *Reproducing Reproduction:
Kinship, Power, and Technological Innovation.* Philadelphia: University of Pennsylvania Press.

Fraser, Gertrude J. 1995. "Modern Bodies, Modern Minds: Midwifery and
Reproductive Change in an African American Community." In *Conceiving the New World Order: The Global Politics of Reproduction,* edited
by Faye D. Ginsburg and Rayna Rapp, 42–58. Berkeley: University of
California Press.

Freundlich, Madelyn. 2000. *Adoption and Ethics: The Market Forces in Adoption.* Washington, D.C.: Child Welfare League of America.

Fried, Marlene Gerber. 1998. "Abortion in the United States—Legal but Inaccessible." In *Abortion Wars: A Half Century of Struggle, 1950–2000,*
edited by Rickie Solinger, 208–26. Berkeley: University of California
Press.

Friedman, Debra, and Doug McAdam, 1992. "Collective Identity and Activism: Networks, Choices, and the Life of a Social Movement." In *Frontiers
in Social Movement Theory,* edited by Aldon D. Morris and Carol Mc-
Clurg Mueller, 156–73. New Haven, Conn.: Yale University Press.

Frierson, Richard I., and Mark W. Binkley. 2001. "Prosecution of Illicit Drug
Use during Pregnancy: *Crystal Ferguson v. City of Charleston.*" *Journal of the American Academy of Psychiatry and the Law* 29, no. 4: 469–
73.

Fuszara, Malgorzata. 1997. "Women's Movements in Poland." In *Transitions,
Environments, Translations: Feminisms in International Politics,* edit-
ed Joan W. Scott, Cora Kaplan, and Debra Keates, 128–42. New York:
Routledge.

Gaber, Milica Antic. 1997. "Politics in Transition." In *Transitions, Environments, Translations: Feminisms in International Politics,* edited by Joan
W. Scott, Cora Kaplan, and Debra Keates, 143–52. New York: Routledge.

Gailey, Christine Ward. 2000. "Ideologies of Motherhood and Kinship in U.S.
Adoption." In *Ideologies and Technologies of Motherhood: Race, Class,
Sexuality, Nationalism,* edited by Heléna Ragoné and France Winddance
Twine, 11–55. New York: Routledge.

Gal, Susan. 1997. "Feminism and Civil Society." In *Transitions, Environments, Translations: Feminisms in International Politics,* edited by Joan
W. Scott, Cora Kaplan, and Debra Keates, 30–45. New York: Routledge.

Galanter, Marc. 1974. "Why the 'Haves' Come out Ahead: Speculations on
the Limits of Legal Change." *Law and Society Review* 9 (Fall): 95–106.

Gallagher, Janet. 1985. "Fetal Personhood and Women's Policy." In *Women,
Biology, and Public Policy,* edited by Virginia Sapiro, 91–116. Beverly
Hills, Calif.: Sage.

———. 1989. "Fetus as Patient." In *Reproductive Laws for the 1990s,* edited
by Sherrill Cohen and Nadine Taub, 185–235. Clifton, N.J.: Humana.

Gardner, Katy. 1981. "Well Woman Clinics: A Positive Approach to Women's Health." In *Women, Health, and Reproduction*, edited by Helen Roberts, 129–43. London: Routledge and Kegan Paul.

Garrow, David J. 1978. *Protest at Selma: Martin Luther King, Jr., and the Voting Rights Act of 1965*. New Haven, Conn.: Yale University Press.

Gates, Elena A. 1994. "Prenatal Genetic Testing: Does It Benefit Pregnant Women?" In *Women and Prenatal Testing: Facing the Challenges of Genetic Technology*, edited by Karen H. Rothenberg and Elizabeth J. Thomson, 183–200. Columbus: Ohio State University Press.

Geller, Gail, Barbara A. Bernhardt, Kathy Helzlsouer, Neil A. Holtzman, Michael Stefanek, and Patti M. Wilcox. 1995. "Correspondence: Informed Consent and BRCA1 Testing." *Nature Genetics* 11, no. 4 (December): 364.

George, Nirmala. 2001. "India Addresses Abortions of Females." Associated Press Online, June 23.

Georges, Eugenia. 1997. "Fetal Ultrasound Imaging and the Production of Authoritative Knowledge in Greece." In *Childbirth and Authoritative Knowledge: Cross-Cultural Perspectives*, edited by Robbie E. Davis-Floyd and Carolyn F. Sargent, 91–112. Berkeley: University of California Press.

Germer, Fawn. 1990. "Women Stress Need, Right to Have Choice." *Rocky Mountain News*, January 22.

Gerstenzang, James. 2001. "Bush Blasts Discrimination Based on Genetic Data." *The State* (Columbia, S.C.), June 24.

Gibbs, W. Wayt. 1995. "Seeking the Criminal Element." *Scientific American* 272, no. 3 (March): 101–7.

Gilbert, Walter. 1992. "A Vision of the Grail." In *The Code of Codes: Scientific and Social Issues in the Human Genome Project*, edited by Daniel J. Kevles and Leroy Hood, 83–97. Cambridge, Mass.: Harvard University Press.

Gilligan, Carol. 1982. *In a Different Voice: Psychological Theory and Women's Development*. Cambridge, Mass.: Harvard University Press.

Gimpel, James G. 1998. "Grassroots Organizations and Equilibrium Cycles in Group Mobilization and Access." In *The Interest Group Connection: Electioneering, Lobbying, and Policymaking in Washington*, edited by Paul S. Herrnson, Ronald G. Shaiko, and Clyde Wilcox, 100–115. Chatham, N.J.: Chatham House.

Ginsburg, Faye. 1989. *Contested Lives*. Berkeley: University of California Press.

———. 1998. "Rescuing the Nation: Operation Rescue and the Rise of Anti-Abortion Militance." In *Abortion Wars: A Half Century of Struggle, 1950–2000*, edited by Rickie Solinger, 227–50. Berkeley: University of California Press.

Ginsburg, Faye D., and Rayna Rapp, eds. 1995. *Conceiving the New World Order: The Global Politics of Reproduction*. Berkeley: University of California Press.

Glantz, Leonard H. 1991. "Criminal Prosecution of Pregnant Drug Users: Bad Law and Worse Health Policy [Editorial]." *Addiction and Recovery* 11, no. 4 (July–August): 3.

Glendon, Mary Ann. 1987. *Abortion and Divorce in Western Law.* Cambridge, Mass.: Harvard University Press.

Glover, Jonathan. 1989. *Ethics of New Reproductive Technologies: The Glover Report to the European Commission.* De Kalb: Northern Illinois University Press.

"God Is Going Back to School." 1997. Columbia Sidewalk Counseling, Press Release, September 2.

Goldsmith, Stephen. 1990. "Prosecution to Enhance Treatment." *Children Today* 19, no. 4 (July–August): 13.

Goldstein, Donna M. 1998. "Nothing Bad Intended: Child Discipline, Punishment, and Survival in a Shantytown in Rio de Janeiro, Brazil." In *Small Wars: The Cultural Politics of Childhood,* edited by Nancy Scheper-Hughes and Carolyn Sargent, 389–415. Berkeley: University of California Press.

Gold-Steinberg, Sharon, and Abigail J. Stewart. 1998. "Psychologies of Abortion: Implications of a Changing Context." In *Abortion Wars: A Half Century of Struggle, 1950–2000,* edited by Rickie Solinger, 356–73. Berkeley: University of California Press.

Gomez, Laura E. 1997. *Misconceiving Mothers: Legislators, Prosecutors, and the Politics of Prenatal Drug Exposure.* Philadelphia: Temple University Press.

Gordon, Linda. 1976. *Woman's Body, Woman's Right: Birth Control in America.* New York: Viking Penguin.

Gorney, Cynthia. 1998. *Articles of Faith: A Frontline History of the Abortion Wars.* New York: Simon and Schuster.

Goslinga-Roy, Gillian M. 2000. "Body Boundaries, Fiction of the Female Self: An Ethnographic Perspective on Power, Feminism, and the Reproductive Technologies." *Feminist Studies* 26, no. 1 (Spring): 113–40.

Gould, Stephen Jay. 1981. *The Mismeasure of Man.* New York: W. W. Norton.

———. 1998. "Dolly's Fashion and Louis's Passion." In *Clones and Clones: Facts and Fantasies about Human Cloning,* edited by Martha C. Nussbaum and Cass R. Sunstein, 41–53. New York: W. W. Norton.

Graber, Mark A. 1996. *Rethinking Abortion: Equal Choice, the Constitution, and Reproductive Politics.* Princeton, N.J.: Princeton University Press.

Graham, Cole Blease, Jr., and William V. Moore. 1994. *South Carolina Politics and Government.* Lincoln: University of Nebraska Press.

Graham, Hillary, and Oakley, Ann. 1981. "Competing Ideologies of Reproduction: Medical and Maternal Perspectives on Pregnancy." In *Women, Health, and Reproduction,* edited by Helen Roberts, 50–74. London: Routledge and Kegan Paul.

Grant, Karen R. 1993. "Perceptions, Attitudes, and Experiences of Prenatal Diagnosis: A Winnipeg Study of Women over Thirty-Five." In *Prenatal Diagnosis: Background and Impact on Individuals,* 185–346. Vol. 12 of Research Studies of the Royal Commission on New Reproductive Technologies. Ottawa, Canada: Minister of Supply and Services.

Grant, Linda. 1994. *Sexing the Millennium: A Political History of the Sexual Revolution.* New York: Grove.

Gray, Virginia, and David Lowery. 1996. "A Niche Theory of Interest Representation." *Journal of Politics* 58, no. 1 (February): 91–111.

Grayson, Deborah R. 1998. "Mediating Intimacy: Black Surrogate Mothers and the Law." *Critical Inquiry* 24, no. 2 (Winter): 525–47.

Greely, Henry T. 1992. "Health Insurance, Employment Discrimination, and the Genetics Revolution." In *The Code of Codes: Scientific and Social Issues in the Human Genome Project*, edited by Daniel J. Kevles and Leroy Hood, 264–80. Cambridge, Mass.: Harvard University Press.

Green, John C., James L. Guth, Corwin E. Smidt, and Lyman A. Kellstedt. 1996. *Religion and the Culture Wars: Dispatches from the Front*. Lanham, Md.: Rowman and Littlefield.

Green, John C., Mark J. Rozell, and Clyde Wilcox, eds. 2000. *Prayers in the Precincts: The Christian Right in the 1998 Elections*. Washington, D.C.: Georgetown University Press.

Green, Valerie. 1993. *Doped Up, Knocked Up, and . . . Locked Up? The Criminal Prosecution of Women Who Use Drugs during Pregnancy*. New York: Garland.

Greene, Melissa Fay. 2000. "The Orphan Ranger." *New Yorker* 76, no. 19 (July 17): 36–45.

Gregg, Robin. 1995. *Pregnancy in a High-Tech Age: Paradoxes of Choice*. New York: New York University Press.

Griffin, Susan. 1978. *Woman and Nature: The Roaring inside Her*. New York: Harper Colophon Books.

Griswold v. Connecticut, 381 U.S. 479, 85 S. Ct. 1678, 14 L.Ed. 2d 510 (1965).

Gupta, Jyotsna Agnihotri. 2000. *New Reproductive Technologies, Women's Health and Autonomy*. New Delhi, India: Sage Publications.

Gusfield, Joseph R. 1981. "Social Movements and Social Change: Perspectives of Linearity and Fluidity." In *Research in Social Movements, Conflict, and Change*, ed. Louis Kriesberg, 317–39. Greenwich, Conn.: JAI Press.

———. 1994. "The Reflexivity of Social Movements: Collective Behavior and Mass Society Theory Revisited." In *New Social Movements: From Ideology to Identity*, edited by Enrique Laraña, Hank Johnston, and Joseph R. Gusfield, 58–78. Philadelphia: Temple University Press.

Gustavsson, Nora S., and Ann E. MacEachron. 1997. "Criminalizing Women's Behavior." *Journal of Drug Issues* 27, no. 3 (Summer): 673–87.

Guth, James L. 1995. "South Carolina: The Christian Right Wins One." In *God at the Grass Roots: The Christian Right in the 1994 Elections*, edited by Mark J. Rozell and Clyde Wilcox, 133–45. Lanham, Md.: Rowman and Littlefield.

Halva-Neubauer, Glen A. 1993. "The States after ROE—No 'Paper Tigers.'" In *Understanding the New Politics of Abortion*, edited by Malcolm L. Goggin, 167–89. Newbury Park, Calif.: Sage.

Halva-Neubauer, Glen A., Raymond Tatalovich, and Byron W. Daynes. 1993. "Locating Abortion Clinics: Aggregate Data and Case Study Approaches to the Implementation Process." Paper presented at the American Political Science Association Annual Meeting, Washington, D.C., September 2–5.

Hanmer, Jalna. 1981. "Sex Predetermination, Artificial Insemination, and the Maintenance of Male-Dominated Culture." In *Women, Health, and Reproduction,* edited by Helen Roberts, 163–90. London: Routledge and Kegan Paul.

———. 1984. "A Womb of One's Own." In *Test-Tube Women: What Future for Motherhood?* edited by Rita Arditti, Renate Duelli Klein, and Shelley Minden, 438–48. London: Pandora.

Haraway, Donna J. 1997. *Modest-Witness@Second-Millennium.FemaleMan© Meets OncoMouse™: Feminism and Technoscience.* New York: Routledge.

Harding, Sandra. 1986. *The Science Question in Feminism.* Ithaca, N.Y.: Cornell University Press.

Harper, Peter S. 1994. "Research Samples from Families with Genetic Diseases: A Proposed Code of Conduct." In *Genetic Counseling: Practice and Principles,* edited by Angus Clarke, 92–93. New York: Routledge, 1994.

Harris, John, and Soren Holm, eds. 1998. *The Future of Human Reproduction: Ethics, Choice, and Regulation.* Oxford: Oxford University Press.

Harrison, Beverly Wildung. 1983. *Our Right to Choose: Toward a New Ethic of Abortion.* Boston: Beacon.

Harrison, M. 1987. "Social Construction of Mary Beth Whitehead." *Gender and Society* 1, no. 3: 300–311.

Harris v. McRae, 448 U.S. 297, 100 S. Ct. 2671, 65 L.Ed. 2d 784 (1980).

Hartmann, Betsy. 1987. *Reproductive Rights and Wrongs: The Global Politics of Population Control and Contraceptive Choice.* New York: Harper and Row.

Hartsock, Nancy C. M. 1998. *The Feminist Standpoint Revisited and Other Essays.* Boulder, Colo.: Westview.

Hayden, Corinne P. 1998. "A Biodiversity Sampler for the Millennium." In *Reproducing Reproduction: Kinship, Power, and Technological Innovations,* edited by Sarah Franklin and Heléna Ragoné, 173–206. Philadelphia: University of Pennsylvania Press.

Hays, Sharon. 1996. *The Cultural Contradictions of Motherhood.* New Haven, Conn.: Yale University Press.

"The Hazards of Genetic Testing." 1996. *Harvard Women's Health Watch* 3, no. 6 (February 6): 6.

Heilbrun, Carolyn G. 1990. "The Politics of Mind: Women, Tradition, and the University." In *Gender in the Classroom: Power and Pedagogy,* edited by Susan L. Gabriel and Isaiah Smithson, 29–40. Urbana: University of Illinois Press.

Hekman, Susan J. 1990. *Gender and Knowledge.* Boston: Northeastern University Press.

Held, Virginia. 1999. "Liberalism and the Ethics of Care." In *On Feminist Ethics and Politics,* edited by Claudia Card, 288–309. Lawrence: University Press of Kansas.

Helmreich, Stefan. 1998. "Replicating Reproduction in Artificial Life: Or, the Essence of Life in the Age of Virtual Electronic Reproduction." In *Repro-*

ducing Reproduction: Kinship, Power, and Technological Innovations, edited by Sarah Franklin and Heléna Ragoné, 207–34. Philadelphia: University of Pennsylvania Press.

Herbert, Bob. 1998. "In The War Zone." *New York Times,* November 8.

Hern, Warren M. 1973. "Abortion: The Need for Rational Policy and Safe Standards." *Denver Post,* May 27.

———. 1984a. *Abortion Practice.* Philadelphia: J. B. Lippincott.

———. 1984b. "The Antiabortion Vigilantes." *New York Times,* December 21.

———. 1984c. "Does the FBI Sanction Terrorism against Abortion Clinics?" *Daily Camera* (Boulder, Colo.), December 9.

———. 1988a. "Abortion Clinics under Siege." *Denver Post,* October 22.

———. 1988b. "Anti-Abortion Campaign Rhetoric Prompts Attacks on Clinics." *Daily Camera* (Boulder, Colo.), September 4.

———. 1991. "Proxemics: The Application of Theory to Conflict Arising from Antiabortion Demonstrations." *Population and Environment: A Journal of Interdisciplinary Studies* 12, no. 4 (Summer): 379–88.

———. 1993. "Florida Doctor's Death Resulted from Twenty Years of Inciting Violence." *Denver Post,* March 20.

———. 1994a. "Anti-Abortion Movement Put Weapon in Slyer's Hand." *Daily Camera* (Boulder, Colo.), March 20.

———. 1994b. "Anti-Abortion Zealots' Grasp for Power." *Rocky Mountain News,* December 19.

———. 1994c. "Life on the Front Lines." *Women's Health Issues* 4, no. 1 (Spring): 48–54.

———. 1995a. "Anti-Abortion Activity at Boulder Abortion Clinic, 1975–1995, in a National Context." Special Report Prepared for Criminal Division, U.S. Department of Justice, Washington, D.C., January 6.

———. 1995b. "'Killing for Life' Is Senseless." *Denver Post,* April 8.

———. 1995c. "Parental Notice Is Bad Legislation: This Discriminates against Young Women." *Colorado Statesman,* March 10.

———. 1995d. "Statement of Warren M. Hern, before the Judiciary Committee of the United States Senate, concerning S. 939 [Partial Birth Abortion Ban]." *Congressional Record,* November 17.

———. 1995e. "Who Wanted to Ban 'Partial Birth Abortion'"? *Daily Camera* (Boulder, Colo.), December 16.

———. 1997. "Abortion Bill Skips the Fine Print." *New York Times,* May 24.

———. 1998. "Life on the Front Lines." In *Abortion Wars: A Half Century of Struggle, 1950–2000,* edited by Rickie Solinger, 307–19. Berkeley: University of California Press.

Hern, Warren M., Marlene R. Gold, and Annagail Oakes. 1977. "Administrative Incongruence and Authority Conflict in Four Abortion Clinics." *Human Organization* 36, no. 4 (Winter): 376–83.

Hertz, Sue. 1991. *Caught in the Crossfire: A Year on Abortion's Front Line.* New York: Prentice Hall.

Hildreth, Anne. 1994. "The Importance of Purposes in 'Purposive' Groups:

Incentives and Participation in the Sanctuary Movement." *American Journal of Political Science* 38, no. 2 (May): 447–63.

Himmelstein, Jerome L. 1990. *To the Right: The Transformation of American Conservatism.* Berkeley: University of California Press.

Hirshman, Linda R., and Jane E. Larson. 1998. *Hard Bargains: The Politics of Sex.* New York: Oxford University Press.

Hodgson, Jane E. 1998. "The Twentieth-Century Gender Battle: Difficulties in Perception." In *Abortion Wars: A Half Century of Struggle, 1950–2000,* edited by Rickie Solinger, 290–306. Berkeley: University of California Press.

Holden, Constance. 1994. "A Cautionary Genetic Tale: The Sobering Story of D2: Alcoholism Research." *Science* 264 (June 17): 1696–97.

Holder, Angela R. 1988. "Surrogate Motherhood and the Best Interest of Children." In *Surrogate Motherhood: Politics and Privacy,* edited by Larry Gostin, 77–87. Bloomington: Indiana University Press.

Hollinger, J. H. 1985. "From Coitus to Commerce: Legal and Social Consequences of Noncoital Reproduction." *University of Michigan Journal of Law Reform* 18, no. 4 (Summer): 865–932.

Holmes, Helen Bequaert. 1995. "Choosing Children's Sex: Challenges to Feminist Ethics." In *Reproduction, Ethics, and the Law: Feminist Perspectives,* edited by Joan C. Callahan, 148–77. Bloomington: Indiana University Press.

———. 1997. "DNA Fingerprints and Rape: A Feminist Assessment." *Policy Sciences* 27: 221–45.

Holmes, Helen Bequaert, and B. B. Hoskins. 1987. "Prenatal and Preconception Sex Choice Technologies: A Path to Femicide?" In *Man-Made Women: How the New Reproductive Technologies Affect Women,* edited by Gena Corea, Jalna Hanmer, Betty Hoskins, Janice Raymond, Renate Duelli Klein, Helen Bequaert Holmes, Madhu Kishwar, Robyn Rowland, and Roberta Steinbacher, 15–29. Bloomington: Indiana University Press.

Homer-Dixon, Thomas F. 1998. "Environmental Scarcities and Violent Conflict: Evidence from Cases." In *Green Planet Blues: Environmental Politics from Stockholm to Kyoto,* 2d ed., edited by Ken Conca and Geoffrey D. Dabelko, 287–97. Boulder, Colo.: Westview.

Honey, Margaret. 1996. "The Maternal Voice in the Technological Universe." In *Representations of Motherhood,* edited by Donna Bassin, Margaret Honey, and Meryle Mahrer Kaplan, 220–39. New Haven, Conn.: Yale University Press.

Hood, Leroy. 1992. "Biology and Medicine in the Twenty-First Century." In *The Code of Codes: Scientific and Social Issues in the Human Genome Project,* edited by Daniel J. Kevles and Leroy Hood, 136–63. Cambridge, Mass.: Harvard University Press.

Horgan, John. 1993. "Trends in Behavioral Genetics: Eugenics Revisited." *Scientific American* 268, no. 6 (June): 123–31.

Horowitz, Craig. 1999. "Time-Bomb Genes." *New York* 32, no. 5 (February 8): 29–33, 89.

Hoskins, Betty B. 1990. "Feminist Understandings and Underpinnings: Reproductive Ethics Re-viewed in the Era of the Human Genome Project." Paper based on lecture to the Theological Opportunities Program, Harvard Divinity School, April 12.

Hoskins, B. B., and H. B. Holmes. 1984. "Technology and Prenatal Femicide." In *Test-Tube Women: What Future for Motherhood?* edited by Rita Arditti, Renate Duelli Klein, and Shelley Minden, 237–55. London: Pandora.

Hrdy, Sarah Blaffer. 1999. *Maternal Instincts and How They Shape the Human Species.* New York: Ballantine Books.

Hubbard, Ruth. 1984. "Personal Courage Is Not Enough: Some Hazards of Childbearing in the 1980s." In *Test-Tube Women: What Future for Motherhood?* edited by Rita Arditti, Renate Duelli Klein, and Shelley Minden, 331–55. London: Pandora.

———. 1995. *Profitable Promises: Essays on Women, Science and Health.* Monroe, Maine: Common Courage.

Hubbard, Ruth, and Elijah Wald. 1993. *Exploding the Gene Myth.* Boston: Beacon.

Hudson, Kathy L., Karen H. Rothenberg, Lori B. Andrews, Mary Jo Ellis Kahn, and Francis S. Collins. 1995. "Genetic Discrimination and Health Insurance: An Urgent Need for Reform." *Science* 270 (October 20): 391–93.

Hughes, Donna M. 1995. "Significant Differences: The Construction of Knowledge, Objectivity, and Dominance." *Women's Studies International Forum* 18, no. 4 (July–August): 395–406.

Humphries, Drew, John Dawson, Valerie Cronin, Phyllis Keating, Chris Wisniewski, and Jennine Eichfeld. 1992. "Mother and Children, Drugs and Crack: Reactions to Maternal Drug Dependency." In *The Criminalization of a Woman's Body*, edited by Clarice Feinman, 203–21. New York: Haworth.

Huxley, Aldous. 1946. *Brave New World.* Cutchogue, N.Y.: Buccaneer Books.

Ikemoto, Lisa. 1992. "The Code of Perfect Pregnancy: At the Intersection of the Ideology of Motherhood, the Practice of Defaulting to Science, and the Interventionist Mindset of Law." *Ohio State Law Journal* 53, no. 4–5 (November): 1205–1306.

Ince, Susan. 1984. "Inside the Surrogate Industry." In *Test-Tube Women: What Future for Motherhood?* edited by Rita Arditti, Renate Duelli Klein, and Shelley Minden, 99–116. London: Pandora.

In the Matter of Baby M, a Pseudonym for an Actual Person, 217 N.J. Super. 313, 525 A.2d 1128 (1987).

In the Matter of Baby M, a Pseudonym for an Actual Person, 109 N.J. 396, 537 A.2d 1227 (1988).

In re A.C., 533 A.2d 611 (1987).

In re A.C., (en banc), 573 A.2d 1235 (1990).

International Union, United Automobile, Aerospace and Agricultural Implement Workers of America, U.A.W., et al. v. Johnson Controls, Inc., 449 U.S. 187 (1991).

Ivers, Gregg. 1998. "Please God, Save This Honorable Court: The Emergence of the Conservative Religious Bar." In *The Interest Group Connection: Electioneering, Lobbying, and Policymaking in Washington,* edited by Paul S. Herrnson, Ronald G. Shaiko, and Clyde Wilcox, 289–301. Chatham, N.J.: Chatham House.

Jaggar, Alison. 1992. "Feminist Ethics." In *Encyclopedia of Ethics,* edited by Lawrence C. Becker and Charlotte B. Becker, 361–70. New York: Garland.

———. 1998. "Regendering the U.S. Abortion Debate." In *Abortion Wars: A Half Century of Struggle, 1950–2000,* edited by Rickie Solinger, 339–55. Berkeley: University of California Press.

Jambai, Amara, and Carol MacCormack. 1997. "Maternal Health, War, and Religious Tradition: Authoritative Knowledge in Pukehun District, Sierra Leone." In *Childbirth and Authoritative Knowledge: Cross-Cultural Perspectives,* edited by Robbie E. Davis-Floyd and Carolyn F. Sargent, 421–40. Berkeley: University of California Press.

James, Joy. 1997. "Ella Baker, 'Black Women's Work,' and Activist Intellectuals." In *Spoils of War: Women of Color, Cultures, and Revolutions,* edited by T. Denean Sharpley-Whiting and Renee T. White, 3–18. Lanham, Md.: Rowman and Littlefield.

Jaquette, Jane S., and Kathleen A. Staudt. 1985. "Women as 'At Risk' Reproducers: Biology, Science, and Population in U.S. Foreign Policy." In *Women, Biology, and Public Policy,* edited by Virginia Sapiro, 235–68. Beverly Hills, Calif.: Sage Publications.

Jaroff, Leon. 1997. "Six Parents, One Orphan." *Time* 150, no. 23 (December 1): 45.

Jessie Mae Jefferson v. Griffin Spalding County Hospital, 247 Ga. 86, 274 S.E.2d 457 (1981).

Joffe, Carole. 1995. *Doctors of Conscience: The Struggle to Provide Abortion before and after Roe v. Wade.* Boston: Beacon.

Joffe, Carole, Patricia Anderson, and Jody Steinauer. 1998. "The Crisis in Abortion Provision and Pro-Choice Medical Activism in the 1990s." In *Abortion Wars: A Half Century of Struggle, 1950–2000,* edited by Rickie Solinger, 320–33. Berkeley: University of California Press.

Johnsen, Dawn E. 1986. "The Creation of Fetal Rights: Conflicts with Women's Constitutional Rights to Liberty, Privacy, and Equal Protection." *Yale Law Journal* 95, no. 3 (January): 599–625.

———. 1992. "Shared Interests: Promoting Healthy Births without Sacrificing Women's Liberty." *Hastings Law Journal* 43, no. 3 (March): 569–614.

Johnson, Kenneth C. 1997. "Randomized Controlled Trials as Authoritative Knowledge: Keeping an Ally from Becoming a Threat to North American Midwifery Practice." In *Childbirth and Authoritative Knowledge: Cross-Cultural Perspectives,* edited by Robbie E. Davis-Floyd and Carolyn F. Sargent, 350–65. Berkeley: University of California Press.

Johnson v. Calvert, 19 Cal. Rptr. 2d 494, 851 P.2d 776 (Cal. 1993).

Johnston, Hank, Enrique Larana, and Joseph R. Gusfield. 1994. "Identities, Grievances, and New Social Movements." In *New Social Movements: From Ideology to Identity,* edited by Enrique Laraña, Hank Johnston, and Joseph R. Gusfield, 3–35. Philadelphia: Temple University Press.

Jordan, Brigitte. 1997. "Authoritative Knowledge and Its Construction." In *Childbirth and Authoritative Knowledge: Cross-Cultural Perspectives,* edited by Robbie E. Davis-Floyd and Carolyn F. Sargent, 55–79. Berkeley: University of California Press.

Jordanova, Ludmilla. 1995. "Interrogating the Concept of Reproduction in the Eighteenth Century." In *Conceiving the New World Order: The Global Politics of Reproduction,* edited by Faye D. Ginsburg and Rayna Rapp, 369–88. Berkeley: University of California Press.

Jos, Philip H., Mary Faith Marshall, and Martin Perlmutter. 1995. "The Charleston Policy on Cocaine Use during Pregnancy: A Cautionary Tale." *Journal of Law, Medicine and Ethics* 23, no. 2 (Summer): 120–28.

Judson, Horace Freeland. 1992. "A History of the Science and Technology behind Gene Mapping and Sequencing." In *The Code of Codes: Scientific and Social Issues in the Human Genome Project,* edited by Daniel J. Kevles and Leroy Hood, 37–80. Cambridge, Mass.: Harvard University Press.

Kahn, Robbie Pfeufer. 1995. *Bearing Meaning: The Language of Birth.* Urbana: University of Illinois Press.

Kamal, Sultana. 1987. "Seizure of Reproductive Rights? A Discussion on Population Control in the Third World and the Emergence of the New Reproductive Technologies in the West." In *Made to Order: The Myth of Reproductive and Genetic Progress,* edited by Patricia Spallone and Deborah Lynn Steinberg, 146–53. New York: Pergamon.

Kane, Elizabeth. 1988. *Birth Mother: The Story of America's First Legal Surrogate Mother.* New York: Harcourt, Brace.

Kaplan, Deborah. 1994. "Prenatal Screening and Diagnosis: The Impact on Persons with Disabilities." In *Women and Prenatal Testing: Facing the Challenges of Genetic Technology,* edited by Karen H. Rothenberg and Elizabeth J. Thomson, 49–61. Columbus: Ohio State University Press.

Kaplan, Laura. 1995. *Jane: The Legendary Underground Feminist Abortion Service.* Chicago: University of Chicago Press.

———. 1998. "Beyond Safe and Legal: The Lessons of Jane." In *Abortion Wars: A Half Century of Struggle, 1950–2000,* edited by Rickie Solinger, 33–41. Berkeley: University of California Press.

Karlin, Elizabeth. 1998. "'We Called It Kindness': Establishing a Feminist Abortion Practice." In *Abortion Wars: A Half Century of Struggle, 1950–2000,* edited by Rickie Solinger, 273–89. Berkeley: University of California Press.

Keller, Evelyn Fox. 1985. *Reflections on Gender and Science.* New Haven, Conn.: Yale University Press.

———. 1992. "Nature, Nurture, and the Human Genome Project." In *The Code of Codes: Scientific and Social Issues in the Human Genome Project,* edited by Daniel J. Kevles and Leroy Hood, 281–99. Cambridge, Mass.: Harvard University Press.

Kelly, James R. 1995. "Beyond Compromise: *Casey,* Common Ground, and the Pro-Life Movement." In *Abortion Politics in American States,* edited by Mary C. Segers and Timothy A. Byrnes, 205–24. Armonk, N.Y.: M. E. Sharpe.

Kenen, Regina H. 1996. "The At-Risk Health Status and Technology: A Diagnostic Invitation and the 'Gift' of Knowing." *Social Science and Medicine* 42, no. 11 (June): 1545–53.

Kesselman, Amy. 1998. "Women versus Connecticut: Conducting a Statewide Hearing on Abortion." In *Abortion Wars: A Half Century of Struggle, 1950–2000,* edited by Rickie Solinger, 42–67. Berkeley: University of California Press.

Ketchum, Sara Anne. 1987. "New Reproductive Technologies and the Definition of Parenthood: A Feminist Perspective." Paper presented at the Feminism and Legal Theory Conference on Intimacy, University of Wisconsin Law School, June.

Kevles, Daniel J. 1992. "Out of Eugenics: The Historical Politics of the Human Genome." In *The Code of Codes: Scientific and Social Issues in the Human Genome Project,* edited by Daniel J. Kevles and Leroy Hood, 3–36. Cambridge, Mass.: Harvard University Press.

Kevles, Daniel J., and Leroy Hood. 1992. "Reflections." In *The Code of Codes: Scientific and Social Issues in the Human Genome Project,* edited by Daniel J. Kevles and Leroy Hood, 300–328. Cambridge, Mass.: Harvard University Press.

Keyserling, Harriet. 1998. *Against the Tide: One Woman's Political Struggle.* Columbia: University of South Carolina Press.

King, Patricia A. 1994. "Ethics and Reproductive Genetic Testing: The Need to Understand the Parent-Child Relationship." In *Women and Prenatal Testing: Facing the Challenges of Genetic Technology,* edited by Karen H. Rothenberg and Elizabeth J. Thomson, 98–104. Columbus: Ohio State University Press.

King, Patricia, and Melinda Beck. 1996. "Persuasion, Not Blame: Now, a 'Kinder, Gentler' Pro-Life Movement." *Newsweek* 127, no. 13 (March 25): 61.

Kishwar, Madhu. 1987. "The Continuing Deficit of Women in India and the Impact of Amniocentesis." In *Man-Made Women: How New Reproductive Technologies Affect Women,* edited by Gena Corea, Jalna Hanmer, Betty Hoskins, Janice Raymond, Renate Duelli Klein, Helen Bequaert Holmes, Madhu Kishwar, Robyn Rowland, and Roberta Steinbacher, 30–37. Bloomington: Indiana University Press.

Kittay, Eva Feder. 1999a. *Love's Labor: Essays on Women, Equality, and Dependency.* New York: Routledge.

———. 1999b. "'Not My Way, Sesha, Your Way, Slowly': 'Maternal Thinking' in the Raising of a Child with Profound Intellectual Disabilities." In *Mother Troubles: Rethinking Contemporary Maternal Dilemmas,* edited by Julia E. Haningberg and Sara Ruddick, 3–27. Boston: Beacon.

Kitzinger, Sheila. 1997. "Authoritative Touch in Childbirth: A Cross-Cultural Approach." In *Childbirth and Authoritative Knowledge: Cross-Cultural Perspectives,* edited by Robbie E. Davis-Floyd and Carolyn F. Sargent, 209–32. Berkeley: University of California Press.

Klein, Renate D. 1987. "What's 'New' about the 'New' Reproductive Technologies." In *Man-Made Women: How the New Reproductive Technologies Affect Women,* edited by Gena Corea, Jalna Hanmer, Betty Hoskins, Janice Raymond, Renate Duelli Klein, Helen Bequaert Holmes, Madhu Kishwar, Robyn Rowland, and Roberta Steinbacher, 64–73. Bloomington: Indiana University Press.

Kligman, Gail. 1995. "Political Demography: The Banning of Abortion in Ceausescu's Romania." In *Conceiving the New World Order: The Global Politics of Reproduction,* edited by Faye D. Ginsburg and Rayna Rapp, 234–55. Berkeley: University of California Press.

Kline, Marlee 1995. "Complicating the Ideology of Motherhood: Child Welfare Law and First Nation Women." In *Mothers in Law: Feminist Theory and the Legal Regulation of Motherhood,* edited by Martha Albertson Fineman and Isabel Karpin, 118–41. New York: Columbia University Press.

Knezevic, Djurdja. 1997. "Affective Nationalism." In *Transitions, Environments, Translations: Feminisms in International Politics,* edited by Joan W. Scott, Cora Kaplan, and Debra Keates, 65–71. New York: Routledge.

Knox, Richard A. 1993. "Gene May Help Explain the Origin of Homosexuality." *Boston Globe,* July 16.

Koenig, Barbara. 1996. "Gene Tests: What You Know Can Hurt You." *New York Times,* Op-Ed, April 6.

Kolata, Gina. 1990. "Under Pressures and Stigma, More Doctors Shun Abortion." *New York Times,* January 8.

———. 1992. "In Late Abortions, Decisions Are Painful and Options Few." *New York Times,* January 5.

———. 1996. "Breaking Ranks, Lab Offers Test to Assess Risk of Breast Cancer." *New York Times,* April 1.

Kolbert, Kathryn, and Andrea Miller. 1998. "Legal Strategies for Abortion Rights in the Twenty-First Century." In *Abortion Wars: A Half Century of Struggle, 1950–2000,* edited by Rickie Solinger, 95–110. Berkeley: University of California Press.

Koppelman, Andrew. 1990. "Forced Labor: A Thirteenth Amendment Defense of Abortion." *Northwestern University Law Review* 84, no. 2 (Winter): 480–535.

Korbin, Jill E. 1998. "'Good Mothers,' 'Babykillers,' and Fatal Child Maltreatment." In *Small Wars: The Cultural Politics of Childhood,* edited by Nancy Scheper-Hughes and Carolyn Sargent, 253–76. Berkeley: University of California Press.

Kunisch, Judith R. 1989. "Electronic Fetal Monitors: Marketing Forces and the Resulting Controversy." In *Healing Technology: Feminist Perspectives,* edited by Kathryn Strother Ratcliff, 41–60. Ann Arbor: University of Michigan Press.

Laborie, Francoise. 1987. "Looking for Mothers, You Only Find Fetuses." In *Made to Order: The Myth of Reproductive and Genetic Progress,* edited by Patricia Spallone and Deborah Lynn Steinberg, 48–57. New York: Pergamon.

Ladd-Taylor, Molly, and Lauri Umansky, eds. 1998. *"Bad" Mothers: The Politics of Blame in Twentieth-Century America.* New York: New York University Press.

Lander, Eric. 1992. "DNA Fingerprinting: Science, Law, and the Ultimate Identifier." In *The Code of Codes: Scientific and Social Issues in the Human Genome Project,* edited by Daniel J. Kevles and Leroy Hood, 191–210. Cambridge, Mass.: Harvard University Press.

Landsman, Gail H. 1998. "Reconstructing Motherhood in the Age of 'Perfect' Babies: Mothers of Infants and Toddlers with Disabilities." *Signs: Journal of Women in Culture and Society* 24, no. 1 (Autumn): 69–99.

———. 1999. "Does God Give Special Kids to Special Parents? Personhood and the Child with Disabilities as Gift and as Giver." In *Transformative Motherhood: On Giving and Getting in a Consumer Culture,* edited by Linda L. Layne, 133–66. New York: New York University Press.

———. 2000. "'Real Motherhood,' Class, and Children with Disabilities." In *Ideologies and Technologies of Motherhood: Race, Class, Sexuality, Nationalism,* edited by Heléna Ragoné and France Winddance Twine, 169–87. New York: Routledge.

Lang, Sabine. 1997. "The NGOization of Feminism: Institutionalization and Institution Building within the German Women's Movements." In *Transitions, Environments, Translations: Feminisms in International Politics,* edited by Joan W. Scott, Cora Kaplan, and Debra Keates, 101–20. New York: Routledge.

Laraña, Enrique, Hank Johnston, and Joseph R. Gusfield, eds. 1994. *New Social Movements: From Ideology to Identity.* Philadelphia: Temple University Press.

Lasker, Judith, and Susan Borg. 1987. *In Search of Parenthood: Coping with Infertility and High-Tech Conception.* Boston: Beacon.

"Late Term Abortion: Speaking Frankly." 1997. *Ms.* 7, no. 6 (May/June): 64–71.

Latour, Bruno, and Steve Woolgar. 1979. *Laboratory Life: The Social Construction of Scientific Facts.* Beverly Hills, Calif.: Sage Publications.

Law, Sylvia. 1984. "Rethinking Sex and the Constitution." *University of Pennsylvania Law Review* 132, no. 5 (June): 955–1040.

Lawson, Annette, and Deborah L. Rhode, eds. 1993. *The Politics of Pregnancy: Adolescent Sexuality and Public Policy.* New Haven, Conn.: Yale University Press.

Layne, Linda L. 1999a. "The Child as Gift: New Directions in the Study of Euro-American Gift Exchange." In *Transformative Motherhood: On Giving and Getting in a Consumer Culture,* edited by Linda L. Layne, 1–27. New York: New York University Press.

———. 1999b. "'True Gifts from God': Motherhood, Sacrifice, and Enrichment in the Case of Pregnancy Loss." In *Transformative Motherhood: On Giving and Getting in a Consumer Culture,* edited by Linda L. Layne, 167–214. New York: New York University Press.

Lazarus, Ellen. 1997. "What Do Women Want? Issues of Choice, Control, and

Class in American Pregnancy and Childbirth." In *Childbirth and Author-itative Knowledge: Cross-Cultural Perspectives*, edited by Robbie E. Davis-Floyd and Carolyn F. Sargent, 132–58. Berkeley: University of California Press.

Lerer, Leonard B. 1998. "Who Is The Rogue? Hunger, Death, and Circumstance in John Mampe Square," In *Small Wars: the Cultural Politics of Childhood*, edited by Nancy Scheper-Hughes and Carolyn Sargent, 228–50. Berkeley: University of California Press.

Levy, Katherine. 1998. "On the Twenty-Fifth Anniversary of *Roe v. Wade*, an Uncertain Future." *AAUW [American Association of University Women] Outlook* 92, no. 1 (Spring): 24–25.

Lewin, Ellen. 1995. "On the Outside Looking In: The Politics of Lesbian Motherhood." In *Conceiving the New World Order: The Global Politics of Reproduction*, edited by Faye D. Ginsburg and Rayna Rapp, 103–21. Berkeley: University of California Press.

Liakos, Ann Marie. 1993. "Baby Jeffrey: Sharing Our Inspiration." *Hydrocephalus News and Notes* 1, no. 1 (January): 1, 19.

———. N.d. "Understanding Hydrocephalus." National Hydrocephalus Foundation, Inc., one-page memo.

Lieberman, Robert C. 1995. "Comment: Social Construction (Continued)." *American Political Science Review* 89, no. 2 (June): 437–41.

Lieske, Joel. 1993. "Regional Subcultures of the United States." *Journal of Politics* 55, no. 4 (November): 888–913.

Lifton, Betty Jean. 1994. *Journey of the Adopted Self: A Quest for Wholeness.* New York: Basic Books.

———. 1998. "Bad/Good, Good/Bad: Birth Mothers and Adoptive Mothers." In *"Bad" Mothers: The Politics of Blame in Twentieth-Century America*, edited by Molly Ladd-Taylor and Lauri Umansky, 191–97. New York: New York University Press.

Lin, Jonathan H. 1998. "Divining and Altering the Future: Implications from the Human Genome Project." *JAMA: The Journal of the American Medical Association* 280, no. 17 (November 4): 1532.

Lippman, Abby. 1994a. "The Genetic Construction of Prenatal Testing: Choice, Consent, or Conformity for Women?" In *Women and Prenatal Testing: Facing the Challenges of Genetic Technology*, edited by Karen H. Rothenberg and Elizabeth J. Thomson, 9–34. Columbus: Ohio State University Press.

———. 1994b. "Prenatal Genetic Testing and Screening: Constructing Needs and Reinforcing Inequities." In *Genetic Counseling: Practice and Principles*, edited by Angus Clarke, 142–86. New York: Routledge.

———. 1998. "The Politics of Health: Geneticization Versus Health Promotion." In *The Politics of Women's Health: Exploring Agency and Autonomy*, edited by Susan Sherwin, 64–82. Philadelphia: Temple University Press.

Little People of America Online. 2001. <http://www.lpaonline.org>. Accessed June 27.

Lock, Margaret. 1998. "Situating Women in the Politics of Health." In *The*

Politics of Women's Health: Exploring Agency and Autonomy, edited by Susan Sherwin, 48–63. Philadelphia: Temple University Press.

Lohmann, Larry. 1998. "Whose Common Future?" In *Green Planet Blues: Environmental Politics from Stockholm to Kyoto,* 2d ed., edited by Ken Conca and Geoffrey D. Dabelko, 240–44. Boulder, Colo.: Westview.

Lopez, Kathryn Jean. 1998. "Egg Heads." *Human Life Review* 24, no. 4 (Fall): 106–10.

Luker, Kristin. 1975. *Taking Chances: Abortion and the Decision Not to Contracept.* Berkeley: University of California Press.

———. 1984. *Abortion and the Politics of Motherhood.* Berkeley: University of California Press.

———. 1996. *Dubious Conceptions: The Politics of Teenage Pregnancy.* Cambridge, Mass.: Harvard University Press.

MacKinnon, Catharine A. 1987. *Feminism Unmodified: Discourses on Life and Law.* Cambridge, Mass.: Harvard University Press.

———. 1991. "Reflections on Sex Equality under Law." *Yale Law Journal* 100, no. 5 (March): 1281–1328.

Macklin, Ruth. 1994. *Surrogates and Other Mothers: The Debates over Assisted Reproduction.* Philadelphia: Temple University Press.

MacNeil-Lehrer News Hour. 1989. Transcript, Public Broadcasting Service, July 3.

Madsen v. Women's Health Center, 512 U.S. 753 (1994).

Maher, Lisa. 1992. "Punishment and Welfare: Crack Cocaine and the Regulation of Mothering." In *The Criminalization of a Woman's Body,* edited by Clarice Feinman, 157–92. New York: Haworth.

Mahowald, Mary B. 1994. "Reproductive Genetics and Gender Justice." In *Women and Prenatal Testing: Facing the Challenges of Genetic Technology,* edited by Karen H. Rothenberg and Elizabeth J. Thomson, 67–87. Columbus: Ohio State University Press.

———. 1995. "Gender Justice and Genetics." In *The Social Power of Ideas,* edited by Yeager Hudson and W. Creighton Peden, 225–52. Lewiston, N.Y.: Edwin Mellen.

Maier, Kelly E. 1989. "Pregnant Women: Fetal Containers or People with Rights?" *Affilia: Journal of Women and Social Work* 4, no. 2 (Summer): 8–20.

Malmsbury, Jeannine. 2001. "Lost Daughters of China." *Coloradan* (February): 19.

Mansbridge, Jane. 1983. *Beyond Adversary Democracy.* Chicago: University of Chicago Press.

———. 1990. "On the Relation of Altruism and Self-Interest." In *Beyond Self-Interest,* edited by Jane J. Mansbridge, 133–43. Chicago: University of Chicago Press.

Marshall, Eliot. 1995a. "Gene Therapy's Growing Pains." *Science* 269 (August 25): 1050–55.

———. 1995b. "Jury Still Out on Pioneering Treatment." *Science* 269 (August 25): 1051.

———. 1995c. "RAC's Identity Crisis." *Science* 269 (August 25): 1054.

———. 1995d. "The Trouble with Vectors." *Science* 269 (August 25): 1052–53.

Marshall, Mary Faith. 1999. "Commentary: Mal-Intentioned Illiteracy, Willful Ignorance, and Fetal Protection Laws: Is There a Lexicologist in the House?" *Journal of Law, Medicine and Ethics* 27, no. 4 (Winter): 343.

Marteau, Theresa, and Harriet Drake. 1995. "Attributions for Disability: The Influence of Genetic Screening." *Social Science and Medicine* 40, no. 8 (April): 1127–32.

Martin, Emily. 1987. *The Woman in the Body: A Cultural Analysis of Reproduction*. Boston: Beacon.

———. 1995. "From Reproduction to HIV: Blurring Categories, Shifting Positions." In *Conceiving the New World Order: The Global Politics of Reproduction*, edited by Faye D. Ginsburg and Rayna Rapp, 256–69. Berkeley: University of California Press.

Martone, Marilyn. 1998. "The Ethics of the Economics of Patenting the Human Genome." *Journal of Business Ethics* 17, no. 15 (November): 1679–84.

Mathieu, Deborah. 1995. "Mandating Treatment for Pregnant Substance Abusers: A Compromise." *Politics and the Life Sciences* 14, no. 2 (August): 199–208.

Maushart, Susan. 2000. *The Mask of Motherhood: How Becoming a Mother Changes Our Lives and Why We Never Talk about It*. New York: Penguin Books.

McAdam, Doug, John D. McCarthy, and Mayer N. Zald. 1996. "Introduction: Opportunities, Mobilizing Structures, and Framing Process—Toward a Synthetic, Comparative Perspective on Social Movements." In *Comparative Perspectives on Social Movements: Political Opportunities, Mobilizing Structures, and Cultural Framings*, edited by Doug McAdam, John D. McCarthy, and Mayer N. Zald, 1–20. New York: Cambridge University Press.

McDonagh, Eileen. 1996. *Breaking the Abortion Deadlock: From Choice to Consent*. New York: Oxford University Press.

McEwen, Angie Godwin. 1999. "So, You're Having Another Woman's Baby: Economics and Exploitation in Gestational Surrogacy." *Vanderbilt Journal of Transnational Law* 32, no. 1 (January): 271–95.

McFarlane, Deborah R., and Kenneth J. Meier. 2001. *The Politics of Fertility Control: Family Planning and Abortion Policies in the American States*. New York: Chatham House.

McGee, Glenn. 1997. *The Perfect Baby: A Pragmatic Approach to Genetics*. Lanham, Md.: Rowman and Littlefield.

McGinnis, Doretta Massardo. 1990. "Prosecution of Mothers of Drug-Exposed Babies: Constitutional and Criminal Theory." *University of Pennsylvania Law Review* 139, no. 2 (December): 505–39.

McGlen, Nancy E., and Karen O'Connor. 1995. *Women, Politics, and American Society*. New York: Prentice Hall.

McGoodwin, Wendy. 1996. "Genie out of the Bottle: Genetic Testing and the Discrimination It's Creating." *Washington Post,* May 5.

McKay, Linda Back. 1998. *Shadow Mothers: Stories of Adoption and Reunion.* St. Cloud, Minn.: North Star.

McLeod, Lisa S. 1999. "Nature, Property, and the Ethic of Care: Anthropocentric and Ecofeminist Approaches to Environmental and Property Rights Protection." Ph.D. diss., University of South Carolina at Columbia.

Mead, Rebecca. 1999. "Annals of Reproduction: Eggs for Sale, Wanted: Highly Accomplished Young Women Willing to Undergo Risky, Painful Medical Procedure for Very Large Sums." *New Yorker* 75, no. 22 (August 9): 56–65.

Mehlman, Maxwell J., and Jeffrey R. Botkin. 1998. *Access to the Genome: The Challenge to Equality.* Washington, D.C.: Georgetown University Press.

Merchant, Carolyn. 1980. *The Death of Nature: Women, Ecology and the Scientific Revolution.* San Francisco: Harper and Row.

Merrick, J. C., and R. H. Blank, eds. 1993. *The Politics of Pregnancy: Policy Dilemmas in the Maternal-Fetal Relationship.* Binghamton, N.Y.: Haworth.

Miglani, Sanjeev. 2001. "India's Missing Girls—High-Tech Victims of Bias." Reuters News Service, Internet, June 16.

Minnich, Elizabeth Kamarck. 1990. *Transforming Knowledge.* Philadelphia: Temple University Press.

Minow, Martha. 1987. "When Difference Has Its Home: Group Homes for the Mentally Retarded, Equal Protection and the Legal Treatment of Difference." *Harvard Civil Rights–Civil Liberties Law Review* 22, no. 1 (Winter): 111–89.

———. 1999. "Child Endangerment, Parental Sacrifice: A Reading of the Binding of Isaac." In *Mother Troubles: Rethinking Contemporary Maternal Dilemmas,* edited by Julia E. Haningberg and Sara Ruddick, 50–58. Boston: Beacon.

Modell, Judith S. 1998. "Rights to the Children: Foster Care and Social Reproduction in Hawai'i." In *Reproducing Reproduction: Kinship, Power, and Technological Innovations,* edited by Sarah Franklin and Heléna Ragoné, 156–72. Philadelphia: University of Pennsylvania Press.

———. 1999. "Freely Given: Open Adoption and the Rhetoric of the Gift." In *Transformative Motherhood: On Giving and Getting in a Consumer Culture,* edited by Linda L. Layne, 29–64. New York: New York University Press.

Mohamad, Mahathir. 1998. "Statement to the U.N. Conference on Environment and Development." In *Green Planet Blues: Environmental Politics from Stockholm to Kyoto,* 2d ed., edited by Ken Conca and Geoffrey D. Dabelko, 325–27. Boulder, Colo.: Westview.

Mohr, James C. 1978. *Abortion in America: The Origins and Evolution of National Policy, 1800–1900.* New York: Oxford University Press.

Mohr, Richard D. 1995. "Anti-Gay Stereotypes." In *Race, Class, and Gender in the United States: An Integrated Study*, 3d ed., edited by Paula Rothenberg, 402–7. New York: St. Martin's.

Monaghan, Peter. 1999. "Making Babies with New Technologies: New Books Examine the Evolving Political Status of the Fetus." *Chronicle of Higher Education* 45, no. 47 (July 30): 10–11.

Moore, Toby. 1992. "'Rescue' Anti-Abortion Demonstration Might Be Held over Weekend." *Greenville News*, March 18.

Morgall, Janine Marie. 1993. *Technology Assessment: A Feminist Perspective*. Philadelphia: Temple University Press.

Morgan, Lynn M. 1998. "Ambiguities Lost: Fashioning the Fetus into a Child in Ecuador and the United States." In *Small Wars: The Cultural Politics of Childhood*, edited by Nancy Scheper-Hughes and Carolyn Sargent, 58–74. Berkeley: University of California Press.

Morsy, Soheir A. 1995. "Deadly Reproduction among Egyptian Women: Maternal Mortality and the Medicalization of Population Control." In *Conceiving the New World Order: The Global Politics of Reproduction*, edited by Faye D. Ginsburg and Rayna Rapp, 162–76. Berkeley: University of California Press.

Moses, Claire Goldberg, and Heidi Hartmann, eds. 1995. *U.S. Women in Struggle: A Feminist Studies Anthology*. Urbana: University of Illinois Press.

Moskowitz, Ellen H., and Bruce Jennings, eds. 1996. *Coerced Contraception? Moral and Policy Challenges of Long-Acting Birth Control*. Washington, D.C.: Georgetown University Press.

"Ms. Whitner Denied Parole." 1999. *South Carolina Advocates for Pregnant Women* 1, no. 2 (June): 1.

Mueller, Carol. 1994. "Conflict Networks and the Origins of Women's Liberation." In *New Social Movements: From Ideology to Identity*, edited by Enrique Larana, Hank Johnston, and Joseph R. Gusfield, 234–63. Philadelphia: Temple University Press.

Mullings, Leith. 1995. "Households Headed by Women: The Politics of Race, Class, and Gender." In *Conceiving the New World Order: The Global Politics of Reproduction*, edited by Faye D. Ginsburg and Rayna Rapp, 122–39. Berkeley: University of California Press.

Muncy, Robyn. 1991. *Creating a Female Dominion in American Reform, 1890–1935*. New York: Oxford University Press.

Murphy, Sheigla, and Marsha Rosenbaum. 1999. *Pregnant Women on Drugs: Combating Stereotypes and Stigma*. New Brunswick, N.J.: Rutgers University Press.

Murphy, Timothy F. 1994. "The Genome Project and the Meaning of Difference." In *Justice and the Human Genome Project*, edited by Timothy F. Murphy and Marc A. Lappe, 1–13. Berkeley: University of California Press.

———. 1997. *Gay Science: The Ethics of Sexual Orientation Research*. New York: Columbia University Press.

National Adoption Information Clearinghouse. 2001. "Cost of Adopting." <http://www.calib.com/naic/pubs>. Accessed June 4.

National Advisory Council for Human Genome Research. 1994. "Commentary: Statement on Use of DNA Testing for Presymptomatic Identification of Cancer Risk." *JAMA: The Journal of the American Medical Association* 271, no. 10 (March 9): 785.

National Association of Alcoholism and Drug Abuse Counselors et al. 1998. "Amicus Brief: *Cornelia Whitner vs. the State of South Carolina.*" *Hastings Women's Law Journal* 9, no. 2: 139–60.

National Bioethics Advisory Commission. 1998. "The Science and Application of Cloning." In *Clones and Clones: Facts and Fantasies about Human Cloning,* edited by Martha C. Nussbaum and Cass R. Sunstein, 29–40. New York: W. W. Norton.

National Breast Cancer Coalition. 1995. "Presymptomatic Genetic Testing for Heritable Breast Cancer Risk." Two-page memo, September.

"National Institutes of Health Workshop Statement, Reproductive Genetic Testing: Impact on Women." 1994. In *Women and Prenatal Testing: Facing the Challenges of Genetic Technology,* edited by Karen H. Rothenberg and Elizabeth J. Thomson, 295–300. Columbus: Ohio State University Press.

National Organization for Women v. Scheidler, 510 U.S. 249 (1994).

National Society of Genetic Counselors. 1991. "Code of Ethics." One-page memo, August.

Nedelsky, Jennifer. 1999. "Dilemmas of Passion, Privilege, and Isolation: Reflections on Mothering in a White, Middle-Class Nuclear Family." In *Mother Troubles: Rethinking Contemporary Maternal Dilemmas,* edited by Julia E. Haningberg and Sara Ruddick, 304–34. Boston: Beacon.

Nelkin, Dorothy. 1992. "The Social Power of Genetic Information." In *The Code of Codes: Scientific and Social Issues in the Human Genome Project,* edited by Daniel J. Kevles and Leroy Hood, 177–90. Cambridge, Mass.: Harvard University Press.

———. 1995. "Biology Is Not Destiny." *New York Times,* September 28.

Nelkin, Dorothy, and Michael S. Brown. 1984. *Workers at Risk: Voices from the Workplace.* Chicago: University of Chicago Press.

Nelkin, Dorothy, and M. Susan Lindee. 1995. "Elvis' DNA: The Gene as a Cultural Icon." *Humanist* 55 (May/June): 10–19.

Nelson, Barbara J., and Najma Chowdhury, eds. 1994. *Women and Politics Worldwide.* New Haven, Conn.: Yale University Press.

"New Study Reveals More Benefits of Folic Acid." 1995. *Amherst Bulletin,* July 28, 17.

Nichols, Eve K. 1988. *Human Gene Therapy: The Facts, the Hopes, the Ethical Concerns Surrounding a Revolutionary Treatment of Inherited Disease.* Cambridge, Mass.: Harvard University Press.

NIH-DOE Joint Working Group on the Ethical, Legal, and Social Implications of Human Genome Research. 1995. "Task Force on Genetic Testing." Factsheet from the National Center for Human Genome Research, September.

Nsiah-Jefferson, Laurie. 1989. "Reproductive Laws, Women of Color, and

Low-Income Women." In *Reproductive Laws for the 1990s,* edited by Sherrill Cohen and Nadine Taub, 23–67. Clifton, N.J.: Humana.

———. 1994. "Reproductive Genetic Services for Low-Income Women and Women of Color: Access and Sociocultural Issues." In *Women and Prenatal Testing: Facing the Challenges of Genetic Technology,* edited by Karen H. Rothenberg and Elizabeth J. Thomson, 234–59. Columbus: Ohio State University Press.

Nsiah-Jefferson, Laurie, and Elaine J. Hall. 1989. "Reproductive Technology: Perspectives and Implications for Low-Income Women and Women of Color." In *Healing Technology: Feminist Perspectives,* edited by Kathryn Strother Ratcliff, 93–117. Ann Arbor: University of Michigan Press.

Oakley, Ann. 1984. *The Captured Womb: A History of the Medical Care of Pregnant Women.* Oxford: Basil Blackwell.

———. 1987. "From Walking Wombs to Test-Tube Babies." In *Reproductive Technologies: Gender, Motherhood, and Medicine,* edited by Michelle Stanworth, 36–56. Minneapolis: University of Minnesota Press.

Oaks, Laury. 1998. "Irishness, Eurocitizens, and Reproductive Rights." In *Reproducing Reproduction: Kinship, Power, and Technological Innovations,* edited by Sarah Franklin and Heléna Ragoné, 132–55. Philadelphia: University of Pennsylvania Press.

———. 2000. "Smoke-Filled Wombs and Fragile Fetuses: The Social Politics of Fetal Representation." *Signs: Journal of Women in Culture and Society* 26, no. 1 (Autumn): 63–108.

O'Brien, Mary. 1981. *The Politics of Reproduction.* Boston: Routledge and Kegan Paul.

O'Connor, Karen. 1996. *No Neutral Ground? Abortion Politics in an Age of Absolutes.* Boulder, Colo.: Westview.

———. 1998. "Lobbying the Justices or Lobbying for Justice?" In *The Interest Group Connection: Electioneering, Lobbying, and Policymaking in Washington,* edited by Paul S. Herrnson, Ronald G. Shaiko, and Clyde Wilcox, 267–88. Chatham, N.J.: Chatham House.

O'Neil, John D., and Patricia Leyland Kaufert. 1995. "*Irniktakpunga!* Sex Determination and the Inuit Struggle for Birthing Rights in Northern Canada." In *Conceiving the New World Order: The Global Politics of Reproduction,* edited by Faye D. Ginsburg and Rayna Rapp, 59–74. Berkeley: University of California Press.

"Online Auction of Model's Eggs Labeled 'Unethical.'" 1999. *The State* (Columbia, S.C.), October 24.

Osakue, Grace, and Adriane Martin-Hilber. 1998. "Women's Sexuality and Fertility in Nigeria: Breaking the Culture of Silence." In *Negotiating Reproductive Rights: Women's Perspectives across Countries and Cultures,* edited by Rosalind P. Petchesky and Karen Judd, 180–216. London: Zed Books.

Overall, Christine. 1987. "Feminism: A Definition." In *Ethics and Human Reproduction: A Feminist Analysis,* edited by Christine Overall, 2–3. Boston: Allen and Unwin.

Paltrow, Lynn M. 1999a. "Pregnant Drug Users, Fetal Persons, and the Threat to *Roe v. Wade*," *Albany Law Review* 62, no. 3 (Spring): 999–1050.

———. 1999b. "Punishment and Prejudice: Judging Drug-Using Pregnant Women." In *Mother Troubles: Rethinking Contemporary Maternal Dilemmas*, edited by Julia E. Haningberg and Sara Ruddick, 59–80. Boston: Beacon.

Pannasch, Jeanann. 1999. "Applause: Light My Fire." *Ms.* 9, no. 3 (April/May): 113.

Parfit, Michael. 1998. "Human Migration." *National Geographic* 195, no. 4 (October): 6–35.

Pateman, Carole. 1988. *The Sexual Contract.* Stanford, Calif.: Stanford University Press.

Pearce, Tola Olu. 1995. "Women's Reproductive Practices and Biomedicine: Cultural Conflicts and Transformations in Nigeria." In *Conceiving the New World Order: The Global Politics of Reproduction*, edited by Faye D. Ginsburg and Rayna Rapp, 195–208. Berkeley: University of California Press.

People with Disabilities Caucus. "The People with Disabilities Caucus Presents Recommendations for Genetic Professionals." 1992. *Genetic Resource* 6, no. 2: 84–85.

Pertman, Adam. 2001. "Preserving Access to Abortion." *Boston Globe*, June 17.

Petchesky, Rosalind Pollack. 1984. *Abortion and Woman's Choice: The State, Sexuality, and Reproductive Freedom.* New York: Longman, 1984.

———. 1987. "Foetal Images: The Power of Visual Culture in the Politics of Reproduction." In *Reproductive Technologies: Gender, Motherhood, and Medicine*, edited by Michelle Stanworth, 57–80. Minneapolis: University of Minnesota Press.

———. 1990. *Abortion and Woman's Choice: The State, Sexuality, and Reproductive Freedom.* Rev. ed. Boston: Northeastern University Press.

———. 1995. "The Body as Property: A Feminist Re-vision." In *Conceiving the New World Order: The Global Politics of Reproduction*, edited by Faye D. Ginsburg and Rayna Rapp, 387–406. Berkeley: University of California Press.

———. 1998a. "Cross-Country Comparisons and Political Visions." In *Negotiating Reproductive Rights: Women's Perspectives across Countries and Cultures*, edited by Rosalind P. Petchesky and Karen Judd, 295–323. London: Zed Books.

———. 1998b. Introduction to *Negotiating Reproductive Rights: Women's Perspectives across Countries and Cultures*, edited by Rosalind P. Petchesky and Karen Judd, 1–30. London: Zed Books.

Peters, June A. 1987. "Feminist Theology and Genetic Counseling: Out of the Closet and into the Clinic." In *Strategies in Genetic Counseling: Religious, Cultural and Ethnic Influences on the Counseling Process*, edited by Barbara Biesecker, Patricia A. Magyari, and Natalie W. Paul, 271–75. White Plains, N.Y.: March of Dimes Birth Defects Foundation.

————. 1993. "Commentary." *Hastings Center Report,* September–October, 30.

Peters, Ted. 1998. "Genes, Theology, and Social Ethics: Are We Playing God?" In *Genetics: Issues of Social Justice,* edited by Ted Peters, 1–45. Cleveland, Ohio: Pilgrim.

Phelan, Shane. 1994. *Getting Specific: Postmodern Lesbian Politics.* Minneapolis: University of Minnesota Press.

Picone, Mary. 1998. "Infanticide, the Spirits of Aborted Fetuses, and the Making of Motherhood in Japan." In *Small Wars: The Cultural Politics of Childhood,* edited by Nancy Scheper-Hughes and Carolyn Sargent, 37–57. Berkeley: University of California Press.

Pigg, Stacy Leigh. 1997. "Authority in Translation: Finding, Knowing, Naming, and Training 'Traditional Birth Attendants' in Nepal." In *Childbirth and Authoritative Knowledge: Cross-Cultural Perspectives,* edited by Robbie E. Davis-Floyd and Carolyn F. Sargent, 233–62. Berkeley: University of California Press.

Pinto-Correia, Clara. 1997. *The Ovary of Eve: Egg and Sperm and Preformation.* Chicago: University of Chicago Press.

Piven, Frances Fox, and Richard A. Cloward. 1977. *Poor People's Movements: Why They Succeed, How They Fail.* New York: Pantheon Books.

————. 1992. "Normalizing Collective Protest." In *Frontiers in Social Movement Theory,* edited by Aldon D. Morris and Carol McClurg Muelle, 301–25. New Haven, Conn.: Yale University Press.

————. 1996. "Welfare Reform and the New Class War." In *Myths about the Powerless: Contesting Social Inequalities,* edited by M. Brinton Lykes, Ali Barauzzi, Ransey Liem, and Michael Morris, 72–86. Philadelphia: Temple University Press.

Planned Parenthood of Central South Carolina and Planned Parenthood of the Low Country. 1996. *State of the State* (newsletter), February–March.

Planned Parenthood of Southeastern Pennsylvania v. Casey, 505 U.S. 833 (1992).

Pollitt, Katha. 1987. "Contracts and Apple Pie: The Strange Case of Baby M." *Nation* 244 (May 23): 667, 682–88.

————. 1995. "Fair Is Fair: What about Unwed Fathers?" *Nation* 260 (January 30): 120.

————. 1997. "Secrets and Lies." *Nation* 264 (March 31): 9.

————. 1999. "Anti-Choice, Anti-Child." *Nation* 269 (November 15): 10.

Pollock, S. 1984. "Refusing to Take Women Seriously: 'Side Effects' and the Politics of Contraception." In *Test-Tube Women: What Future for Motherhood?* edited by Rita Arditti, Renate Duelli Klein, and Shelley Minden, 138–52. London: Pandora.

Powledge, Tabitha M. 1981. "Unnatural Selection: On Choosing Children's Sex." In *The Custom-Made Child? Women-Centered Perspectives,* edited by Helen B. Holmes, Betty B. Hoskins, and Michael Gross, 193–99. Clifton, N.J.: Humana.

————. 1993. "The Genetic Fabric of Human Behavior: Do Single Genes or

Interacting Genes Determine the Patterns of Human Actions?" *Bioscience* 43, no. 6 (June): 362–67.

———. 1996. "Genetics and the Control of Crime: Experts Say Other Fields of Research May Be More Useful in Dealing with Certain Social Problems." *Bioscience* 46, no. 1 (January): 7–10.

Press, Andrea L., and Elizabeth R. Cole. 1999. *Speaking of Abortion: Television and Authority in the Lives of Women.* Chicago: University of Chicago Press.

Press, Nancy Anne, and Carole H. Browner. 1994. "Collective Silences, Collective Fictions: How Prenatal Diagnostic Testing Became Part of Routine Prenatal Care." In *Women and Prenatal Testing: Facing the Challenges of Genetic Technology,* edited by Karen H. Rothenberg and Elizabeth J. Thomson, 201–18. Columbus: Ohio State University Press.

Press, Nancy, Carole H. Browner, Diem Tran, Christine Morton, and Barbara Le Master. 1998. "Provisional Normalcy and 'Perfect Babies': Pregnant Women's Attitudes toward Disability in the Context of Prenatal Testing." In *Reproducing Reproduction: Kinship, Power, and Technological Innovations,* edited by Sarah Franklin and Heléna Ragoné, 46–65. Philadelphia: University of Pennsylvania Press.

Preston, Richard. 2000. "The Genome Warrior: Craig Venter Has Grabbed the Lead in the Quest for Biology's Holy Grail." *New Yorker* 76, no. 15 (June 12): 66–83.

Pryse, Marjorie. 2000. "Trans/Feminist Methodology: Bridges to Interdisciplinary Thinking." *NWSA Journal* 12, no. 2 (Summer): 105–18.

Quindlen, Anna. 2001. "Playing God on No Sleep." *Newsweek* 138, no. 1 (July 2): 64.

Radin, Margaret J. 1987. "Market-Inalienability." *Harvard Law Review* 100, no. 8 (June): 1849–1937.

———. 1990. "The Pragmatist and the Feminist." *Southern California Law Review* 63, no. 6 (September): 1699–1726.

Ragoné, Heléna. 1996. "Chasing the Blood Tie: Surrogate Mothers, Adoptive Mothers and Fathers." *American Ethnologist* 23, no. 2 (May): 352–65.

———. 1998. "Incontestable Motivations." In *Reproducing Reproduction: Kinship, Power, and Technological Innovations,* edited by Sarah Franklin and Heléna Ragoné, 118–31. Philadelphia: University of Pennsylvania Press.

———. 1999. "The Gift of Life: Surrogate Motherhood, Gamete Donation, and Constructions of Altruism." In *Transformative Motherhood: On Giving and Getting in a Consumer Culture,* edited by Linda L. Layne, 65–88. New York: New York University Press.

———. 2000. "Of Likeness and Difference: How Race Is Being Transfigured by Gestational Surrogacy." In *Ideologies and Technologies of Motherhood: Race, Class, Sexuality, Nationalism,* edited by Heléna Ragoné and France Winddance Twine, 56–75. New York: Routledge.

Ragoné, Heléna, and France Winddance Twine. 2000. "Introduction: Motherhood on the Fault Lines." In *Ideologies and Technologies of Mother-*

hood: Race, Class, Sexuality, Nationalism, edited by Heléna Ragoné and France Winddance Twine, 1–8. New York: Routledge.

Raj, Rita, Chee Heng Leng, and Rashidah Shuib. 1998. "Between Modernization and Patriarchal Revivalism: Reproductive Negotiations among Women in Peninsular Malaysia." In *Negotiating Reproductive Rights: Women's Perspectives across Countries and Cultures*, edited by Rosalind P. Petchesky and Karen Judd, 108–44. London: Zed Books.

Rapp, Rayna. 1984. "XYLO: A True Story." In *Test-Tube Women: What Future for Motherhood?* edited by Rita Arditti, Renate Duelli Klein, and Shelley Minden, 313–28. London: Pandora.

———. 1994a. "The Power of 'Positive' Diagnosis: Medical and Maternal Discourses on Amniocentesis." In *Representations of Motherhood*, edited by Donna Bassin, Margaret Honey, and Meryle Mahrer Kaplan, 204–19. New Haven, Conn.: Yale University Press.

———. 1994b. "Women's Responses to Prenatal Diagnosis: A Sociocultural Perspective on Diversity." In *Women and Prenatal Testing: Facing the Challenges of Genetic Technology*, edited by Karen H. Rothenberg and Elizabeth J. Thomson, 219–33. Columbus: Ohio State University Press.

———. 1999. Foreword to *Transformative Motherhood: On Giving and Getting in a Consumer Culture*, edited by Linda L. Layne, xi–xix. New York: New York University Press.

———. 2000. Foreword to *Ideologies and Technologies of Motherhood: Race, Class, Sexuality, Nationalism*, edited by Heléna Ragoné and France Winddance Twine, xii–xvi. New York: Routledge.

Raymond, Janice. 1984. "Feminist Ethics, Ecology, and Vision." In *Test-Tube Women: What Future for Motherhood?* edited by Rita Arditti, Renate Duelli Klein, and Shelley Minden, 427–37. London: Pandora.

———. 1987. Preface to *Man-Made Women: How the New Reproductive Technologies Affect Women*, edited by Gena Corea, Jalna Hanmer, Betty Hoskins, Janice Raymond, Renate Duelli Klein, Helen Bequaert Holmes, Madhu Kishwar, Robyn Rowland, and Roberta Steinbacher, 9–13. Bloomington: Indiana University Press.

———. 1993. *Women as Wombs: Reproductive Technologies and the Battle over Women's Freedom.* New York: HarperCollins.

Reagan, Leslie J. 1997. *When Abortion Was a Crime: Women, Medicine, and Law in the United States, 1867–1973.* Berkeley: University of California Press.

———. 2000. "Crossing the Border for Abortions: California Activists, Mexican Clinics, and the Creation of a Feminist Health Agency in the 1960s." *Feminist Studies* 26, no. 2 (Summer): 323–47.

Reid, T. R. 1998. "Feeding the Planet." *National Geographic* 195, no. 4 (October): 56–74.

"Results from First Human Gene Therapy Clinical Trial." 1995. In *Progress*, four-page memo from the National Center for Human Genome Research, National Institutes of Health, October 19.

Rhode, Deborah L. 1993. "Adolescent Pregnancy and Public Policy." In *The

Politics of Pregnancy: Adolescent Sexuality and Public Policy, edited by Annette Lawson and Deborah L. Rhode, 301–35. New Haven, Conn.: Yale University Press.

Rhode, Deborah L., and Annette Lawson. 1993. Introduction to *The Politics of Pregnancy: Adolescent Sexuality and Public Policy,* edited by Annette Lawson and Deborah L. Rhode, 1–19. New Haven, Conn.: Yale University Press.

Rich, Adrienne. 1976. *Of Women Born: Motherhood as Experience and Institution.* New York: W. W. Norton.

Richard, P. B. 1989. "Fetal Research Policy." In *Biomedical Technology and Public Policy,* edited by Robert H. Blank, 57–72. Westport, Conn.: Greenwood.

Ridley, Matt. 1999. *Genome: The Autobiography of a Species in Twenty-Three Chapters.* New York: HarperCollins.

Rifkin, Jeremy. 1998. *The Biotech Century: Harnessing the Gene and Remaking the World.* New York: Putnam.

Risen, James, and Judy L. Thomas. 1998. *Wrath of Angels: The American Abortion War.* New York: Basic Books.

Robbins, Jim. 2001. "Where Adoption Is Suddenly an Open Book." *New York Times,* May 7.

Roberts, Dorothy E. 1991. "Punishing Drug Addicts Who Have Babies: Women of Color, Equality, and the Right of Privacy." *Harvard Law Review* 104, no. 7 (May): 1419–82.

———. 1995. "Racism and Patriarchy in the Meaning of Motherhood." In *Mothers in Law: Feminist Theory and the Legal Regulation of Motherhood,* edited by Martha Albertson Fineman and Isabel Karpin, 224–49. New York: Columbia University Press.

———. 1998. "Punishing Drug Addicts Who Have Babies: Women of Color, Equality, and the Right of Privacy." In *Abortion Wars: A Half Century of Struggle, 1950–2000,* edited by Rickie Solinger, 124–55. Berkeley: University of California Press.

———. 1999. "Mothers Who Fail to Protect Their Children: Accounting for Private and Public Responsibility." In *Mother Troubles: Rethinking Contemporary Maternal Dilemmas,* edited by Julia E. Haningberg and Sara Ruddick, 31–49. Boston: Beacon.

Roberts, Elizabeth F. S. 1998. "Examining Surrogacy Discourses: Between Feminine Power and Exploitation." In *Small Wars: The Cultural Politics of Childhood,* edited by Nancy Scheper-Hughes and Carolyn Sargent, 93–110. Berkeley: University of California Press.

Robertson, John A. 1983. "Procreative Liberty and the Control of Conception, Pregnancy, and Childbirth." *Virginia Law Review* 69, no. 3 (April): 405–64.

———. 1986. "Embryos, Families, and Procreative Liberty: The Legal Structure of the New Reproduction." *Southern California Law Review* 59, no. 5 (July): 939–1041.

Robey, Renate. 1988. "Shots Fired at Boulder Abortion Clinic." *Denver Post,* February 6.

Rochon, Thomas R. 1998. *Culture Moves: Ideas, Activism and Changing Values*. Princeton, N.J.: Princeton University Press.

Roe v. Wade, 410 U.S. 113, 93 S. Ct. 705, 35 L.Ed. 2d 147 (1973).

Roggenkamp, Viola. 1984. "Abortion of a Special Kind: Male Sex Selection in India." In *Test-Tube Women: What Future for Motherhood?* edited by Rita Arditti, Renate Duelli Klein, and Shelley Minden, 266–77. London: Pandora.

Roiphe, A. 1989. "What's a Mother to Do?" *Ms.* 17, no. 10 (May): 26–27.

"Romania Suspends International Adoptions." 2001. *New York Times*, June 22.

Rose, Hilary. 1994. *Love, Power and Knowledge: Towards a Feminist Transformation of the Sciences*. Bloomington: Indiana University Press.

Rosenberg, Gerald N. 1991. *The Hollow Hope: Can Courts Bring about Social Change?* Chicago: University of Chicago Press.

Ross, Loretta J. 1998. "African-American Women and Abortion." In *Abortion Wars: A Half Century of Struggle, 1950–2000*, edited by Rickie Solinger, 161–207. Berkeley: University of California Press.

Rosser, Sue. 1986. *Teaching Science and Health from a Feminist Perspective*. New York: Pergamon.

———. ed. 1989. "Feminism and Science: In Memory of Ruth Bleier." *Women's Studies International Forum* 12, special issue.

Rothenberg, Karen H., and Elizabeth J. Thomson. 1994. "Introduction: Women and Prenatal Testing: An Introduction to the Issues." In *Women and Prenatal Testing: Facing the Challenges of Genetic Technology*, edited by Karen H. Rothenberg and Elizabeth J. Thomson, 1–4. Columbus: Ohio State University Press.

Rothman, Barbara Katz. 1982. *In Labour: Women and Power in the Birthplace*. New York: W. W. Norton.

———. 1984. "The Meanings of Choice in Reproductive Technology." In *Man-Made Women: How the New Reproductive Technologies Affect Women*, edited by Gena Corea, Jalna Hanmer, Betty Hoskins, Janice Raymond, Renate Duelli Klein, Helen Bequaert Holmes, Madhu Kishwar, Robyn Rowland, and Roberta Steinbacher, 23–33. Bloomington: Indiana University Press.

———. 1986. *The Tentative Pregnancy: Prenatal Diagnosis and the Future of Motherhood*. New York: Viking.

———. 1989. *Recreating Motherhood: Ideology and Technology in a Patriarchal Society*. New York: W. W. Norton.

———. 1994. "The Tentative Pregnancy: Then and Now." In *Women and Prenatal Testing: Facing the Challenges of Genetic Technology*, edited by Karen H. Rothenberg and Elizabeth J. Thomson, 260–70. Columbus: Ohio State University Press.

———. 1995. "Of Maps and Imaginations: Sociology Confronts the Genome." *Social Problems* 42, no. 1 (February): 1–10.

———. 1998. *Genetic Maps and Human Imaginations: The Limits of Science in Understanding Who We Are*. New York: W. W. Norton.

Rothman, Sheila M. 1978. *Woman's Proper Place: A History of Changing Ideals and Practices, 1870 to the Present.* New York: Basic Books.

Rothschild, Joan. 1983. "Introduction: Why Machina Ex Dea?" In *Machina Ex Dea: Feminist Perspectives on Technology,* edited by Joan Rothschild, ix–xxix. New York: Pergamon.

Rowland, Robyn. 1987. "Technology and Motherhood: Reproductive Choice Reconsidered." *Signs: Journal of Women in Culture and Society* 12, no. 3 (Spring): 512–28.

———. 1992. *Living Laboratories: Women and Reproductive Technologies.* Bloomington: University of Indiana Press.

Roy, Ina. 1999. "Defending Abortion: Should We Treat the Body as Property?" *Public Affairs Quarterly* 13, no. 4 (October): 309–29.

Ruddick, Sara. 1980. "Maternal Thinking." *Feminist Studies* 6, no. 1: 432–67.

———. 1994. "Thinking Mothers/Conceiving Birth." In *Representations of Motherhood,* edited by Donna Bassin, Margaret Honey, and Meryle Mahrer Kaplan, 29–45. New Haven, Conn.: Yale University Press.

Russell, Andrew, and Mary S. Thompson. 2000. "Introduction: Contraception across Cultures." In *Contraception across Cultures: Technologies, Choices, Constraints,* edited by Andrew Russell, Elisa Sobo, and Mary Thompson, 3–25. Oxford: Berg.

Rust v. Sullivan, 500 U.S. 173 (1991).

Salecl, Renata. 1997. "The Postsocialist Moral Majority." In *Transitions, Environments, Translations: Feminisms in International Politics,* edited by Joan W. Scott, Cora Kaplan, and Debra Keates, 79–97. New York: Routledge.

Saletan, William. 1998. "Electoral Politics and Abortion: Narrowing the Message." In *Abortion Wars: A Half Century of Struggle, 1950–2000,* edited by Rickie Solinger, 111–23. Berkeley: University of California Press.

Saltzman, Russell E. 1998. "A Fear of Abandonment: Adoption versus Abortion." *First Things: A Monthly Journal of Religion and Public Life,* no. 80 (February): 16–19.

Sandel, Michael J. 1997. "The Baby Bazaar: Surrogate Motherhood, the Hard Questions." *New Republic* 217, no. 16 (October 20): 25.

Sanger, Carol. 1996. "Separating from Children." *Columbia Law Review* 96, no. 2 (March): 375–517.

Sargent, Carolyn F., and Grace Bascope. 1997. "Ways of Knowing about Birth in Three Cultures." In *Childbirth and Authoritative Knowledge: Cross-Cultural Perspectives,* edited by Robbie E. Davis-Floyd and Carolyn F. Sargent, 183–208. Berkeley: University of California Press.

Saxton, Marsha. 1984. "Born and Unborn: The Implications of Reproductive Technologies for People with Disabilities." In *Test-Tube Women: What Future for Motherhood?* edited by Rita Arditti, Renate Duelli Klein, and Shelley Minden, 298–312. London: Pandora.

———. 1998. "Disability Rights and Selective Abortion." In *Abortion Wars: A Half Century of Struggle, 1950–2000,* edited by Rickie Solinger, 374–93. Berkeley: University of California Press.

Scheper-Hughes, Nancy, and Carolyn Sargent. 1998. Introduction to *Small Wars: The Cultural Politics of Childhood*, edited by Nancy Scheper-Hughes and Carolyn Sargent, 1–33. Berkeley: University of California Press.

Schlozman, Kay Lehman, Nancy Burns, and Sidney Verba. 1999. "'What Happened at Work Today?' A Multistage Model of Gender, Employment, and Political Participation." *Journal of Politics* 61, no. 1 (February): 29–53.

Schmidt, Karen F. 1992. "The Dark Legacy of Fatherhood: It's Not Just Prospective Mothers Whose Habits Can Damage the Health of Their Children." *U.S. News and World Report* 113, no. 23 (December 14): 47–48.

Schneider, Anne, and Helen Ingram. 1993. "The Social Construction of Target Populations: Implications for Politics and Policy." *American Political cal Science Review* 87, no. 2 (June): 334–47.

———. 1995. "Response to Robert C. Liberman." *American Political Science Review* 89, no. 2 (June): 441–46.

Schneider, Mark, and Paul Teske. 1993. "The Antigrowth Entrepreneur: Challenging the 'Equilibrium' of the Growth Machine." *Journal of Politics* 55, no. 3 (August): 720–36.

Schneider, Peter, and Jane Schneider. 1995. "Coitus Interruptus and Family Respectability in Catholic Europe: A Sicilian Case Study." In *Conceiving the New World Order: The Global Politics of Reproduction*, edited by Faye D. Ginsburg and Rayna Rapp, 177–94. Berkeley: University of California Press.

Schoen, Johanna. 2000. "Reconceiving Abortion: Medical Practice, Women's Access, and Feminist Politics before and after *Roe v. Wade*." *Feminist Studies* 26, no. 2 (Summer): 349–76.

Schroedel, Jean Reith. 2000. *Is the Fetus a Person? A Comparison of Policies across the Fifty States*. Ithaca, N.Y.: Cornell University Press.

Schroedel, Jean Reith, Pamela Fiber, and Bruce D. Snyder. 2000. "Women's Rights and Fetal Personhood in Criminal Law." Paper presented at the Western Political Science Association Annual Meeting, San Jose, California, March 24–26.

Schwartz, Adria. 1994. "Taking the Nature out of Mother." In *Representations of Motherhood*, edited by Donna Bassin, Margaret Honey, and Meryle Mahrer Kaplan, 240–55. New Haven, Conn.: Yale University Press.

Scoppe, Cindi Ross. 1992. "Operation Rescue Plans S.C. Blockades." *The State* (Columbia, S.C.), February 16.

———. 1996. "Abortion Rules Face Rewrite: Opponents Don't Want DHEC to Get Medical Records Access." *The State* (Columbia, S.C.), March 22.

———. 1997a. "House Rejects 'Partial-Birth' Abortion: Ban Procedure in S.C., Lawmakers Say." *The State* (Columbia, S.C.), February 28.

———. 1997b. "'Partial-Birth' Ban Passes in Senate: S.C. Sixth in Outlawing Abortion Procedure." *The State* (Columbia, S.C.), March 14.

Segers, Mary C. 1995. "The Pro-Choice Movement Post-*Casey*: Preserving Access." In *Abortion Politics in American States*, edited by Mary C. Segers and Timothy A. Byrnes, 225–45. Armonk, N.Y.: M. E. Sharpe.

Segers, Mary C., and Timothy A. Byrnes. 1995. "Introduction: Abortion Politics in American States." In *Abortion Politics in American States*, edited by Mary C. Segers and Timothy A. Byrnes, 1–15. Armonk, N.Y.: M. E. Sharpe.

Sen, Gita. 1998. "Women, Poverty, and Population: Issues for the Concerned Environmentalist." In *Green Planet Blues: Environmental Politics from Stockholm to Kyoto*, 2d ed., edited by Ken Conca and Geoffrey D. Dabelko, 328–36. Boulder, Colo.: Westview.

Sesia, Paola M. 1997. "'Women Come Here on Their Own When They Need To': Prenatal Care, Authoritative Knowledge, and Maternal Health in Oaxaca." In *Childbirth and Authoritative Knowledge: Cross-Cultural Perspectives*, edited by Robbie E. Davis-Floyd and Carolyn F. Sargent, 397–420. Berkeley: University of California Press.

Sevenhuijsen, Selma, and Petra de Vries. 1984. "The Women's Movement and Motherhood." In *A Creative Tension: Key Issues of Socialist-Feminism*, edited by Anja Meulenbelt, 9–25. Boston: South End.

Shalev, Carmel. 1989. *Birth Power: The Case for Surrogacy*. New Haven, Conn.: Yale University Press.

Shanley, Mary Lyndon. 1993. "'Surrogate Motherhood' and Women's Freedom: A Critique of Contracts for Human Reproduction." *Signs: Journal of Women in Culture and Society* 18, no. 3 (Spring): 618–39.

———. 1999. "Lesbian Families: Dilemmas in Grounding Legal Recognition of Parenthood." In *Mother Troubles: Rethinking Contemporary Maternal Dilemmas*, edited by Julia E. Haningberg and Sara Ruddick, 178–207. Boston: Beacon.

Shapiro, Thomas M. 1985. *Population Control Politics: Women, Sterilization, and Reproductive Choice*. Philadelphia: Temple University Press.

Sharp, Elaine B. 1994. "The Dynamics of Issue Expansion: Cases from Disability Rights and Fetal Research Controversy." *Journal of Politics* 56, no. 4 (November): 919–39.

———. 1996. "Culture Wars and City Politics: Local Government's Role in Social Conflict." *Urban Affairs Review* 31, no. 6 (July): 738–58.

———. 1998. "A Comparative Anatomy of Urban Social Conflict." *Political Research Quarterly* 50, no. 2 (June): 261–80.

———. 1999. *Culture Wars and Local Politics*. Lawrence: University Press of Kansas.

Sherman, R. 1988a. "'Fetal Rights' Cases Draw Little Attention." *National Law Journal* 11, no. 4 (October 3): 25.

———. 1988b. "Keeping Baby Safe from Mom." *National Law Journal* 11, no. 4 (October 3): 1, 24, 26.

Sherrill, George R., and Robert H. Stoudemire. 1950. *Municipal Government in South Carolina*. Columbia: University of South Carolina Press.

Sherwin, Susan. 1992. *No Longer Patient: Feminist Ethics and Health Care*. Philadelphia: Temple University Press.

———, ed. 1998. *The Politics of Women's Health: Exploring Agency and Autonomy*. Philadelphia: Temple University Press.

Shin, Annys. 1999. "Feds Revisit Clinic Violence." *Ms.* 9, no. 3 (April/May): 30–31.

Shoop, Julie Gannon. 1992. "States Cannot Punish Pregnant Women for 'Fetal Abuse,' Courts Say." *Trial* 28 (May): 11–14.

Shreeve, James. 1999. "Secrets of the Gene." *National Geographic* 196, no. 4 (October): 42–75.

Siegel, Reva. 1992. "Reasoning from the Body: A Historical Perspective on Abortion Regulation and Questions of Equal Protection." *Stanford Law Review* 44, no. 1–3 (January): 261–381.

Silverstein, Helena. 1999. "Road Closed: Evaluating the Judicial Bypass Provision of the Pennsylvania Abortion Control Act." *Law and Social Inquiry* 24, no. 1 (Winter): 73–96.

Simon, Rita J. 1998. *Abortion: Statutes, Policies, and Public Attitudes the World Over.* Westport, Conn.: Praeger.

Simon, Rita J., and Howard Altstein. 2000. *Adoption across Borders: Serving the Children in Transracial and Intercountry Adoptions.* Lanham, Md.: Rowman and Littlefield.

Simonds, Wendy. 1996. *Abortion at Work: Ideology and Practice in a Feminist Clinic.* New Brunswick, N.J.: Rutgers University Press.

Skocpol, Theda. 1992. *Protecting Soldiers and Mothers: The Political Origins of Social Policy in the United States.* Cambridge, Mass.: Harvard University Press.

Skocpol, Theda, M. Abend-Wein, C. Howard, and S. G. Lehmann. 1993. "Women's Associations and the Enactment of Mothers' Pensions in the United States." *American Political Science Review* 87, no. 3 (September): 686–701.

Slaughter, M. M. 1995. "The Legal Construction of 'Mother.'" In *Mothers in Law: Feminist Theory and the Legal Regulation of Motherhood,* edited by Martha Albertson Fineman and Isabel Karpin, 73–100. New York: Columbia University Press.

Sly, Karen Marie. 1982–83. "Baby-Sitting Consideration: Surrogate Mother's Right to 'Rent Her Womb' for a Fee." *Gonzaga Law Review* 18, no. 3 (Summer): 539–65.

Smith, Oran P. 1997. *The Rise of Baptist Republicanism.* New York: New York University Press.

Snow, D. A., and R. D. Benford. 1992. "Master Frames and Cycles of Protest." In *Frontiers in Social Movement Theory,* edited by Aldon D. Morris and Carol McClurg Mueller, 133–55. New Haven, Conn.: Yale University Press.

Snow, D. A., E. B. Rochford Jr., S. K. Worden, and R. D. Benford. 1986. "Frame Alignment Processes, Micromobilization, and Movement Participation." *American Sociological Review* 51, no. 4 (August): 464–81.

Solinger, Rickie. 1992. *Wake up Little Susie: Single Pregnancy and Race before Roe v. Wade.* New York: Routledge.

———. 1994. *The Abortionist: A Woman against the Law.* New York: Free Press.

————. 1998. "Pregnancy and Power before *Roe v. Wade, 1950–1970.*" In *Abortion Wars: A Half Century of Struggle, 1950–2000*, edited by Rickie Solinger, 15–32. Berkeley: University of California Press.

Solomon, Alison. 1988. "Integrating Infertility Crisis Counseling into Feminist Practice." *Reproductive and Genetic Engineering: Journal of International Feminist Analysis* 1, no. 1: 41–49.

Sorenson, James R. 1993. "Genetic Counseling: Values That Have Mattered." In *Prescribing Our Future: Ethical Challenges In Genetic Counseling*, edited by Dianne M. Bartels, Bonnie S. LeRoy, and Arthur L. Caplan, 3–14. New York: Aldine de Gruyter.

Spallone, Patricia, and Deborah Lynn Steinberg. 1987. Introduction to *Made to Order: The Myth of Reproductive and Genetic Progress*, edited by Patricia Spallone and Deborah Lynn Steinberg, 13–17. New York: Pergamon.

Spalter-Roth, Roberta, and Ronnie Schreiber. 1995. "Outsider Issues and Insider Tactics: Strategic Tensions in the Women's Policy Network during the 1980s." In *Feminist Organizations: Harvest of the New Women's Movement*, edited by Myra Marx Ferree and Patricia Yancey Martin, 105–27. Philadelphia: Temple University Press.

Sprague, Joey, and Margaret Greer. 1998. "Standpoints and the Discourse on Abortion: The Reproductive Debate." *Women and Politics* 19, no. 3: 49–80.

Stack, Carol. 1974. *All Our Kin: Strategies for Survival in a Black Community*. New York: Harper and Row.

Staggenborg, Suzanne. 1991. *The Pro-Choice Movement: Organization and Activism in the Abortion Conflict*. New York: Oxford University Press.

————. 1996. "The Survival of the Women's Movement: Turnover and Continuity in Bloomington, Indiana." *Mobilization: An International Journal* 1, no. 2 (November): 143–58.

Stanworth, Michelle, ed. 1987. *Reproductive Technologies: Gender, Motherhood, and Medicine*. Minneapolis: University of Minnesota Press.

State of South Carolina v. Brenda Kay Peppers, Supreme Court of South Carolina, Case #98-GS-30-0809. Oral arguments June 20, 2001.

Steinbacher, Roberta. 1981. "Futuristic Implications of Sex Preselection." In *The Custom-Made Child? Women-Centered Perspectives*, edited by Helen B. Holmes, Betty B. Hoskins, and Michael Gross, 187–91. Clifton, N.J.: Humana.

Steinbacher, Roberta, and Helen Bequaert Holmes. 1987. "Sex Choice: Survival and Sisterhood." In *Man-Made Women: How the New Reproductive Technologies Affect Women*, edited by Gena Corea, Jalna Hanmer, Betty Hoskins, Janice Raymond, Renate Duelli Klein, Helen Bequaert Holmes, Madhu Kishwar, Robyn Rowland, and Roberta Steinbacher, 52–63. Bloomington: Indiana University Press.

Steiner, Gilbert Y., ed. 1983. *The Abortion Dispute and the American System*. Washington, D.C.: Brookings Institution.

Stephens, Sharon. 1995. "Physical and Cultural Reproduction in a Post-Chernobyl Norwegian Sami Community." In *Conceiving the New World Order: The Global Politics of Reproduction*, edited by Faye D. Ginsburg and Rayna Rapp, 270–88. Berkeley: University of California Press.

Stetson, Dorothy McBride. 1991. *Women's Rights in the U.S.A.: Policy Debates and Gender Roles*. Pacific Grove, Calif.: Brooks/Cole.

Stewart, Abigail J., and Sharon Gold-Steinberg. 1996. "Women's Abortion Experiences as Sources of Political Mobilization." In *Myths about the Powerless: Contesting Social Inequalities*, edited by M. Brinton Lykes, Ali Banuazizi, Ramsay Liem, and Michael Morris, 275–95. Philadelphia: Temple University Press.

Stoller, Debbie. 1999. "There's Got to Be a Morning After." *Ms.* 9, no. 3 (April/May): 91–93.

Stormer, Nathan. 2000. "Prenatal Space." *Signs: Journal of Women in Culture and Society* 26, no. 1 (Autumn): 109–44.

St. Peter, C. 1989. "Feminist Discourse, Infertility, and Reproductive Technologies." *NWSA Journal* 1, no. 3 (Spring): 353–67.

Strathern, Marilyn. 1992. *Reproducing the Future: Essays on Anthropology, Kinship, and the New Reproductive Technologies*. New York: Routledge.

———. 1995. "Displacing Knowledge: Technology and the Consequences for Kinship." In *Conceiving the New World Order: The Global Politics of Reproduction*, edited by Faye D. Ginsburg and Rayna Rapp, 346–64. Berkeley: University of California Press.

Styron, William. 1979. *Sophie's Choice*. New York: Random House.

Sullivan, Randall. 2001a. "The Bastard Chronicles: Part I: Helen Hill's Crusade." *Rolling Stone*, no. 862 (February 15): 53–61, 89.

———. 2001b. "The Bastard Chronicles: Part II: The Birth Mother's Story." *Rolling Stone*, no. 863 (March 1): 41–48, 61.

"Surrogate Parenthood." 1987. *American Bar Association Journal* 73 (June 1): 38–39.

Swerdlow, Joel L. 1998. "Population." *National Geographic* 195, no. 4 (October): 2–4.

Szurek, Jane. 1997. "Resistance to Technology-Enhanced Childbirth in Tuscany: The Political Economy of Italian Birth." In *Childbirth and Authoritative Knowledge: Cross-Cultural Perspectives*, edited by Robbie E. Davis-Floyd and Carolyn F. Sargent, 287–314. Berkeley: University of California Press.

Tarrow, Sidney. 1992. "Mentalities, Political Cultures, and Collective Action Frames: Constructing Meanings through Action." In *Frontiers in Social Movement Theory*, edited by Aldon D. Morris and Carol McClurg Mueller, 174–202. New Haven, Conn.: Yale University Press.

———. 1994. *Power in Movement: Social Movements, Collective Action, and Politics*. Cambridge: Cambridge University Press.

Tatalovich, Raymond, and Bryan Daynes. 1988. *Social Regulatory Policy: Moral Controversies in American Politics*. Boulder, Colo.: Westview.

Tax, Meredith. 1998. "For the People Hear Us Singing, 'Bread and Roses! Bread and Roses!'" In *The Feminist Memoir Project: Voices from Women's Lib-*

eration, edited by Rachel Blau DuPlessis and Ann Snitow, 311–23. New York: Three Rivers.

Taylor, Janelle S. 1998. "Image of Contradiction: Obstetrical Ultrasound in American Culture." In *Reproducing Reproduction: Kinship, Power, and Technological Innovations,* edited by Sarah Franklin and Heléna Ragoné, 15–45. Philadelphia: University of Pennsylvania Press.

———. 2000. "Of Sonograms and Baby Prams: Prenatal Diagnosis, Pregnancy, and Consumption." *Feminist Studies* 26, no. 2 (Summer): 391–418.

Teich, Albert H., ed. 1990. *Technology and the Future.* 5th ed. New York: St. Martin's.

Terry, Jennifer. 1998. "'Momism' and the Making of Treasonous Homosexuals." In *"Bad" Mothers: The Politics of Blame in Twentieth-Century America,* edited by Molly Ladd-Taylor and Lauri Umansky, 169–90. New York: New York University Press.

Thom, Mary. 1999. "Hearts and Minds: Women Are Becoming More Religious, Does that Mean They Are Becoming More Conservative?" *Ms.* 9, no. 3 (April/May): 72–77.

Thomson, Elizabeth J. 1994. "Communicating Complex Genetic Information." In *Genes and Human Self-Knowledge: Historical and Philosophical Reflections on Modern Genetics,* edited by Robert F. Weir, Susan C. Lawrence, and Evan Fales, 172–77. Iowa City: University of Iowa Press.

Thornburgh v. American College of Obstetricians and Gynecologists, 476 U.S. 747 (1986).

Tobias, Sheila. 1997. *Faces of Feminism: An Activist's Reflections on the Women's Movement.* Boulder, Colo.: Westview.

Tobin, Richard J. 1989. "Environment, Population, and Development in the Third World." In *Environmental Policy in the 1990s,* edited by Norman J. Vig and Michael E. Kraft, 279–300. Washington, D.C.: Congressional Quarterly.

Tong, Rosemarie Putnam. 1998. *Feminist Thought: A More Comprehensive Introduction.* 2d ed. Boulder, Colo.: Westview.

Tracy, David. 1998. "Human Cloning and the Public Realm: A Defense of Intuitions of the Good." In *Clones and Clones: Facts and Fantasies about Human Cloning,* edited by Martha C. Nussbaum and Cass R. Sunstein, 190–203. New York: W. W. Norton.

Trevathan, Wenda R. 1997. "An Evolutionary Perspective on Authoritative Knowledge about Birth." In *Childbirth and Authoritative Knowledge: Cross-Cultural Perspectives,* edited by Robbie E. Davis-Floyd and Carolyn F. Sargent, 80–88. Berkeley: University of California Press.

Tronto, Joan C. 1993. *Moral Boundaries: A Political Argument for an Ethic of Care.* New York: Routledge.

Tubert, Silvia. 1992. "How IVF Exploits the Wish to Be a Mother: A Psychoanalyst's Account." *Genders* 14, no. 33: 17+.

Turnock v. Ragsdale, 493 U.S. 987 (1989).

U.S. General Accounting Office. 1998. Abortion Clinics: Information on the Effectiveness of the Freedom of Access to Clinic Entrances Act. Washington, D.C.: General Accounting Office.

U.S. House of Representatives, Committee on Government Operations. 1992. *Designing Genetic Information Policy: The Need for an Independent Policy Review of the Ethical, Legal, and Social Implications of the Human Genome Project.* Washington, D.C.: Government Printing Office.

Vames, Steven, and W. Wayt Gibbs. 1995. "The Tangled Roots of Violence." *Scientific American* 272, no. 3 (March): 104–5.

Vetri, D. 1988. "Reproductive Technologies and United States Law." *International and Comparative Law Quarterly* 37, no. 3 (July): 505–34.

VHL Family Alliance. n.d. "Von Hippel-Lindau Syndrome (VHL)." Two-page memo.

Wagner, Marsden. 1997. "Confessions of a Dissident." In *Childbirth and Authoritative Knowledge: Cross-Cultural Perspectives,* edited by Robbie E. Davis-Floyd and Carolyn F. Sargent, 366–93. Berkeley: University of California Press.

Wang, Caroline. 1992. "Culture, Meaning and Disability: Injury Prevention Campaigns and the Production of Stigma." *Social Science and Medicine* 35, no. 9 (November): 1093–1102.

———. 1998. "Portraying Stigmatized Conditions: Disabling Images in Public Health." *Journal of Health Communication* 3: 149–59.

Wang, Vivian Ota. 1994. "Cultural Competency in Genetic Counseling." *Journal of Genetic Counseling* 3, no. 4 (December): 267–77.

Ward, Martha C. 1995. "Early Childbearing: What Is the Problem and Who Owns It?" In *Conceiving the New World Order: The Global Politics of Reproduction,* edited by Faye D. Ginsburg and Rayna Rapp, 140–58. Berkeley: University of California Press.

Warren, M. A. 1985. *Gendercide: The Implications of Sex Selection.* Totowa, N.J.: Rowman and Allanheld.

Watson, James D. 1992. "A Personal View of the Project." In *The Code of Codes: Scientific and Social Issues in the Human Genome Project,* edited by Daniel J. Kevles and Leroy Hood, 164–73. Cambridge, Mass.: Harvard University Press.

Webber, Tammy. 2001. "Fortified Foods Credited with Decline in Birth Defects." *The State* (Columbia, S.C.), June 20.

Weber, Lynn. 2000. *Understanding Race, Class, Gender, and Sexuality: A Conceptual Framework.* Boston: McGraw Hill.

Webster v. Reproductive Health Services, Inc., 492 U.S. 490, 109 S. Ct. 3040, 106 L.Ed. 2d 410 (1989).

Weiner, Annette B. 1995. "Reassessing Reproduction in Social Theory." In *Conceiving the New World Order: The Global Politics of Reproduction,* edited by Faye D. Ginsburg and Rayna Rapp, 407–24. Berkeley: University of California Press.

Weisman, S. R. 1988. "State in India Bars Fetus Sex-Testing." *New York Times,* July 20.

Weiss, Meira. 1998. "Ethical Reflections: Taking a Walk on the Wild Side." In *Small Wars: The Cultural Politics of Childhood,* edited by Nancy Scheper-Hughes and Carolyn Sargent, 149–62. Berkeley: University of California Press.

Weiss, Suzanne. 1989. "124 Protesters Arrested: Blockade of Boulder Abortion Clinic Ends Peacefully." *Rocky Mountain News,* April 30.

Wertz, Dorothy C. 1992. "How Parents of Affected Children View Selective Abortion." In *Issues in Reproductive Technology,* edited by Helen Bequaert Holmes, 171–89. New York: Garland.

Wertz, Dorothy C., and John C. Fletcher. 1993. "A Critique of Some Feminist Challenges to Prenatal Diagnosis." *Journal of Women's Health* 2, no. 2: 173–88.

West, Guida, and Rhoda Lois Blumberg. 1990. "Reconstructing Social Protest from a Feminist Perspective." In *Women and Social Protest,* edited by Guida West and Rhoda Lois Blumberg, 3–35. New York: Oxford University Press.

Wetzstein, Cheryl. 1998. "Adoption Advocates Encouraged by Big Response to Internet Sites." *Insight on the News* 14, no. 4 (February 2): 2.

Wexler, Alice. 1995. *Mapping Fate: A Memoir of Family, Risk, and Genetic Research.* Berkeley: University of California Press.

Wexler, Nancy. 1975. "Living out the Dying: HD, Grief and Death." *ERIC Reports.* Washington, D.C.: National Institute of Education.

———. 1979. "Genetic 'Russian Roulette': The Experience of Being at Risk for Huntington's Disease.'" In *Genetic Counseling: Psychological Dimensions,* edited by Seymour Kessler, 199–220. New York: Academic.

———. 1992. "Clairvoyance and Caution: Repercussions from the Human Genome Project." In *The Code of Codes: Scientific and Social Issues in the Human Genome Project,* edited by Daniel J. Kevles and Leroy Hood, 211–43. Cambridge, Mass.: Harvard University Press.

Wheeler, David L. 1999. "For Biologists, the Postgenomic World Promises Vast and Thrilling New Knowledge." *Chronicle of Higher Education* 45, no. 49 (August 13): 17–18.

Whitehead, Mary Beth. 1989. *A Mother's Story: The Truth about the Baby M Case.* New York: St. Martin's.

"The Whitner Update: SCAPW Spreading the Word." 1999. *South Carolina Advocates for Pregnant Women* 1, no. 2 (June): 1.

Whitner v. State of South Carolina, 492 S.E.2d 777 (S.C. 1997), cert. Denied, 118 S. Ct 1957 (1998).

Wiesel, Torsten N. 1994. "Genetics and Behavior: Editorial." *Science* 264 (June 17): 1647.

Wikler, Norma J. 1986. "Society's Response to the New Reproductive Technologies: The Feminist Perspectives." *Southern California Law Review* 59, no. 5 (July): 1043–57.

Wilcox, Clyde, Matthew DeBell, and Lee Sigelman. 1999. "The Second Coming of the New Christian Right: Patterns of Popular Support in 1984 and 1996." *Social Science Quarterly* 80, no. 1 (March): 181–92.

Wilder, Marcy J. 1998. "The Rule of Law, the Rise of Violence, and the Role of Morality: Reframing America's Abortion Debate." In *Abortion Wars: A Half Century of Struggle, 1950–2000,* edited by Rickie Solinger, 73–94. Berkeley: University of California Press.

Wilkie, Tom. 1993. *Perilous Knowledge: The Human Genome Project and Its Implications*. Berkeley: University of California Press.

Williams, Joan. 1991. "Gender Wars: Selfless Women in the Republic of Choice." *New York University Law Review* 66, nos. 4–6 (December): 1559–1634.

Williams, Patricia J. 1988. "On Being the Object of Property." *Signs: Journal of Women in Culture and Society* 14, no. 1 (Autumn): 5–24.

———. 1991. *The Alchemy of Race and Rights: Diary of a Law Professor*. Cambridge, Mass.: Harvard University Press.

———. 2000. "Dust and Destiny." *Nation* 271, no. 3 (July 17): 11.

Williams, Rhys H., and Jeffrey Blackburn. 1996. "Many Are Called but Few Obey: Ideological Commitment and Activism in Operation Rescue." In *Disruptive Religion: The Force of Faith in Social Movement Activism*, edited by Christian Smith, 167–85. New York: Routledge.

Willis, Ellen. 1983. "Is a Woman a Person?" In *Powers of Desire*, edited by Ann Snitow, Christine Stansell, and Sharon Thompson, 471–76. New York: Monthly Review.

Wingerter, Rex B. 1987. "Fetal Protection Becomes Assault on Motherhood." *In These Times*, June 10–23.

Winiarski, Kathryn. 2001. "S.C. in Forefront of Efforts to Legislative Morality." *The State* (Columbia, S.C.), May 6.

Winslow, Barbara. 1998. "Primary and Secondary Contradictions in Seattle: 1967–1969." In *The Feminist Memoir Project: Voices from Women's Liberation*, edited by Rachel Blau DuPlessis and Ann Snitow, 225–48. New York: Three Rivers.

Wolbrecht, Christina. 2000. *The Politics of Women's Rights*. Princeton, N.J.: Princeton University Press.

Wolf, Naomi. 1995. "Our Bodies, Our Souls: Rethinking Pro-Choice Rhetoric." *New Republic* 213, no. 4 (October 16): 26–29, 32–35.

Wolfson, Alice J. 1998. "Clenched Fist, Open Heart." In *The Feminist Memoir Project: Voices from Women's Liberation*, edited by Rachel Blau DuPlessis and Ann Snitow, 268–83. New York: Three Rivers.

Woliver, Laura R. 1987. Review of Judith Lasker and Susan Borg's *In Search of Parenthood: Coping with Infertility and High-Tech Conception. Women's Review of Books* 5, no. 3 (December): 25.

———. 1988. "The Equal Rights Amendment and the Limits of Liberal Legal Reform." *Polity* 21, no. 1 (Fall): 183–200.

———. 1989a. "The Deflective Power of Reproductive Technologies: The Impact on Women." *Women and Politics* 9, no. 3: 17–47.

———. 1989b. "The Medicalization of Gestation and Women's Rights." Paper presented at the American Political Science Association Annual Meeting, Atlanta, Georgia, August 31–September 3.

———. 1989c. "New Reproductive Technologies: Challenges to Women's Control of Gestation and Birth." In *Biomedical Technology and Public Policy*, edited by Robert Blank and Miriam K. Mills, 43–56. New York: Greenwood.

————. 1990a. "The Marginalization of Women in Reproductive Technologies and Surrogacy." Paper presented at the 1990 Feminism and Legal Theory Conference, University of Wisconsin Law School, June 18–22.

————. 1990b. "Mobilizing a Silent Majority: Pro-Choice Interests after *Webster.*" Paper presented at the American Political Science Association Annual Meeting, San Francisco, California, August 30–September 2.

————. 1990c. "Reproductive Technologies and Surrogacy: Policy Concerns for Women." *Politics and the Life Sciences* 8, no. 2 (February): 185–93.

————. 1990d. Review of Barbara Katz Rothman's *Recreating Motherhood: Ideology and Technology in a Patriarchal Society. Women's Studies International Forum* 13, no. 5 (September/October): 529–30.

————. 1991a. "The Influence of Technology on the Politics of Motherhood: An Overview of the United States." *Women's Studies International Forum* 14, no. 5 (December): 479–90.

————. 1991b. "Lobbying the Supreme Court: Coalitions of Abortion Interests and the *Webster* Decision." Paper presented at the Southern Political Science Association Annual Meeting, Tampa, Florida, November 6–9.

————. 1991c. "Mobilizing the Pro-Choice Movement in South Carolina." Paper presented at the Midwest Political Science Association Annual Meeting, Chicago, Illinois, April 17–20.

————. 1992a. "Rhetoric and Symbols in the Pro-Life Amicus Briefs in the *Webster* Case." Paper presented at the American Political Science Association Annual Meeting, Chicago, Illinois, September 3–6.

————. 1992b. "Symbols and Rhetoric in Pro-Choice Amicus Briefs." Paper presented at the Southern Political Science Association Annual Meeting, Atlanta, Georgia, November 5–7.

————. 1993a. *From Outrage to Action: The Politics of Grass-Roots Dissent.* Urbana: University of Illinois Press.

————. 1993b. "Representation and Abortion Politics in the American Medical Profession." Paper presented at the American Political Science Association Annual Meeting, Washington, D.C., September 2–5.

————. 1993c. Review of *Surrogate Motherhood: Politics and Privacy,* edited by Larry Gostin. *Women's Studies International Forum* 16, no. 3 (May–June): 306.

————. 1995. "Reproductive Technologies, Surrogacy Arrangements, and the Politics of Motherhood." In *Mothers in Law: Feminist Theory and the Legal Regulation of Motherhood,* edited by Martha Albertson Fineman and Isabel Karpin, 346–59. New York: Columbia University Press,

————. 1996a. "Local Diligence: The Impact of Fluid Social Movements on Abortion Politics." Paper presented at the Midwest Political Science Association Annual Meeting, Chicago, Illinois, April 18–21.

————. 1996b. "Mobilizing and Sustaining Grass-Roots Dissent." *Journal of Social Issues* 52, no. 1 (Spring): 139–51.

————. 1996c. "Policies to Assist Pregnant Women and Children Should Include Complete Assessment of the Realities of Women's Lives." *Politics and the Life Sciences* 15, no. 1 (March): 75–77.

———. 1996d. "The Politics of the Human Genome Project: Gender Rights and Reproductive Policy." Paper presented at the Southern Political Science Association Annual Meeting, Atlanta, Georgia, November 7–9.

———. 1996e. "The Politics of Surrogacy." In *Encyclopedia of U.S. Biomedical Policy*, edited by Robert Blank and Janna C. Merrick, 296–98. Westport, Conn.: Greenwood.

———. 1996f. "Rhetoric and Symbols in American Abortion Politics." In *Abortion Politics: Public Policy in Cross Cultural Perspective*, edited by Marianne Githens and Dorothy Stetson, 5–28. New York: Routledge.

———. 1997a. "Grass-Roots Coalitions and Abortion Politics." Paper presented at the Midwest Political Science Association Annual Meeting, Chicago, Illinois, April 10–12.

———. 1997b. Review of Eileen McDonagh's *Breaking the Abortion Deadlock. Law and Politics Book Review*, April, 171–73.

———. 1998a. "Abortion Interests: From the Usual Suspects to Expanded Coalitions." In *Interest Group Politics*, edited by Allan J. Cigler and Burdett A. Loomis, 327–42. Washington, D.C.: Congressional Quarterly.

———. 1998b. Review of *Coerced Contraception? Moral and Policy Challenges of Long-Acting Birth Control*, edited by Ellen H. Moskowitz and Bruce Jennings. *Politics and the Life Sciences* 17, no. 1 (March): 101–2.

———. 1998c. "Social Movements and Abortion Law." In *Social Movements and American Political Institutions*, edited by Anne N. Costain and Andrew S. McFarland, 233–47. Armonk, N.Y.: Rowman and Littlefield.

———. 1999a. "Abortion Conflicts, City Governments, and Culture Wars: Continually Negotiating Coexistence in South Carolina." In *Culture Wars and Local Politics*, edited by Elaine Sharp, 21–42. Lawrence: University of Kansas Press.

———. 1999b. "Designer Genes: Cultural Shifting on Reproductive Values and the Impact on Gender, Race, Class and Sexualities." Paper presented at the Southern Political Science Association Annual Meeting, Savannah, Georgia, November 3–6.

———. 1999c. "Terrains of Reproductive Power." Paper presented at the American Political Science Association Annual Meeting, September 2–5.

———. 2000. "Social Controls and Reproductive Politics: The Punitive Monitoring of Pregnant Women." Paper presented at the Western Political Science Association Annual Meeting, San Jose, California, March 24–26.

Woliver, Laura R., and Kathryn Bryant. 1997a. "Deviant, Martyr, or Ghost? Media Images of Women Involved in Abortion and Adoption." Paper presented at the Southern Political Science Association Annual Meeting, Norfolk, Virginia, November 6–8.

———. 1997b. "Invisible and Visible Women: Media Images of Pregnant Women Who Experience Adoption, Abortion, and Social Motherhood." Paper presented at the Western Political Science Association Annual Meeting, Tucson, Arizona, March 13–15.

Woliver, Laura R., and Angela Ledford. 2001. "Policing Mifepristone in South Carolina." Paper presented at the 2001 Politics and the Life Sciences Convention, Charleston, South Carolina, October 18–21.

Woliver, Laura R., and Patricia Tangney. 1995. "Comparative Abortion Policies and Practices." Paper presented at the Southern Political Science Association Annual Meeting, Tampa, Florida, November 1–4.

———. Forthcoming. "Comparative Abortion Policies and Practices." *Asian Women.*

"Women Give Most Care to Dying, Study Finds." 1999. *The State* (Columbia, S.C.), September 23.

Wozniak, Danielle F. 1999. "Gifts and Burdens: The Social and Familial Context of Foster Mothering." In *Transformative Motherhood: On Giving and Getting in a Consumer Culture,* edited by Linda L. Layne, 89–133. New York: New York University Press.

Wyman, Scott. 1996a. "Suburbs Won't See Olympic Flame: Run Organizers Will Keep Torch out of View from Greenville County Line to City Limits in Response to Anti-Gay Resolution." *Greenville (S.C.) News,* 25 June.

———. 1996b. "Greenville County's Image Tested by Olympic Rebuke." *Greenville (S.C.) News,* 26 June.

Young, Iris Marion. 1999. "Public Address as a Sign of Political Inclusion." In *On Feminist Ethics and Politics,* edited by Claudia Card, 103–15. Lawrence: University Press of Kansas.

Zihlman, Adrienne L. 1995. "Misreading Darwin on Reproduction: Reductionism in Evolutionary Theory." In *Conceiving the New World Order: The Global Politics of Reproduction,* edited by Faye D. Ginsburg and Rayna Rapp, 425–44. Berkeley: University of California Press.

Zorza, Joan. 1992. "The Criminal Law of Misdemeanor Domestic Violence, 1970–1990." *Journal of Criminal Law and Criminology* 83, no. 1 (Spring): 46–72.

Zwingle, Erla. 1998. "Women and Population." *National Geographic* 195, no. 4 (October): 36–55.

INDEX

Abate, Tom, 47

abortion: access to, 96–102; back-alley, 89–90; breaking the silence about, 87–88, 112; and civil disobedience, 100, 101–2, 104–7; and the courts, 8, 38–39, 85–92; and culture wars, 96–102; and equality, 91, 156; and equal protection, 91, 109–11; and genetic testing, 9, 32–34, 36, 39–40, 53, 54–56, 61, 63–65, 70–71, 78, 83; and grass-roots politics, 96–102; history of, 8, 15, 16, 58, 84–92, 109–13; and local government, 96–107; public funding for, 78, 86, 110–11; and reproductive technologies, 9, 30, 32–34, 36–39, 54–55, 61, 70, 83; rhetoric, 5, 16–17, 22–23, 37–39, 83, 89–90, 92–93, 102–3; for sex selection, 2, 35–36, 44, 52; and social movements, 97–109, 109–12; and social services, 32–33, 70, 78, 110–11; speak outs, 87–88; therapeutic, 83, 88–89, 108; women's choices of, 4, 8, 32–34, 39, 54–56, 70, 78, 157–58. *See also* abortion politics; illegal abortion; late-term abortions; partial-birth abortions; selective abortions

abortion clinic regulations: in South Carolina, 102

abortion politics: anti–legal abortion, 21–22, 37–39, 86, 92–93, 98–109; framing of, 5, 15–17, 37–39, 54–55, 109–11; pro-choice, 109–11; in South Carolina, 3, 96–107

Abzug, Bella, 68

actuarial thinking, 49, 63–65

Adams, Greg D., 98, 101

adoption, 2, 4, 5, 115–20, 132–33; "Adoption, Not Abortion" slogan, 4, 25, 116, 131; and birthmothers, 5, 14, 22, 115–20, 132–33; and conflicts of interest, 116–17; experiences, 4, 118–20, 132–33; and genetic testing, 58; history of, 8, 15, 16, 58, 84–92, 109–13; international, 4, 5, 117–20, 131–32; markets, 4, 115–20, 132–33; and money, 4, 9, 115–20, 132–33; open, 5, 131; and reproductive technologies, 41; and social class, 4, 9, 115–20, 132–33; and social structures, 4, 9, 115–20, 131–32; and South Korea, 4

adult adoptees, 4, 116

African Americans: and genetic research, 55–56, 78; and medical care, 53, 78. *See also* African American women

African American women: and abortion, 91, 109–11, 140–41; and adoption, 118–20, 130–31; and birth control, 15, 53, 78; and the courts, 33–34, 91, 138–47, 154n1; and medical care, 34, 53, 78, 91, 138–47; as single mothers, 118–20, 130–31

Ahern, David W., 101

Aho, James, 99

Akhtar, Farida, 35

Akron v. Akron Center for Reproductive Health (1983), 38

alternative medicine, 24

Altstein, Howard, 117, 118

Alzheimer's disease, 48, 51, 60

American Association of University Women, 86–87

LAURA R. WOLIVER is a professor of political science in the Department of Government and International Studies and the associate director of the Women's Studies Program at the University of South Carolina. She is the author of *From Outrage to Action: The Politics of Grass-Roots Dissent* and numerous articles on women's rights, civil rights, legal issues, activism, and reproductive politics.

The University of Illinois Press
is a founding member of the
Association of American University Presses.

———————————————————————

Composed in 9.5/12.5 Trump Mediaeval
with Trump Mediaeval display
at the University of Illinois Press
Manufactured by Maple-Vail Book Manufacturing Group

University of Illinois Press
1325 South Oak Street
Champaign, IL 61820-6903
www.press.uillinois.edu